DARK HORSE OCCULT THEATRE UNVEILS

The Superb Supernatural Spectacle!

LAZARUS JACK™

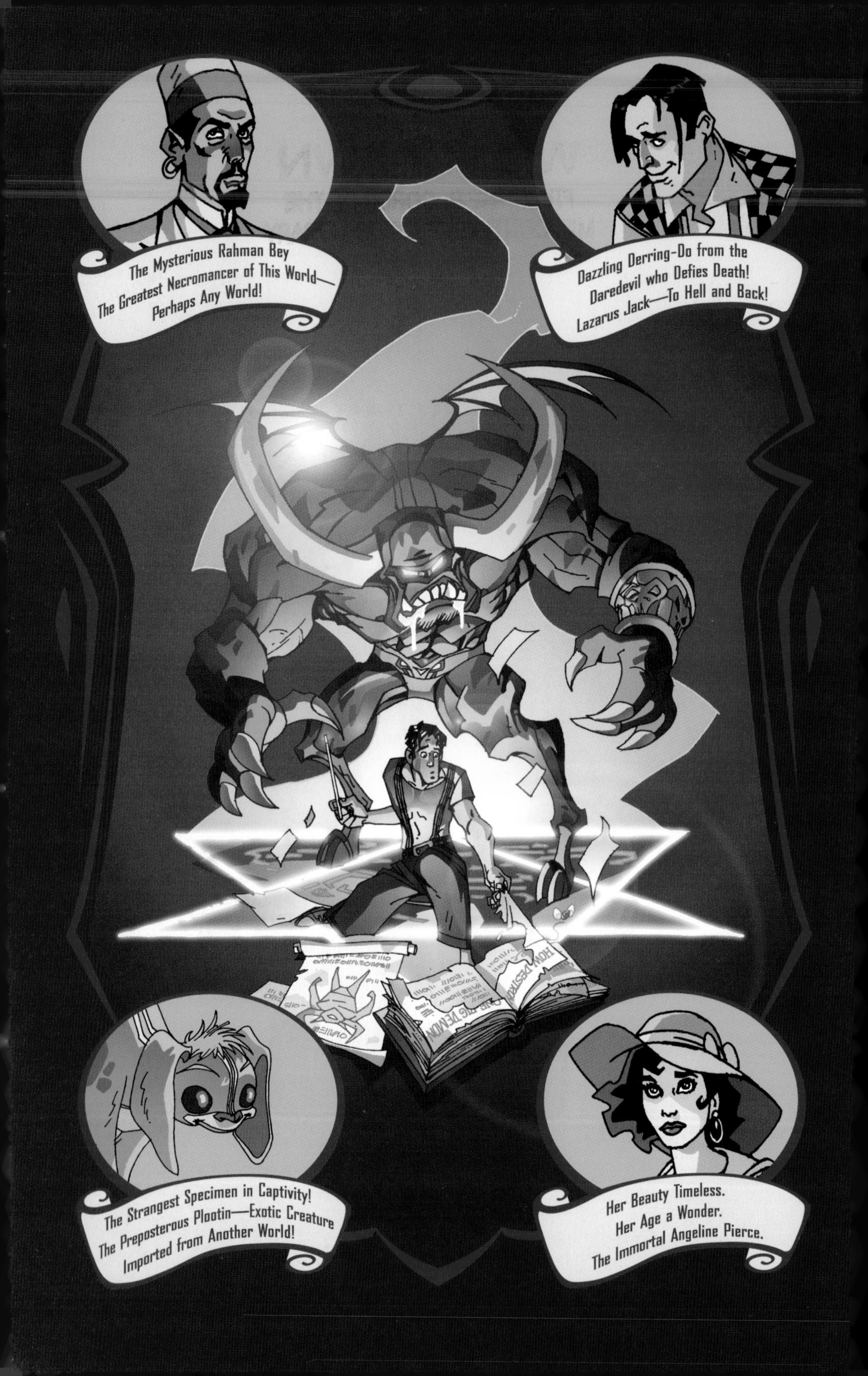
The Mysterious Rahman Bey
The Greatest Necromancer of This World—
Perhaps Any World!
Dazzling Derring-Do from the
Daredevil who Defies Death!
Lazarus Jack—To Hell and Back!
The Strangest Specimen in Captivity!
The Preposterous Plootin—Exotic Creature
Imported from Another World!
Her Beauty Timeless.
Her Age a Wonder.
The Immortal Angeline Pierce.

PRESENTING

THE MOST DIFFICULT AND DANGEROUS FEATS EVER DEVISED

BY HUMAN OR DEMONIC INGENUITY

FROM THE IMAGINATION OF

MARK & HORACIO
RICKETTS DOMINGUES

Phantasmagorists without Parallel!

Fainting couches provided in the lobby

DARK HORSE BOOKS™

EDITOR **SCOTT ALLIE**   ASSISTANT EDITOR **MATT DRYER**
DESIGNER **AMY ARENDTS**   ART DIRECTOR **LIA RIBACCHI**
PUBLISHER **MIKE RICHARDSON**

SPECIAL THANKS TO THE AMAZING ESCAPIST, **DAN JACKSON**

Published by
Dark Horse Books
A division of
Dark Horse Comics, Inc.
10956 SE Main Street
Milwaukie, OR 97222

First Edition: September 2004
ISBN: 1-59307-097-7

1 3 5 7 9 10 8 6 4 2
Printed in China

Horacio would like to thank Mario Fernandez,
Omar Francia, and Nano Pereyra for their hard work,
and the artist extends his very special thanks
to Darío Brizuela.

Mark would like to salute the tireless efforts of
Acme Straitjacket, Manacles-R-Us, Craig's House of
Magical Gloves, and The Otherworld Travel Agency.

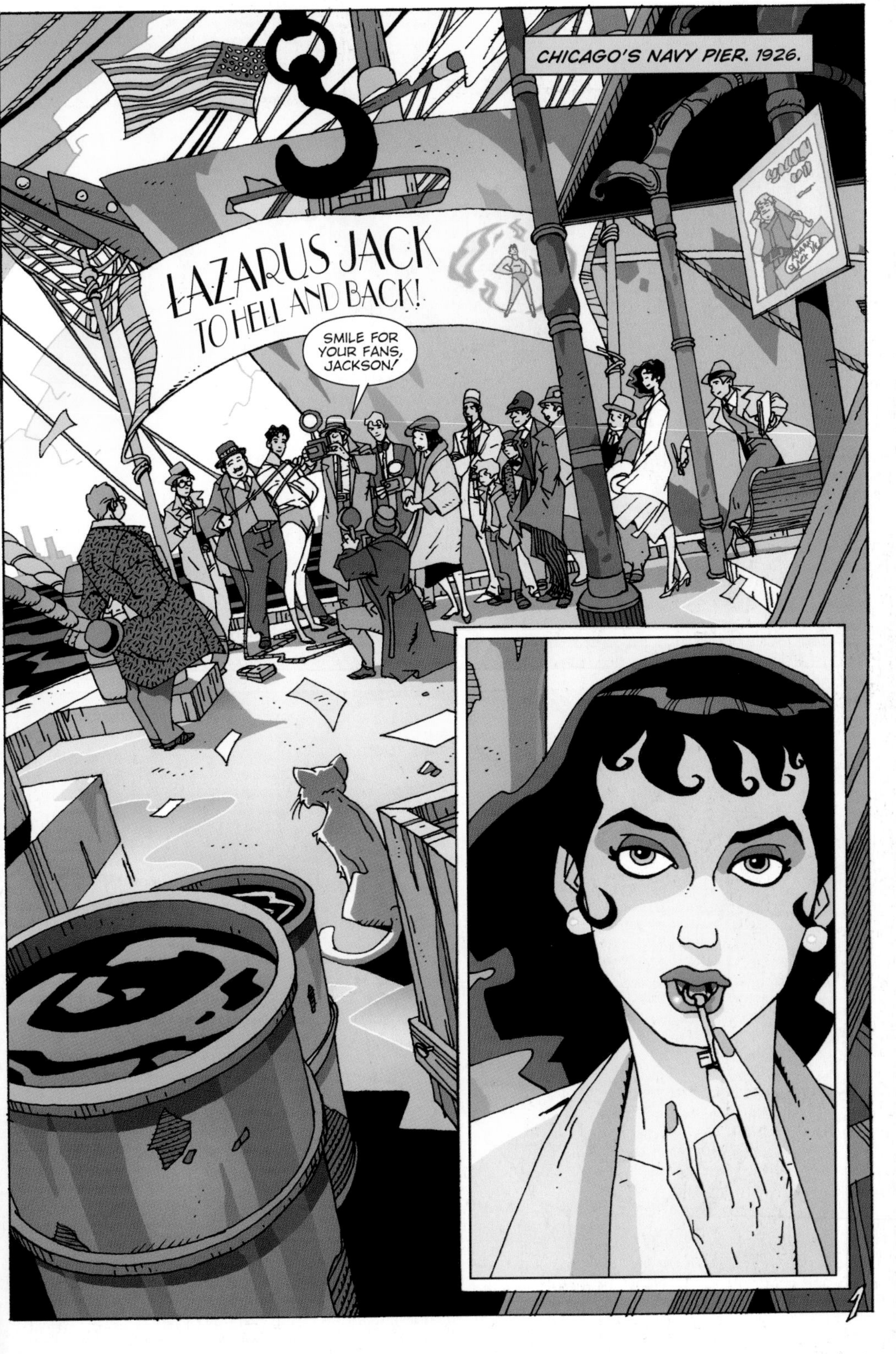
CHICAGO'S NAVY PIER. 1926.
LAZARUS JACK
TO HELL AND BACK!
SMILE FOR YOUR FANS, JACKSON!

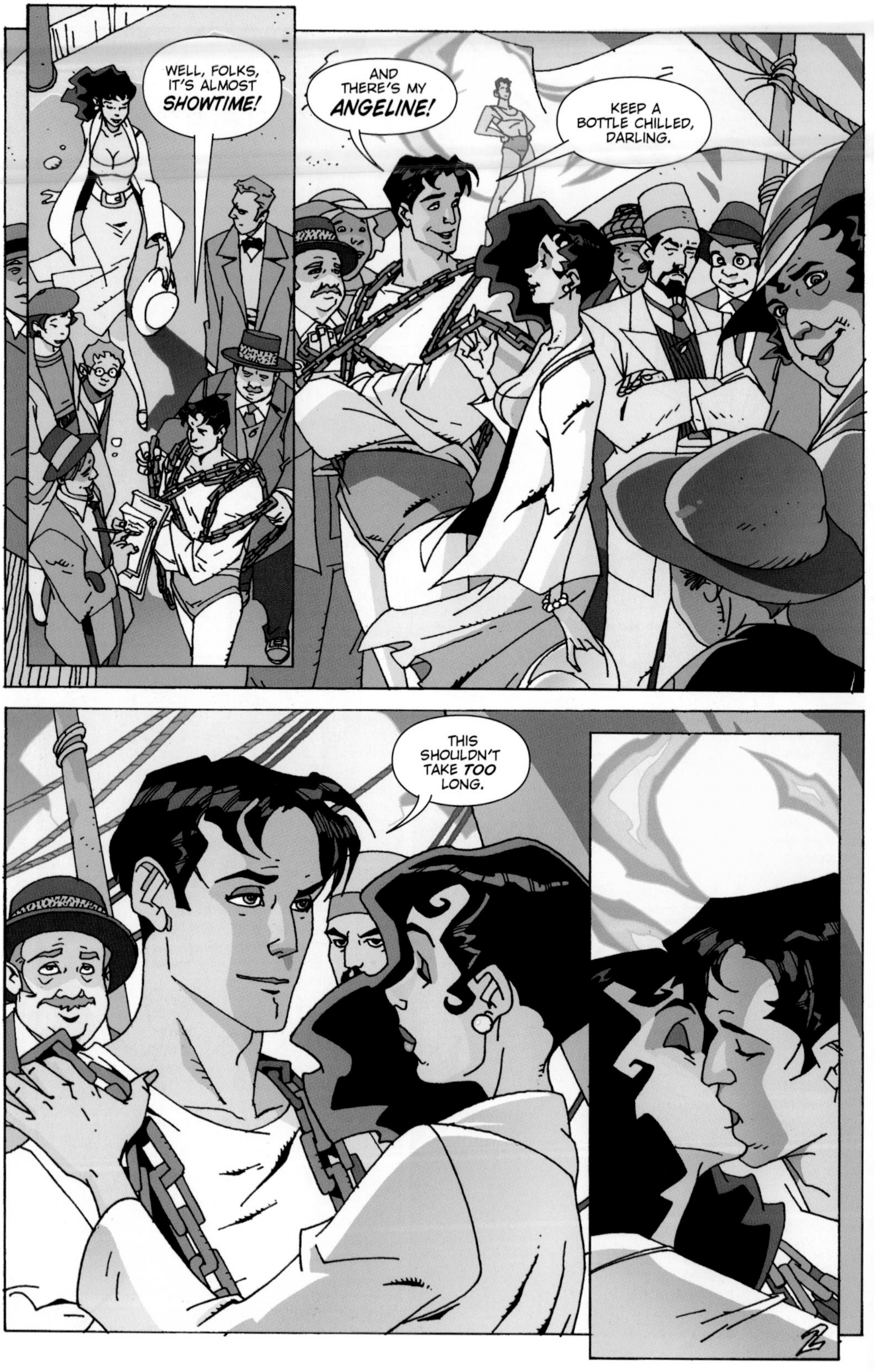

WELL, FOLKS, IT'S ALMOST *SHOWTIME!*
AND THERE'S MY *ANGELINE!*
KEEP A BOTTLE CHILLED, DARLING.
THIS SHOULDN'T TAKE *TOO* LONG.

YOU SEEM WORRIED, ANGELINE.

FRANKLY, RAHMAN, JACKSON'S PUSHING HIMSELF *TOO* HARD.

THE SHADOW OF HOUDINI.

HE'S *OBSESSED*.

HE'S EVEN TURNED TO A GROUP OF SATANISTS FOR ASSISTANCE.

PLEASE, RAHMAN, PERSUADE HIM TO CHANGE HIS COURSE.

AS YOU WISH, MY DEAR.

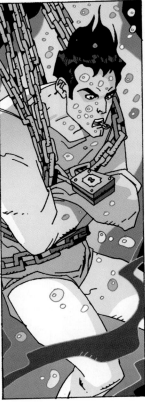

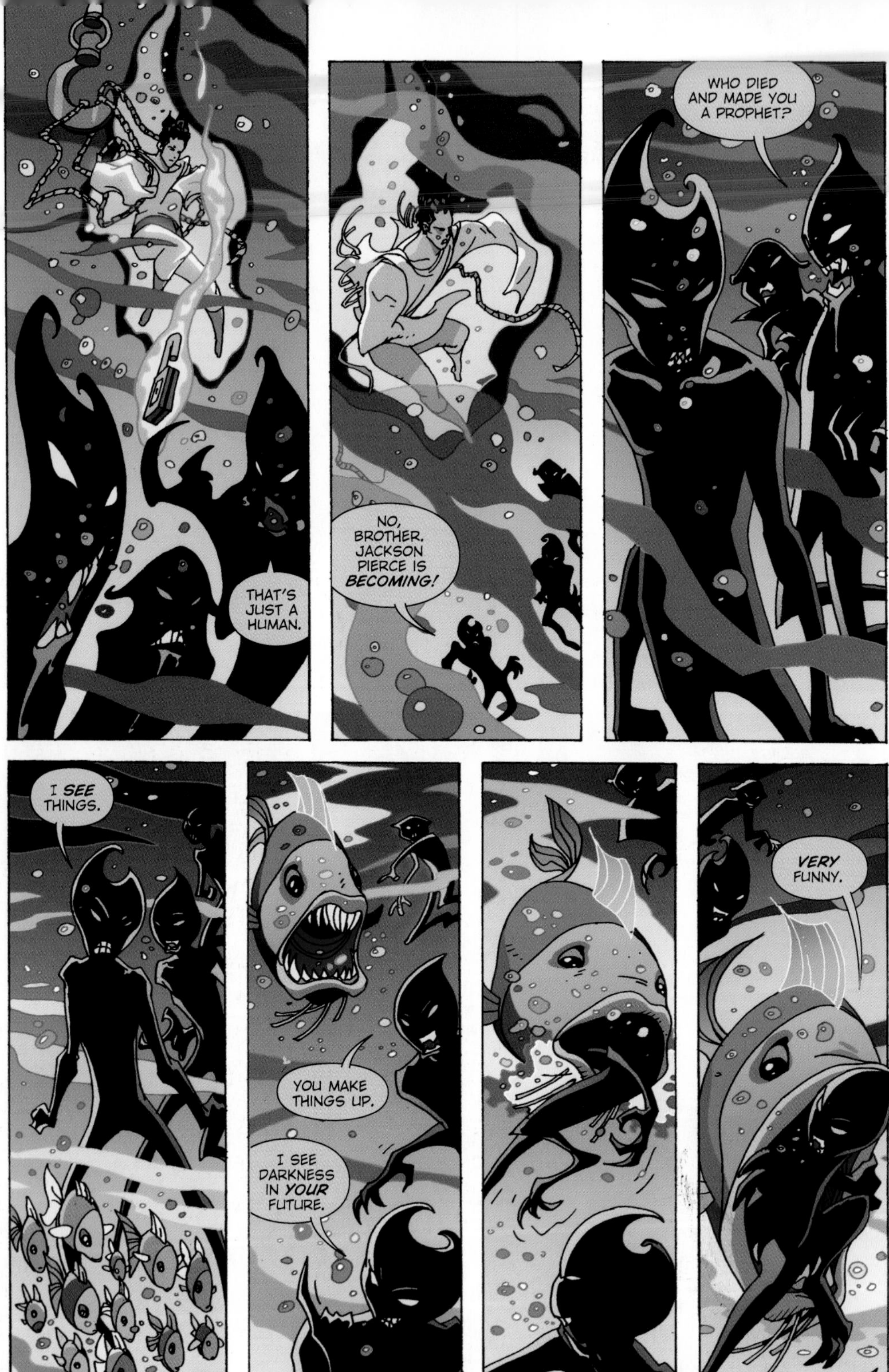
THAT'S JUST A HUMAN.
NO, BROTHER. JACKSON PIERCE IS **BECOMING!**
WHO DIED AND MADE YOU A PROPHET?
I **SEE** THINGS.
YOU MAKE THINGS UP.
I SEE DARKNESS IN **YOUR** FUTURE.
VERY FUNNY.

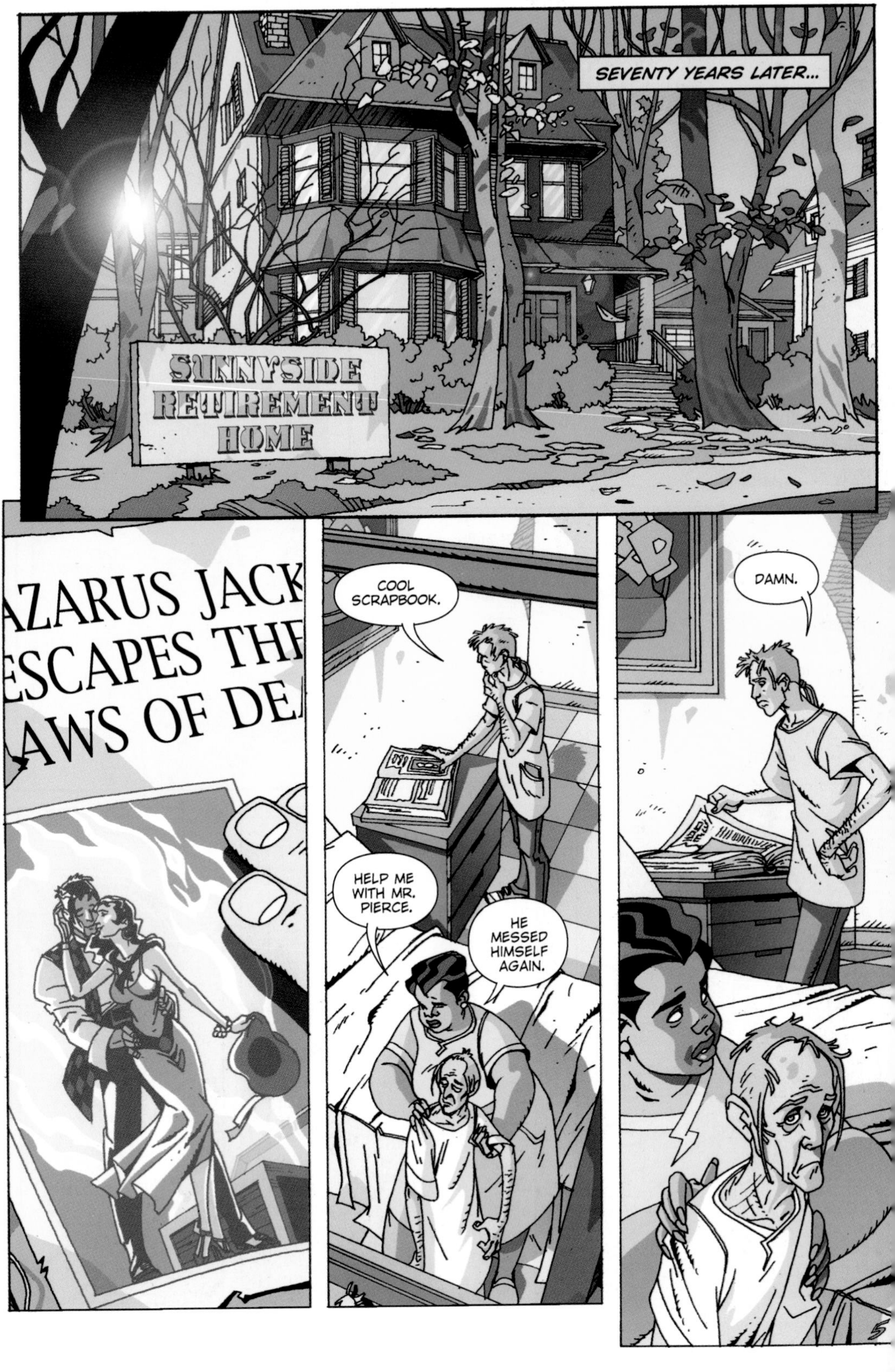
SEVENTY YEARS LATER...
SUNNYSIDE RETIREMENT HOME
AZARUS JACK ESCAPES THE AWS OF DE
COOL SCRAPBOOK.
HELP ME WITH MR. PIERCE.
HE MESSED HIMSELF AGAIN.
DAMN.

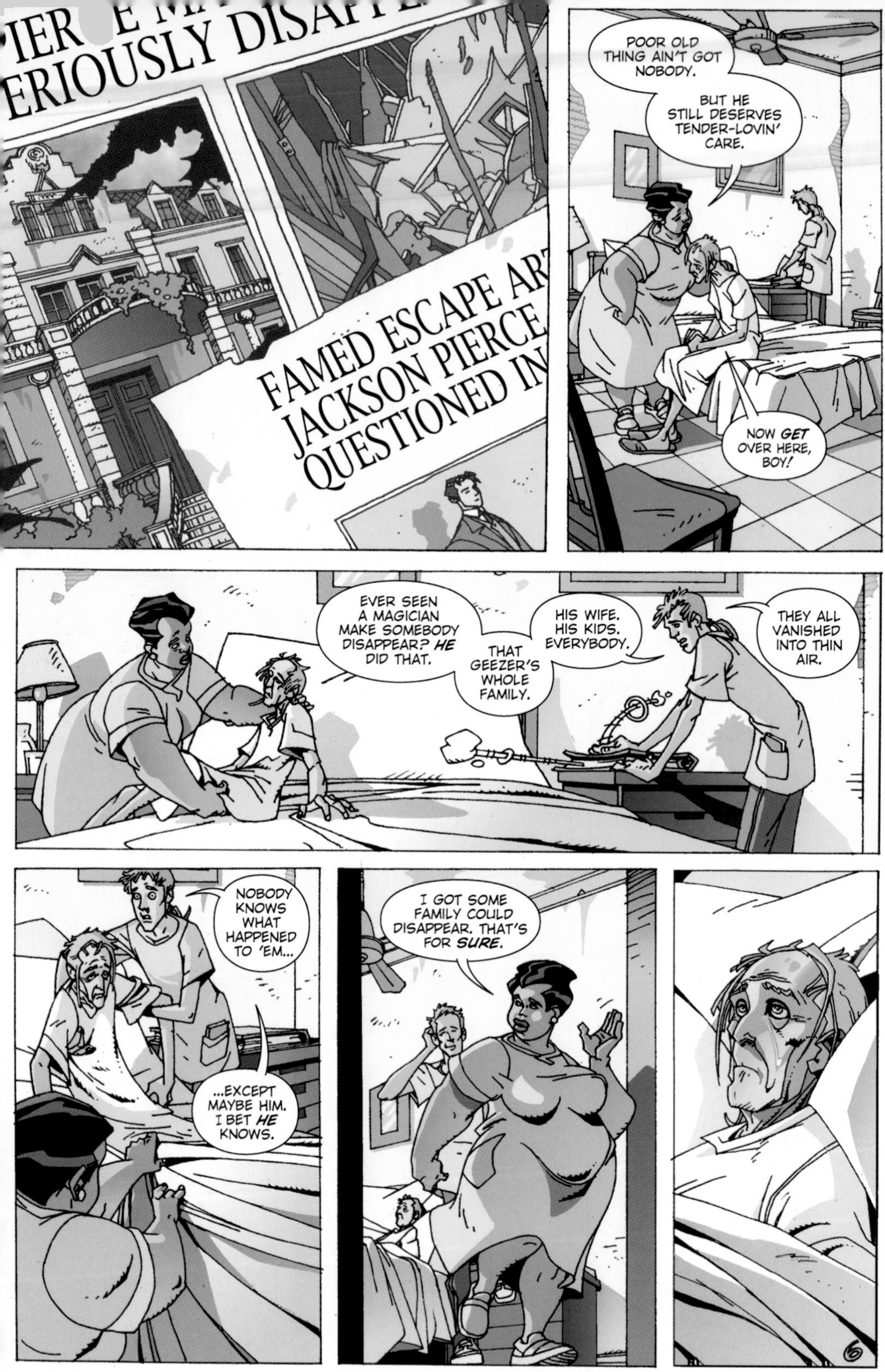

PIER E M
ERIOUSLY DISAPPE
FAMED ESCAPE ART
JACKSON PIERCE
QUESTIONED IN
POOR OLD THING AIN'T GOT NOBODY.
BUT HE STILL DESERVES TENDER-LOVIN' CARE.
NOW GET OVER HERE, BOY!
EVER SEEN A MAGICIAN MAKE SOMEBODY DISAPPEAR? HE DID THAT.
THAT GEEZER'S WHOLE FAMILY.
HIS WIFE. HIS KIDS. EVERYBODY.
THEY ALL VANISHED INTO THIN AIR.
NOBODY KNOWS WHAT HAPPENED TO 'EM...
...EXCEPT MAYBE HIM. I BET HE KNOWS.
I GOT SOME FAMILY COULD DISAPPEAR. THAT'S FOR SURE.
6

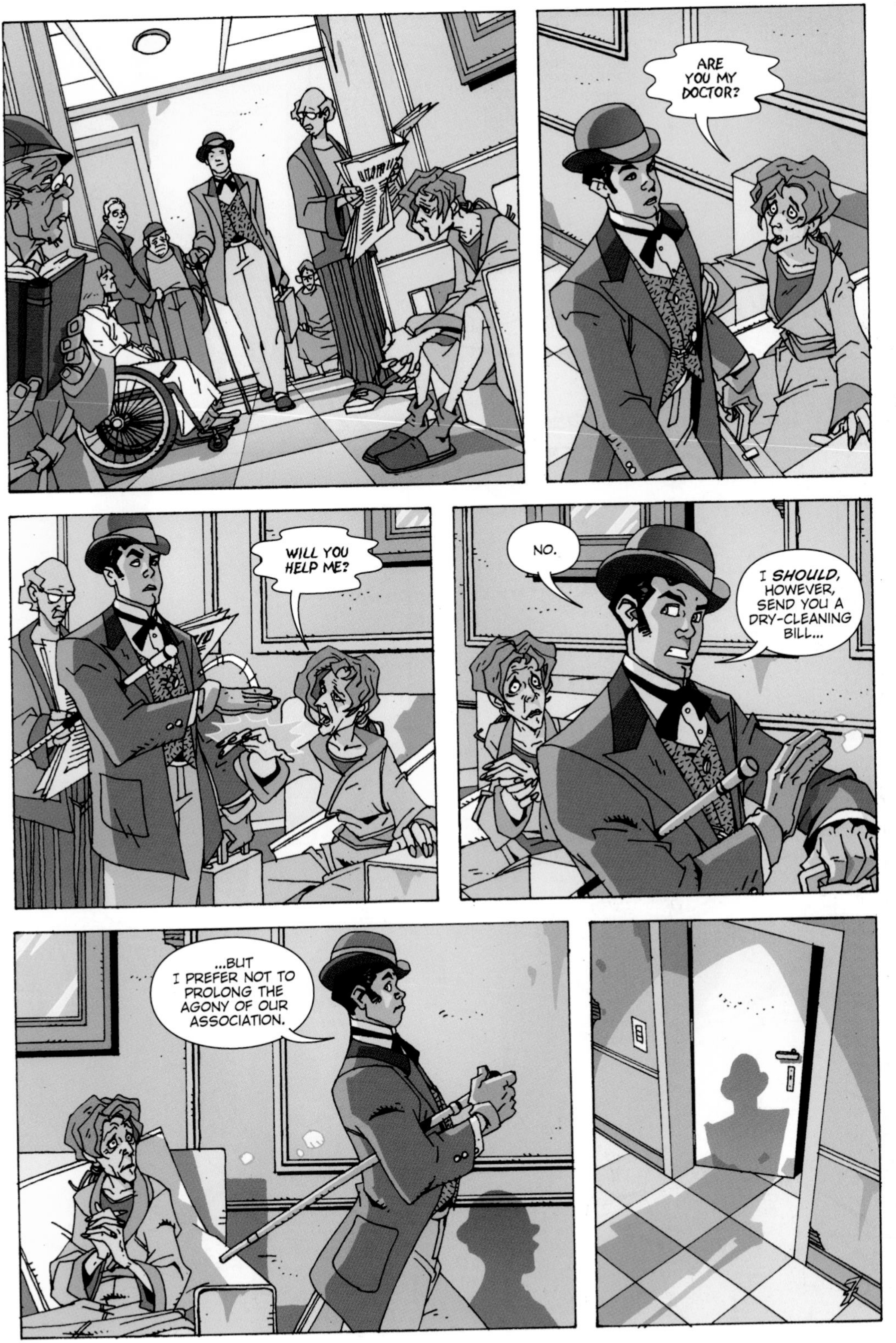
ARE YOU MY DOCTOR?
WILL YOU HELP ME?
NO.
I SHOULD, HOWEVER, SEND YOU A DRY-CLEANING BILL...
...BUT I PREFER NOT TO PROLONG THE AGONY OF OUR ASSOCIATION.

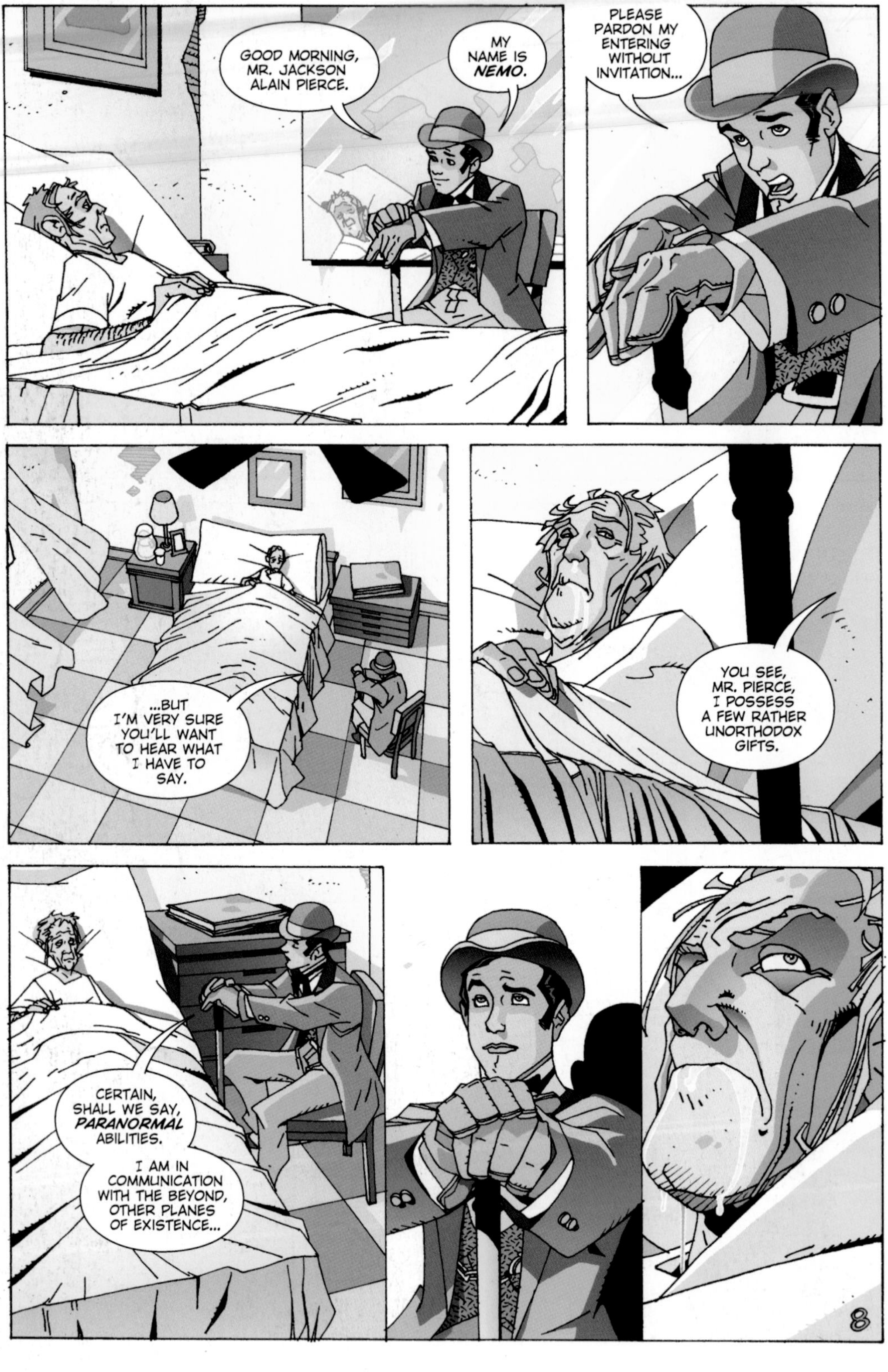
GOOD MORNING, MR. JACKSON ALAIN PIERCE.
MY NAME IS ***NEMO***.
PLEASE PARDON MY ENTERING WITHOUT INVITATION...
...BUT I'M VERY SURE YOU'LL WANT TO HEAR WHAT I HAVE TO SAY.
YOU SEE, MR. PIERCE, I POSSESS A FEW RATHER UNORTHODOX GIFTS.
CERTAIN, SHALL WE SAY, ***PARANORMAL*** ABILITIES.
I AM IN COMMUNICATION WITH THE BEYOND, OTHER PLANES OF EXISTENCE...
8

BEFORE YOU WRITE ME OFF AS A CHARLATAN...

...I SHOULD TELL YOU THAT I'M *CURRENTLY* IN CONTACT WITH YOUR ESTRANGED *WIFE.*

AND I KNOW *ALL* YOUR SECRETS.

ON OCTOBER *24TH, 1926,* WHILE INVOKING THE POWERS OF THE DEMON VERDELET, YOU ACCIDENTLY *TORE OPEN* A PORTAL INTO ANOTHER DIMENSION.

BELIEVE ME, IT'S NOT MY INTENTION TO STIR *DARK* MEMORIES OR OPEN OLD WOUNDS.

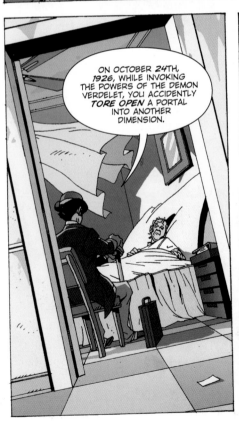

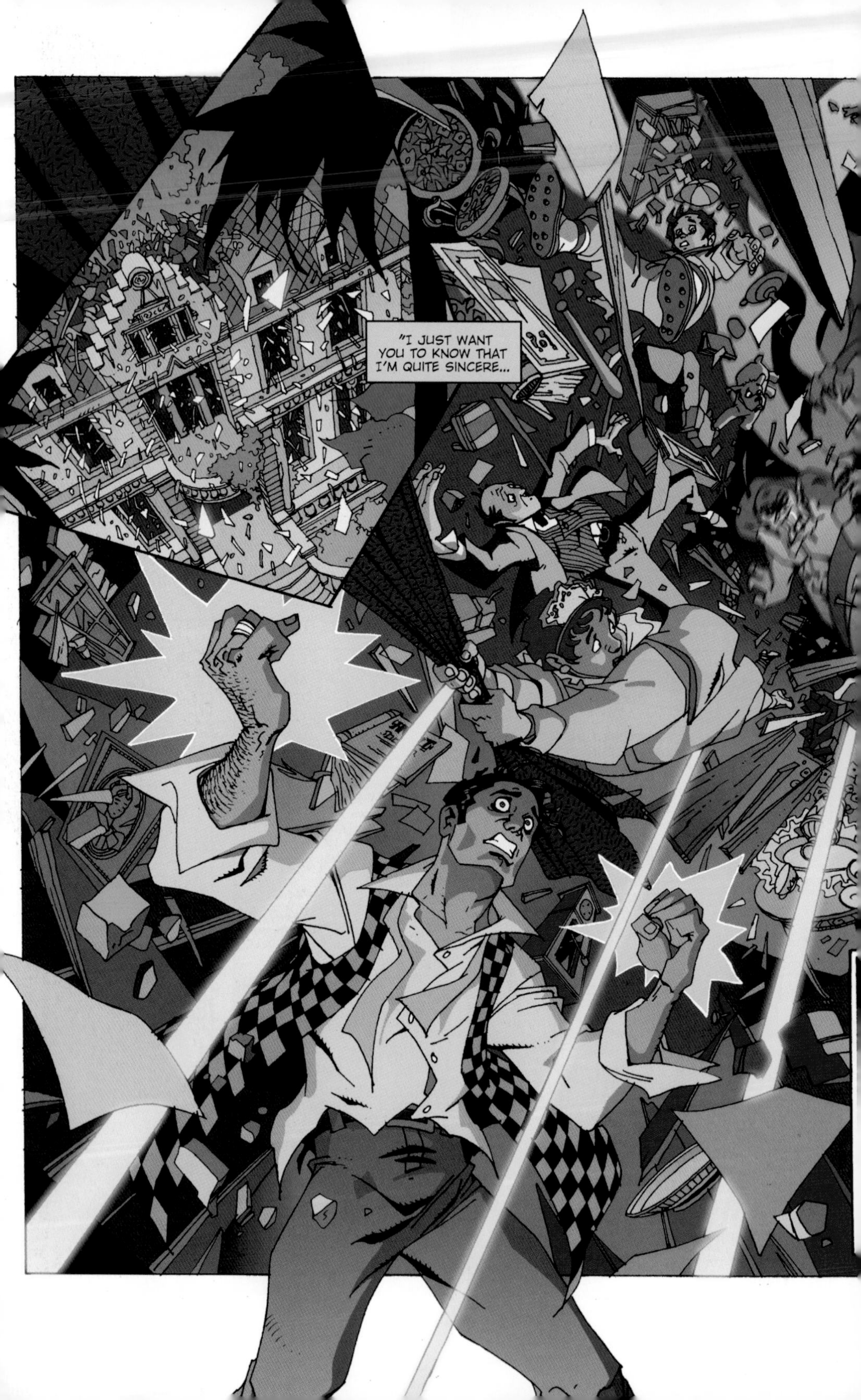
"I JUST WANT YOU TO KNOW THAT I'M QUITE SINCERE...

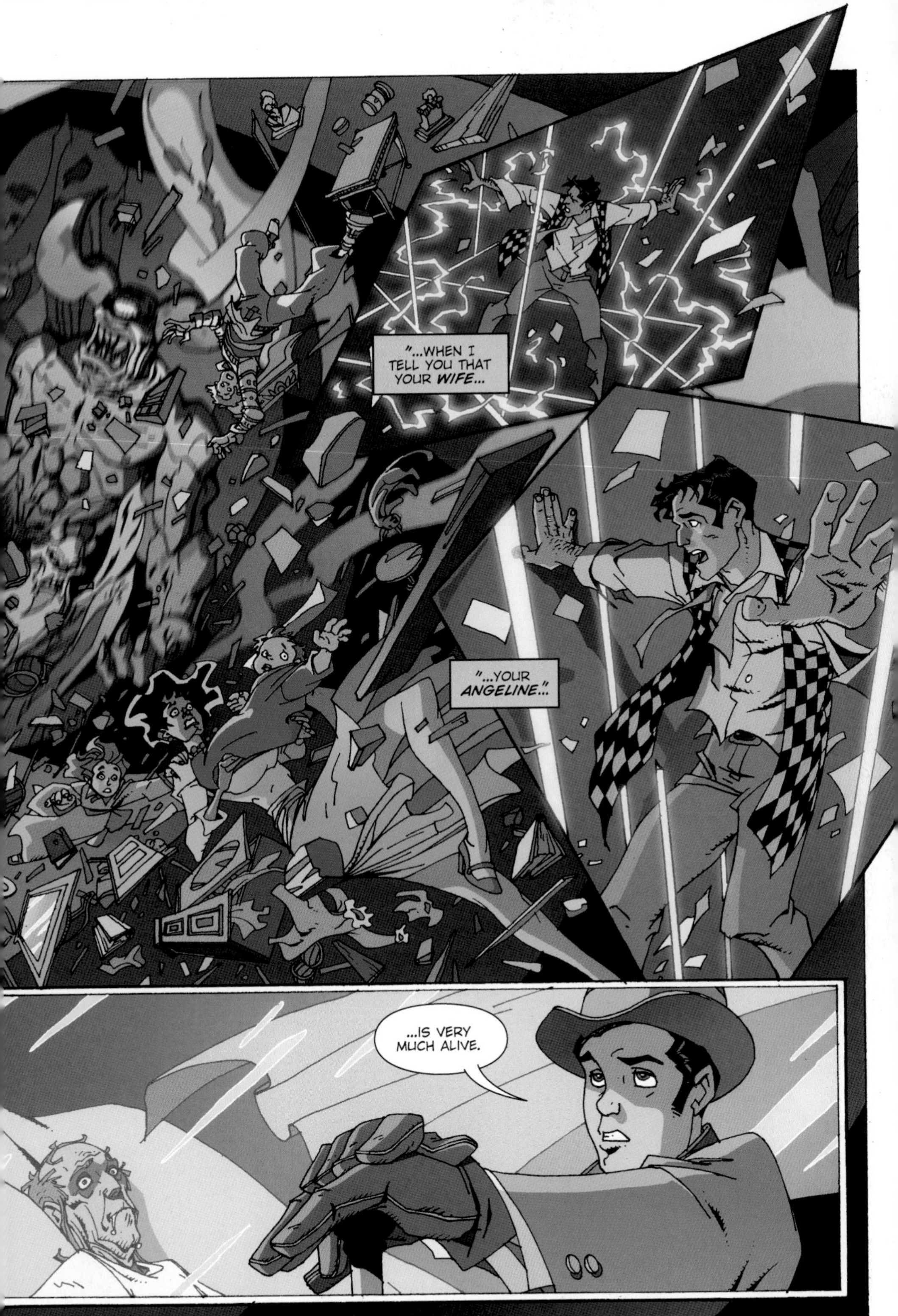
"...WHEN I TELL YOU THAT YOUR WIFE...
"...YOUR ANGELINE..."
...IS VERY MUCH ALIVE.

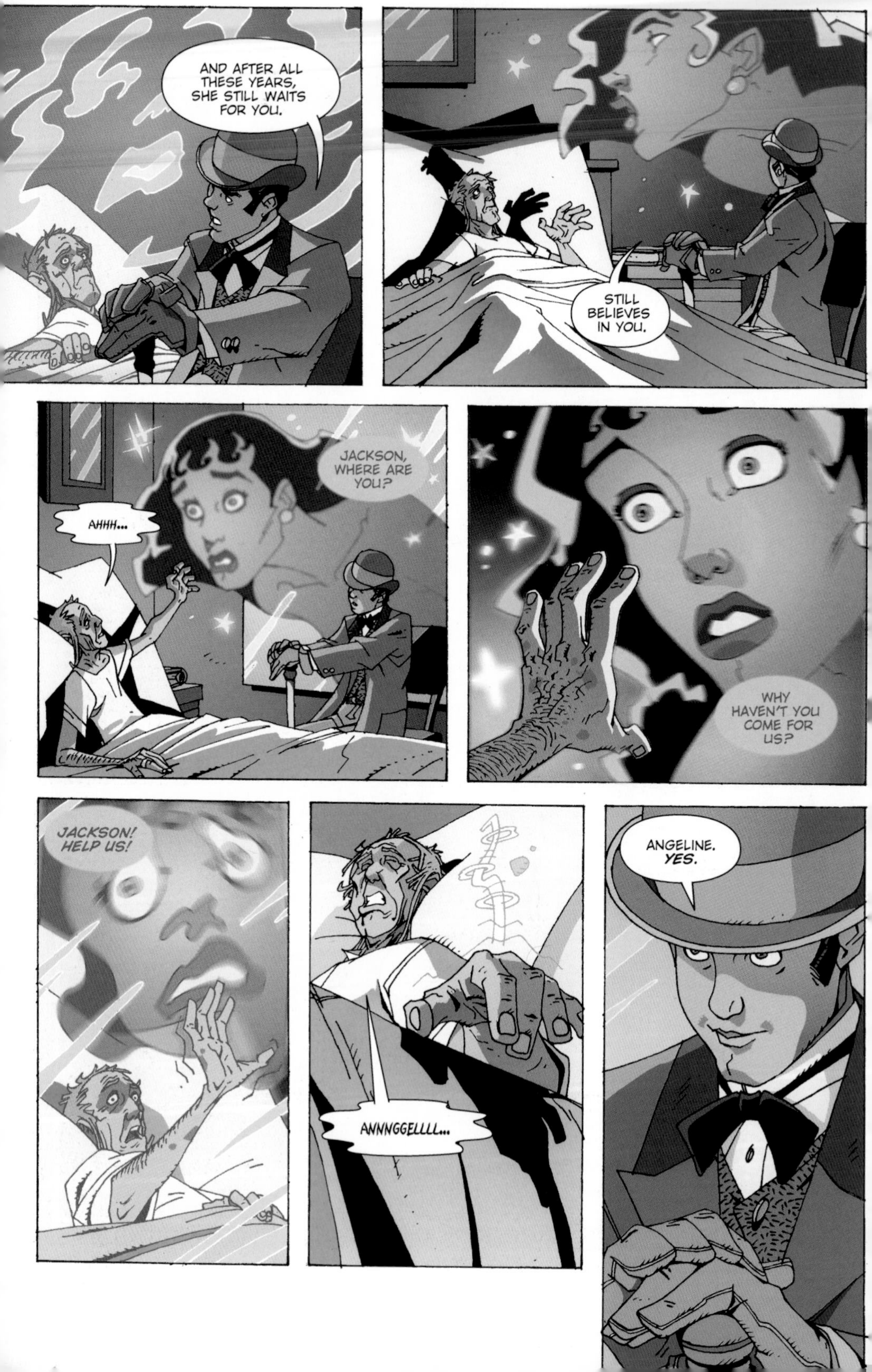
AND AFTER ALL THESE YEARS, SHE STILL WAITS FOR YOU.
STILL BELIEVES IN YOU.
JACKSON, WHERE ARE YOU?
AHHH...
WHY HAVEN'T YOU COME FOR US?
JACKSON! HELP US!
ANNNGGELLLL...
ANGELINE. YES.

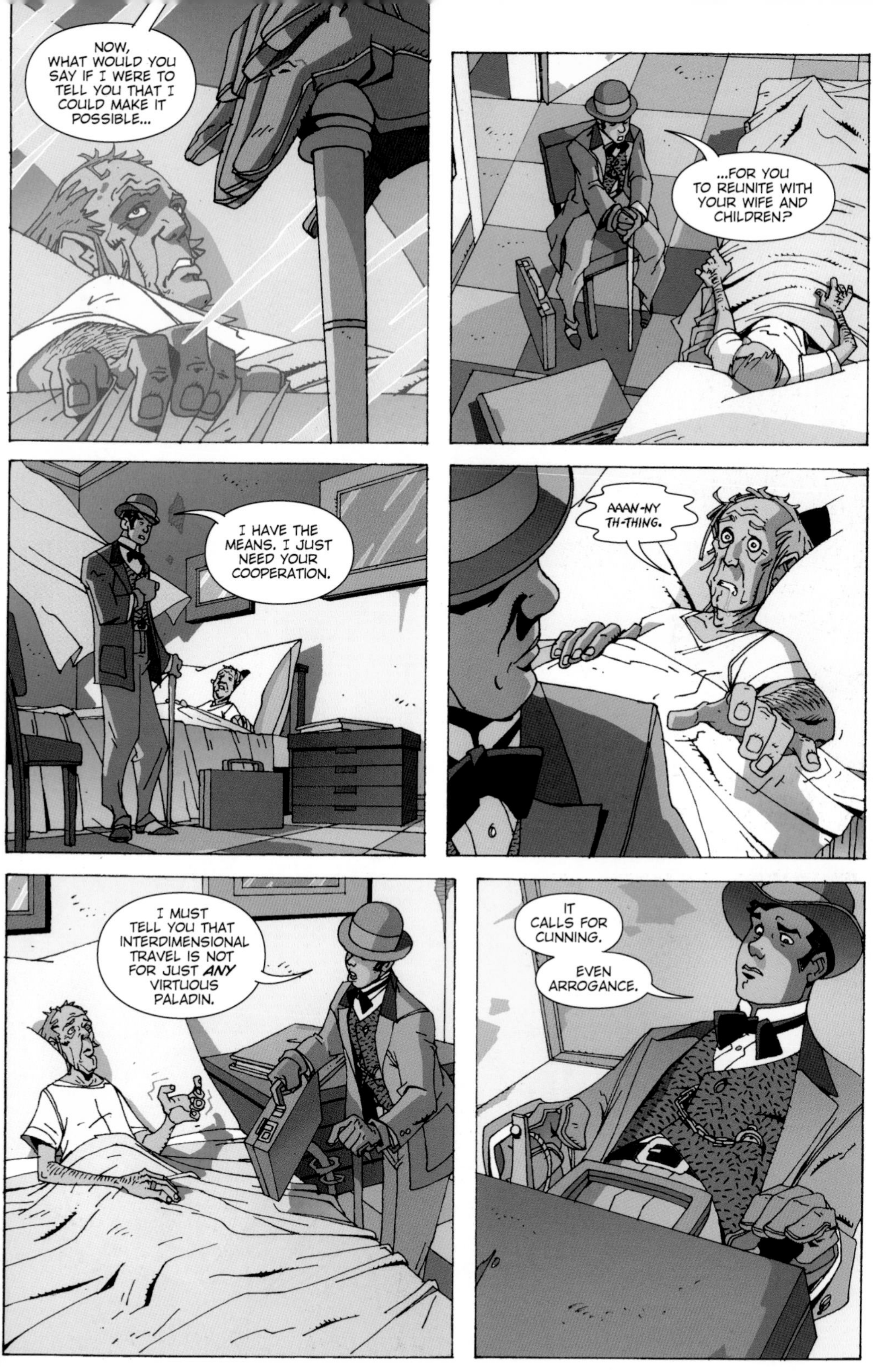
NOW, WHAT WOULD YOU SAY IF I WERE TO TELL YOU THAT I COULD MAKE IT POSSIBLE...
...FOR YOU TO REUNITE WITH YOUR WIFE AND CHILDREN?
I HAVE THE MEANS. I JUST NEED YOUR COOPERATION.
AAAN-NY TH-THING.
I MUST TELL YOU THAT INTERDIMENSIONAL TRAVEL IS NOT FOR JUST *ANY* VIRTUOUS PALADIN.
IT CALLS FOR CUNNING.
EVEN ARROGANCE.

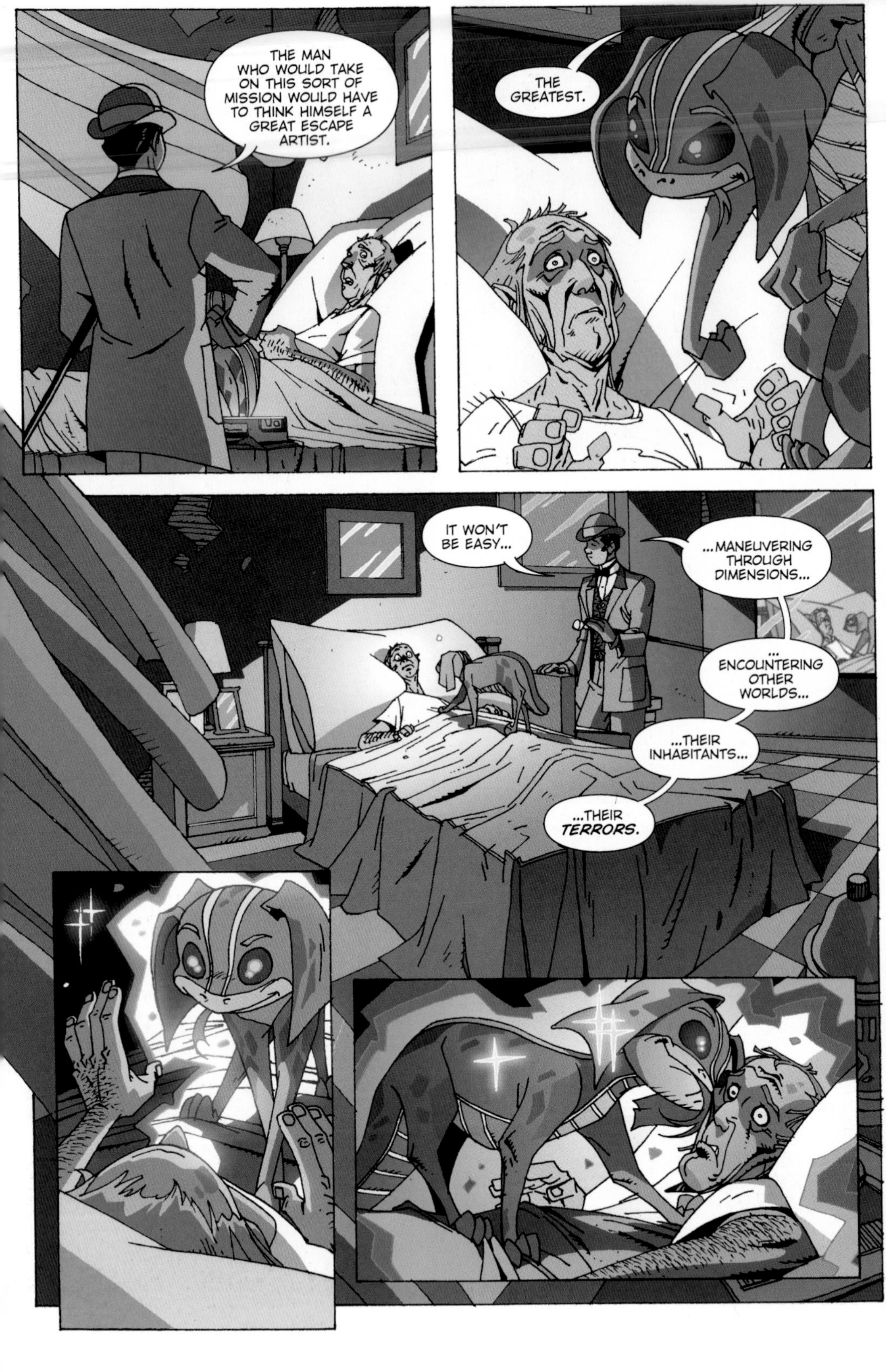
THE MAN WHO WOULD TAKE ON THIS SORT OF MISSION WOULD HAVE TO THINK HIMSELF A GREAT ESCAPE ARTIST.
THE GREATEST.
IT WON'T BE EASY...
...MANEUVERING THROUGH DIMENSIONS...
... ENCOUNTERING OTHER WORLDS...
...THEIR INHABITANTS...
...THEIR *TERRORS*.

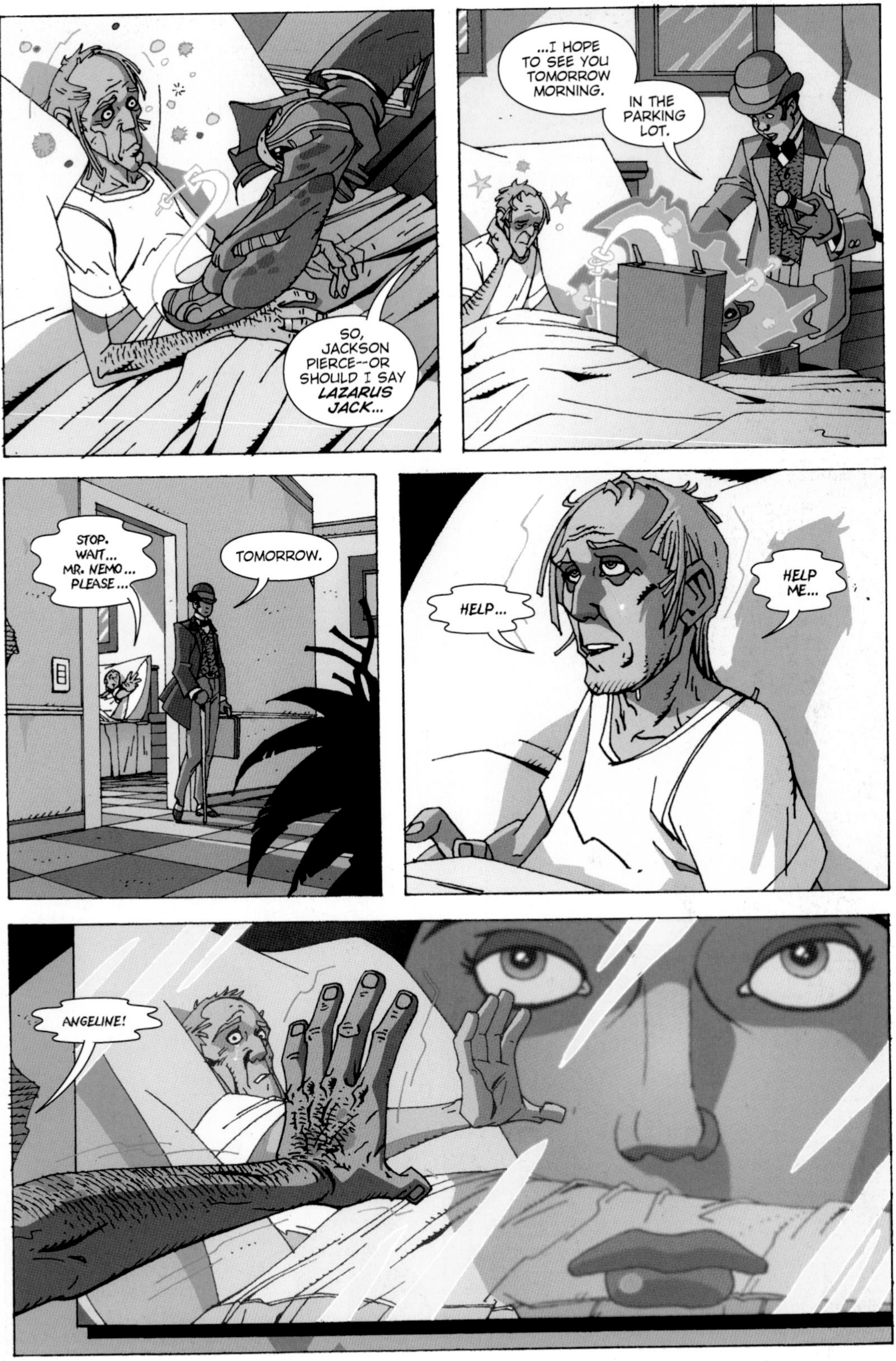
SO, JACKSON PIERCE--OR SHOULD I SAY *LAZARUS JACK*...
...I HOPE TO SEE YOU TOMORROW MORNING.
IN THE PARKING LOT.
STOP. WAIT... MR. NEMO... PLEASE...
TOMORROW.
HELP...
HELP ME...
ANGELINE!

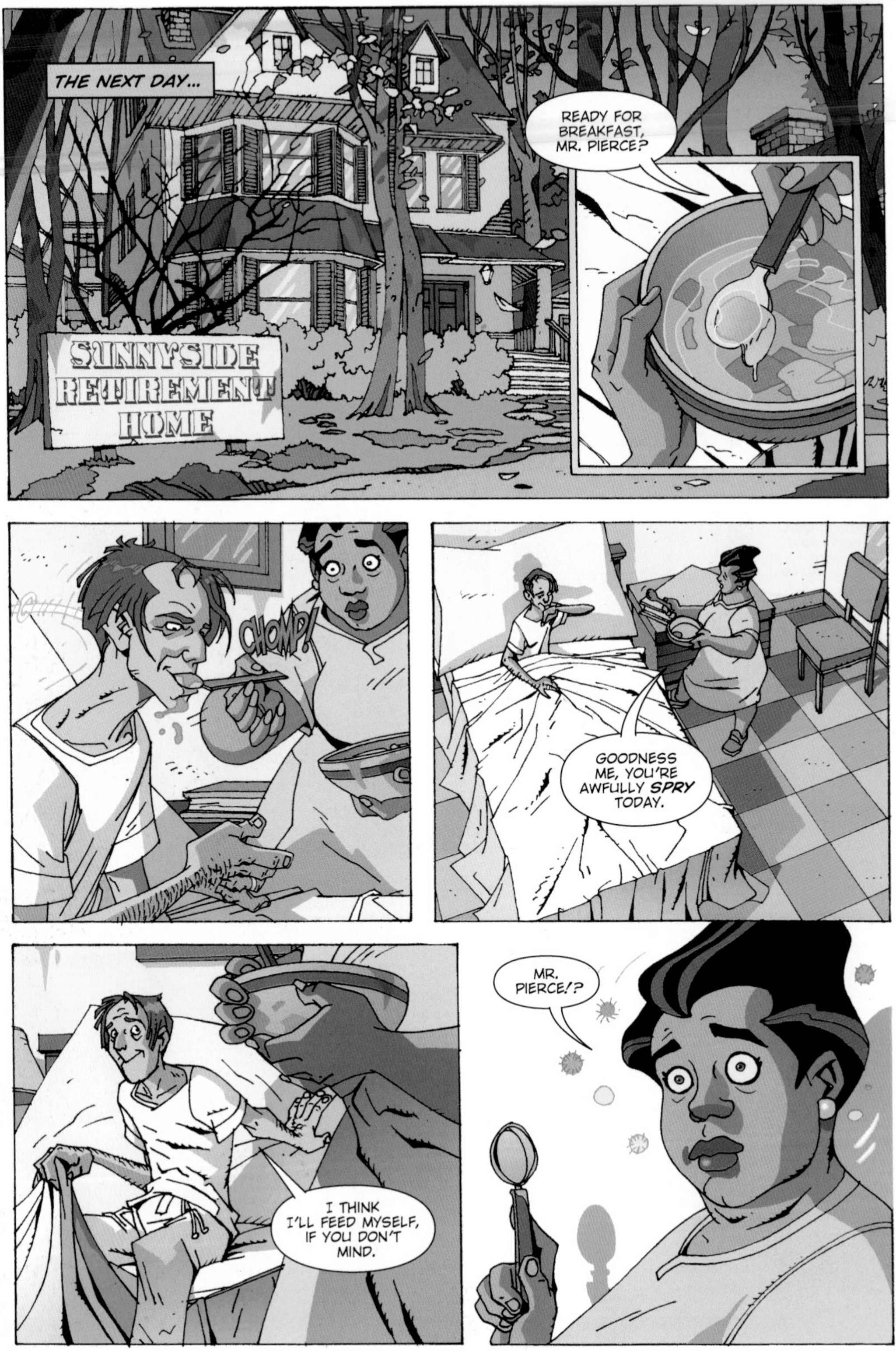
THE NEXT DAY...
SUNNYSIDE RETIREMENT HOME
READY FOR BREAKFAST, MR. PIERCE?
CHOMP!
GOODNESS ME, YOU'RE AWFULLY SPRY TODAY.
I THINK I'LL FEED MYSELF, IF YOU DON'T MIND.
MR. PIERCE!?

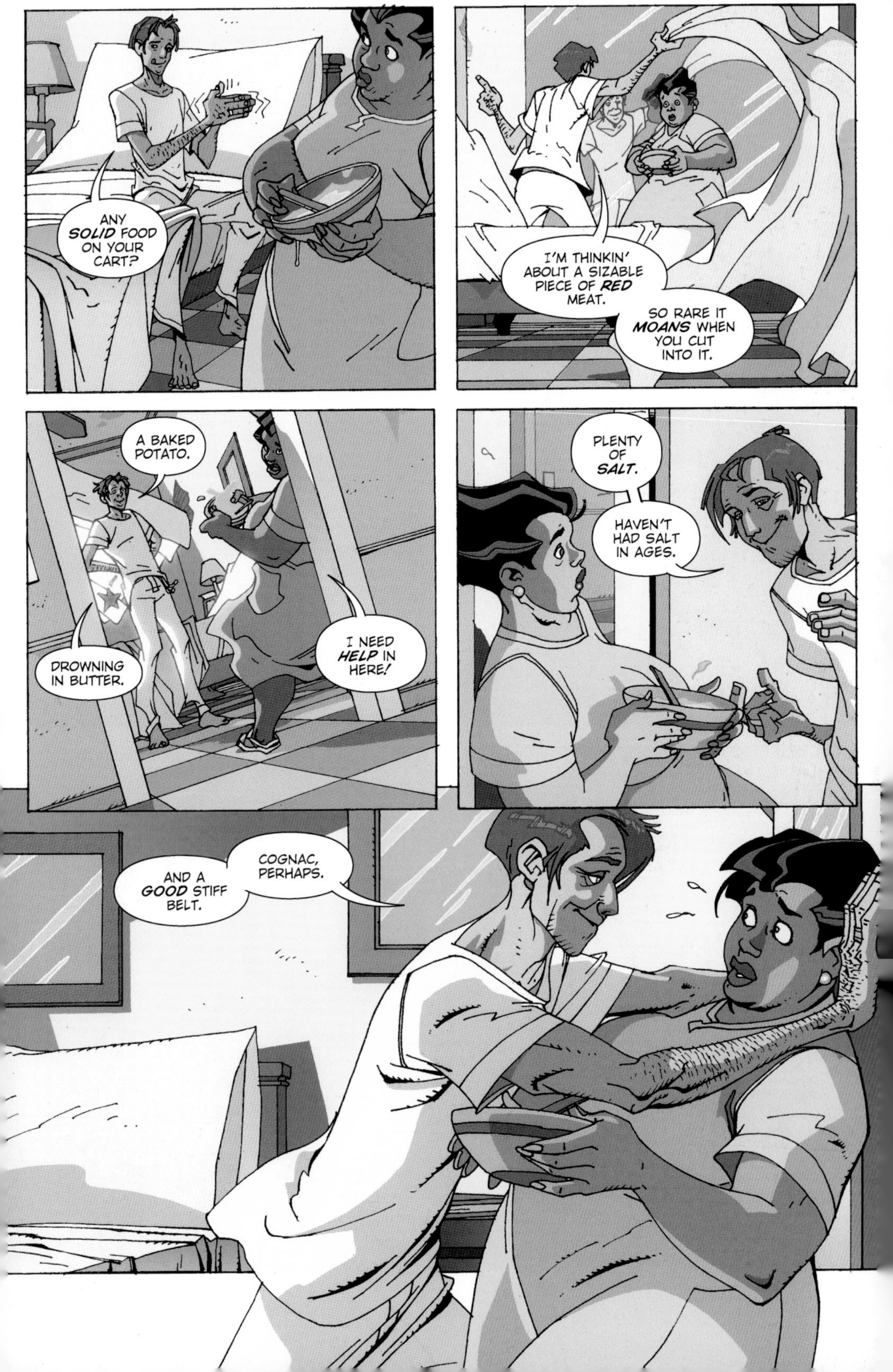
ANY *SOLID* FOOD ON YOUR CART?
I'M THINKIN' ABOUT A SIZABLE PIECE OF *RED* MEAT.
SO RARE IT *MOANS* WHEN YOU CUT INTO IT.
A BAKED POTATO.
DROWNING IN BUTTER.
I NEED *HELP* IN HERE!
PLENTY OF *SALT*.
HAVEN'T HAD SALT IN AGES.
AND A *GOOD* STIFF BELT.
COGNAC, PERHAPS.

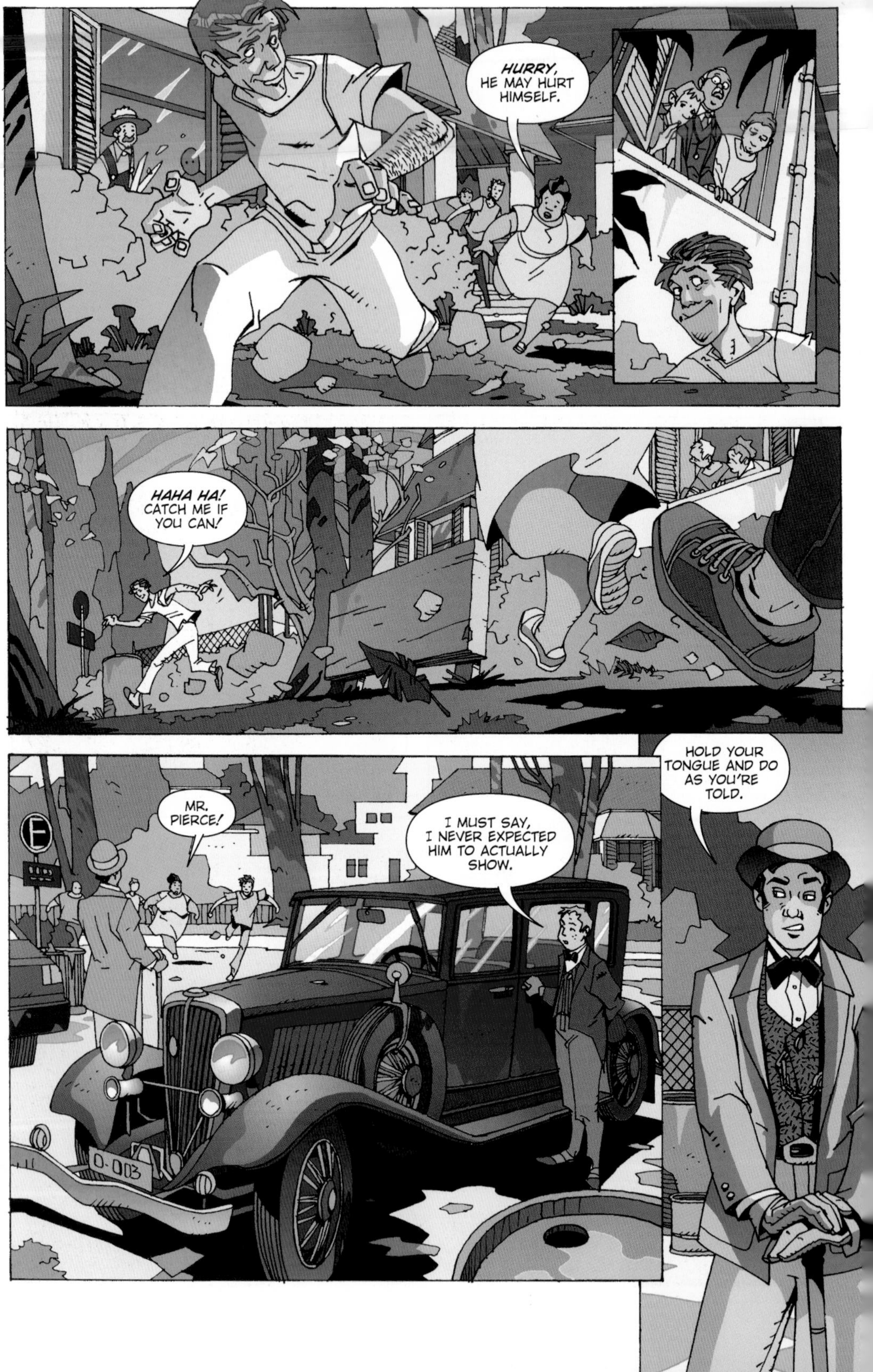
HURRY, HE MAY HURT HIMSELF.
HAHA HA! CATCH ME IF YOU CAN!
MR. PIERCE!
I MUST SAY, I NEVER EXPECTED HIM TO ACTUALLY SHOW.
HOLD YOUR TONGUE AND DO AS YOU'RE TOLD.
O-003

THIS IS *AMAZING!*

YOU *OKAY*, MR. PIERCE?

THAT CAN'T BE HIM.

I DON'T KNOW HOW YOU DID THIS, MR. NEMO...

...BUT I'M *YOUNG* AGAIN...

...I HAVE *HOPE,* AND I'M TRULY GRATEFUL.

MR. JACKSON ALAIN PIERCE, IF YOU WOULD, SIR...

CALL ME JACKSON.

...PLEASE *SIGN* THE DOTTED LINE.

THIS IS YOUR REASON FOR HELPING ME?

YOU WANT ME TO BRING BACK SOME KINDA *GLOVE?*

A RELIC. A UNIQUE ARTIFACT. THAT'S WHAT I REQUIRE.

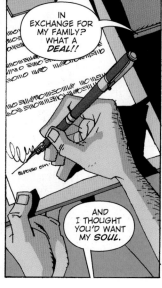

IN EXCHANGE FOR MY FAMILY? WHAT A *DEAL!!*

AND I THOUGHT YOU'D WANT MY *SOUL.*

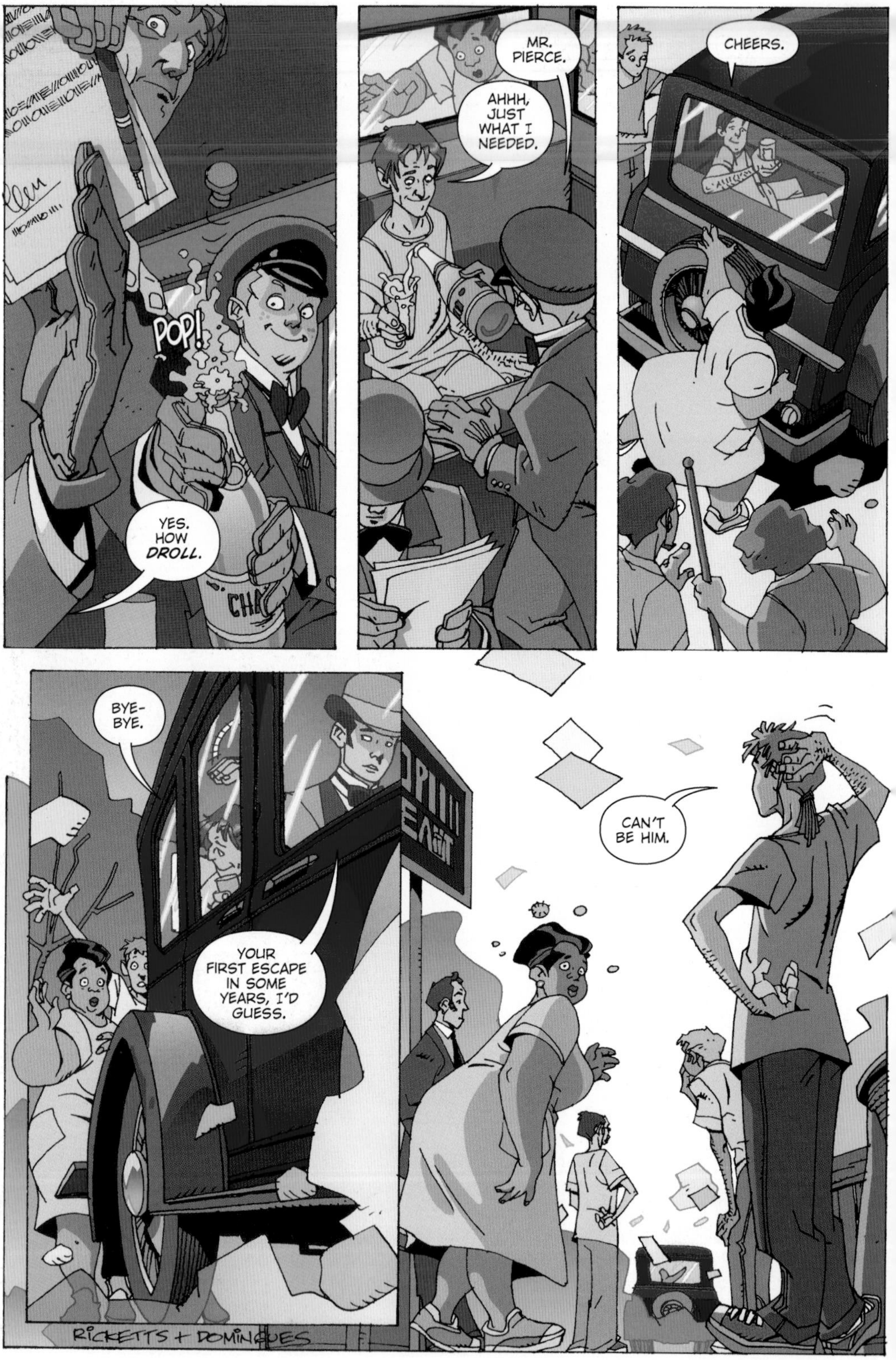

POP!
YES. HOW *DROLL*.
MR. PIERCE.
AHHH, JUST WHAT I NEEDED.
CHEERS.
BYE-BYE.
YOUR FIRST ESCAPE IN SOME YEARS, I'D GUESS.
CAN'T BE HIM.
RICKETTS + DOMINGUES

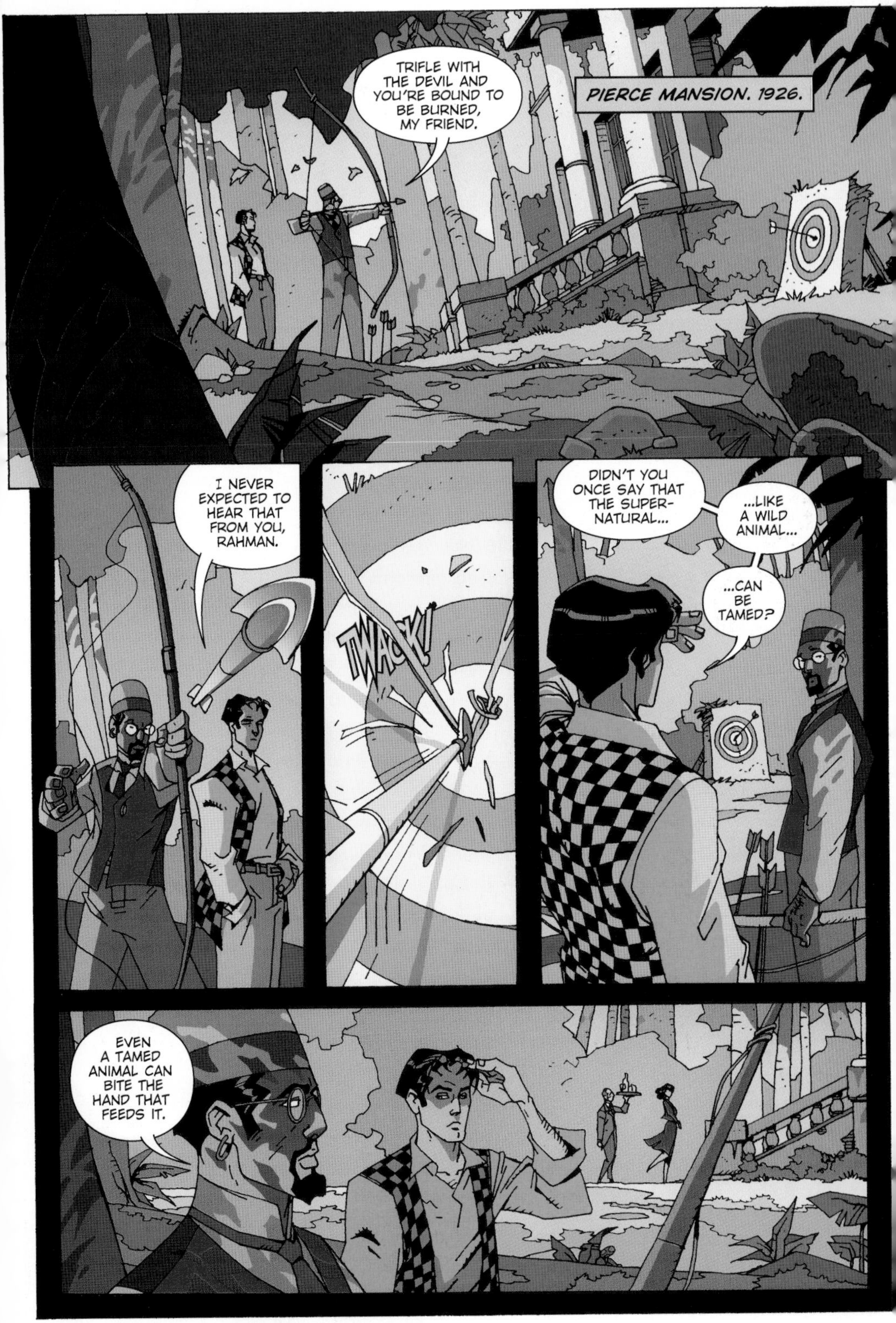
PIERCE MANSION. 1926.
TRIFLE WITH THE DEVIL AND YOU'RE BOUND TO BE BURNED, MY FRIEND.
I NEVER EXPECTED TO HEAR THAT FROM YOU, RAHMAN.
TWACK!
DIDN'T YOU ONCE SAY THAT THE SUPER-NATURAL...
...LIKE A WILD ANIMAL...
...CAN BE TAMED?
EVEN A TAMED ANIMAL CAN BITE THE HAND THAT FEEDS IT.

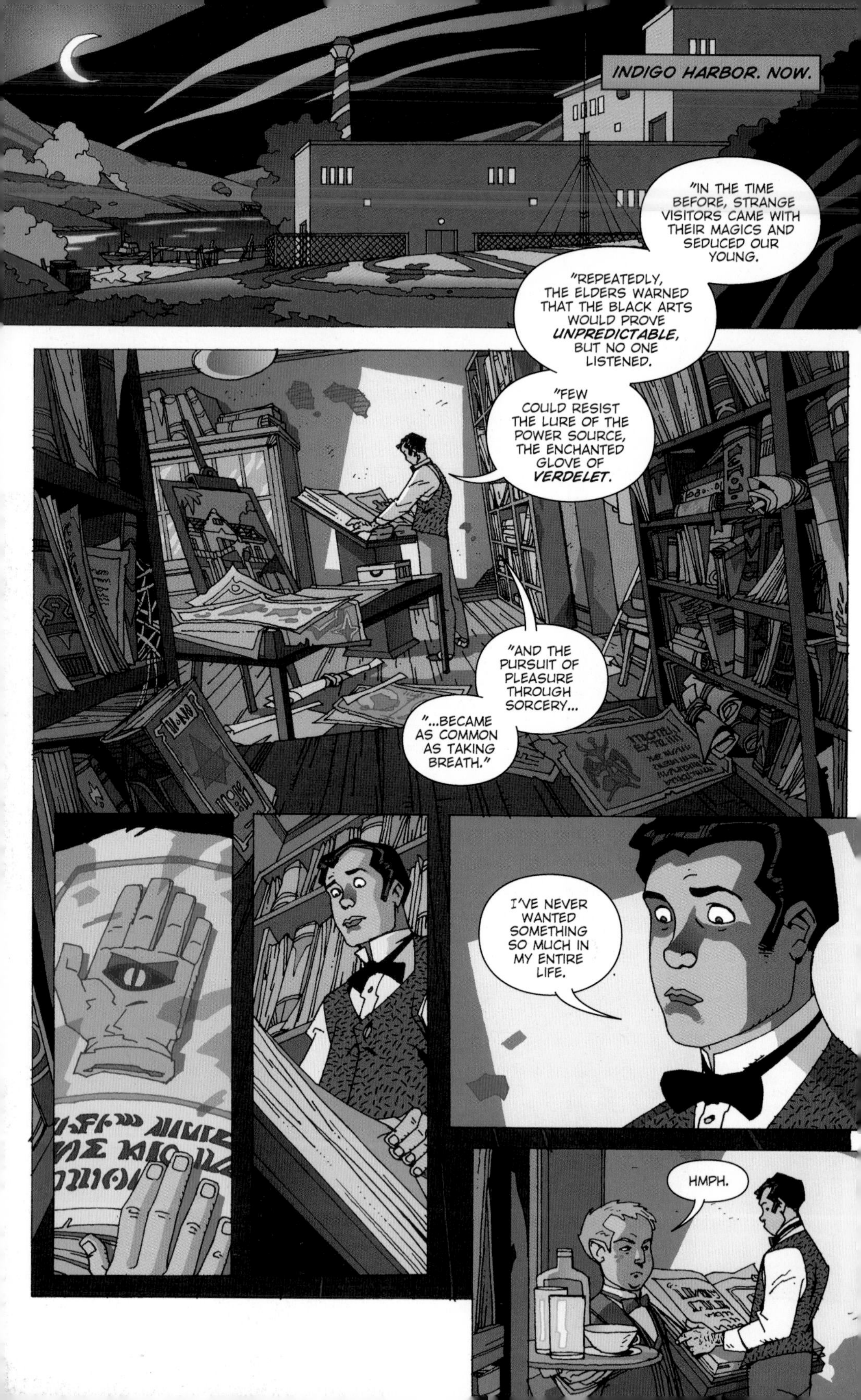
INDIGO HARBOR. NOW.
"IN THE TIME BEFORE, STRANGE VISITORS CAME WITH THEIR MAGICS AND SEDUCED OUR YOUNG.
"REPEATEDLY, THE ELDERS WARNED THAT THE BLACK ARTS WOULD PROVE UNPREDICTABLE, BUT NO ONE LISTENED.
"FEW COULD RESIST THE LURE OF THE POWER SOURCE, THE ENCHANTED GLOVE OF VERDELET.
"AND THE PURSUIT OF PLEASURE THROUGH SORCERY...
"...BECAME AS COMMON AS TAKING BREATH."
I'VE NEVER WANTED SOMETHING SO MUCH IN MY ENTIRE LIFE.
HMPH.

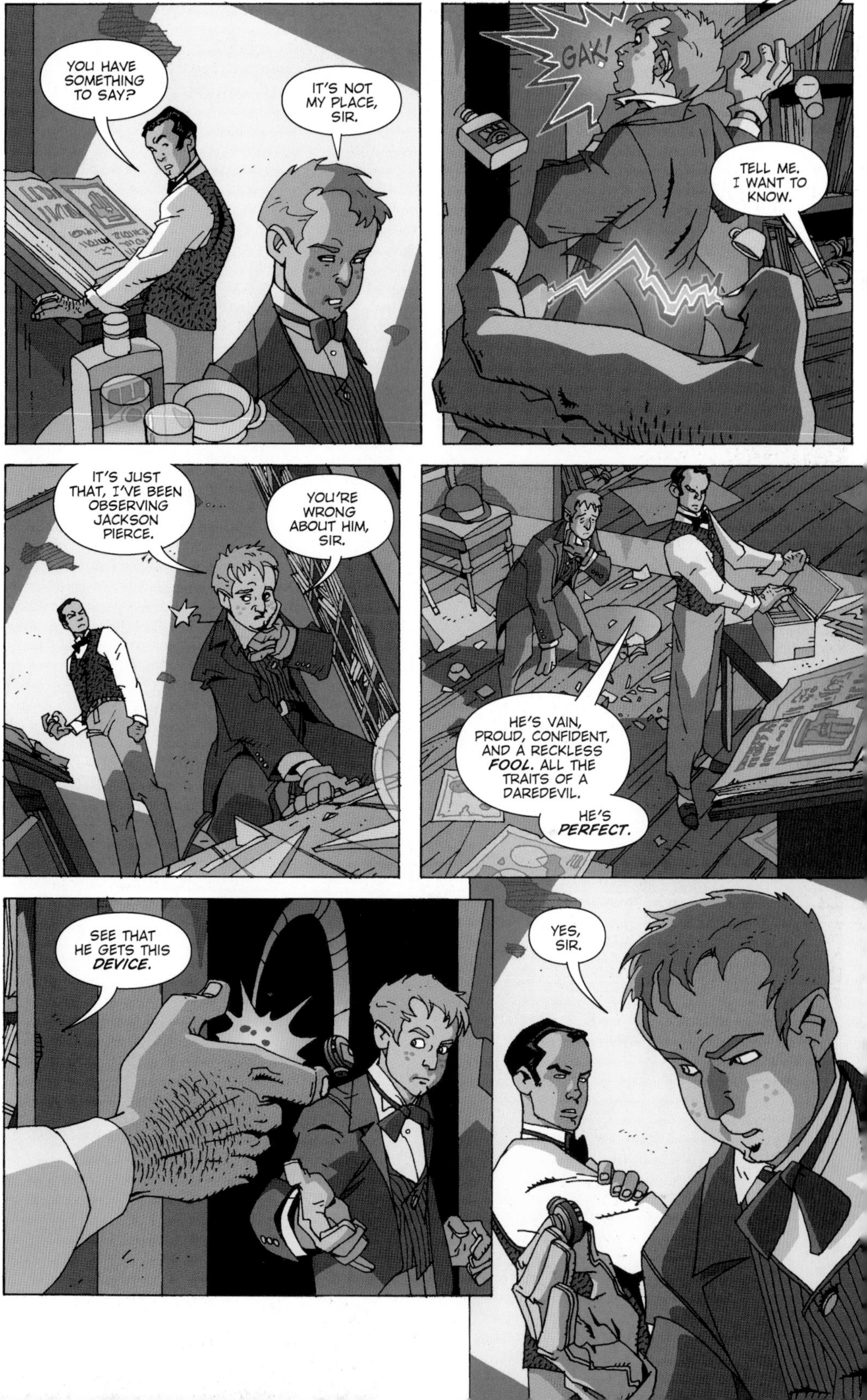
YOU HAVE SOMETHING TO SAY?
IT'S NOT MY PLACE, SIR.
GAK!
TELL ME. I WANT TO KNOW.
IT'S JUST THAT, I'VE BEEN OBSERVING JACKSON PIERCE.
YOU'RE WRONG ABOUT HIM, SIR.
HE'S VAIN, PROUD, CONFIDENT, AND A RECKLESS FOOL. ALL THE TRAITS OF A DAREDEVIL.
HE'S PERFECT.
SEE THAT HE GETS THIS DEVICE.
YES, SIR.

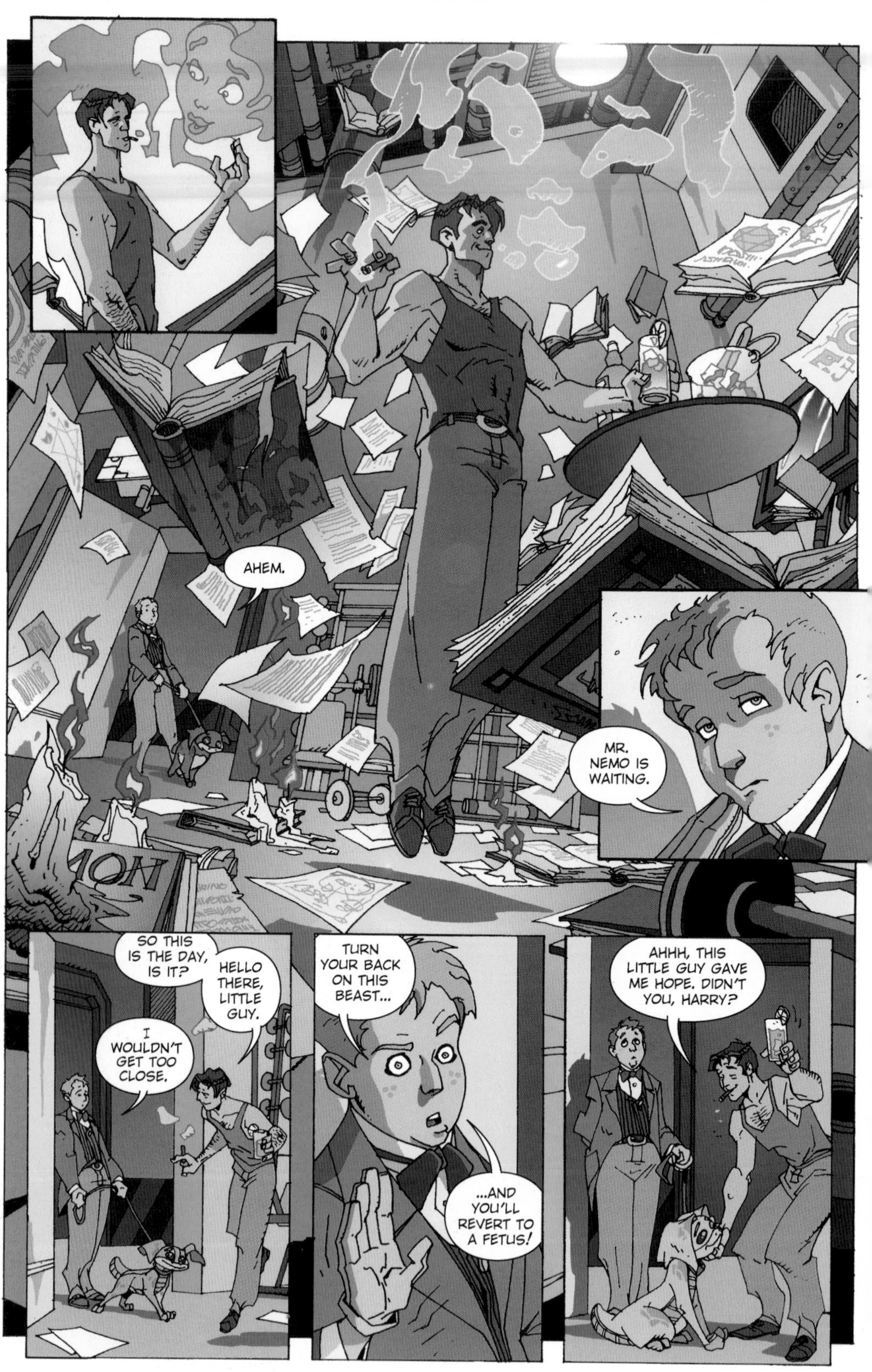
AHEM.
MR. NEMO IS WAITING.
SO THIS IS THE DAY, IS IT?
HELLO THERE, LITTLE GUY.
I WOULDN'T GET TOO CLOSE.
TURN YOUR BACK ON THIS BEAST...
...AND YOU'LL REVERT TO A FETUS!
AHHH, THIS LITTLE GUY GAVE ME HOPE. DIDN'T YOU, HARRY?

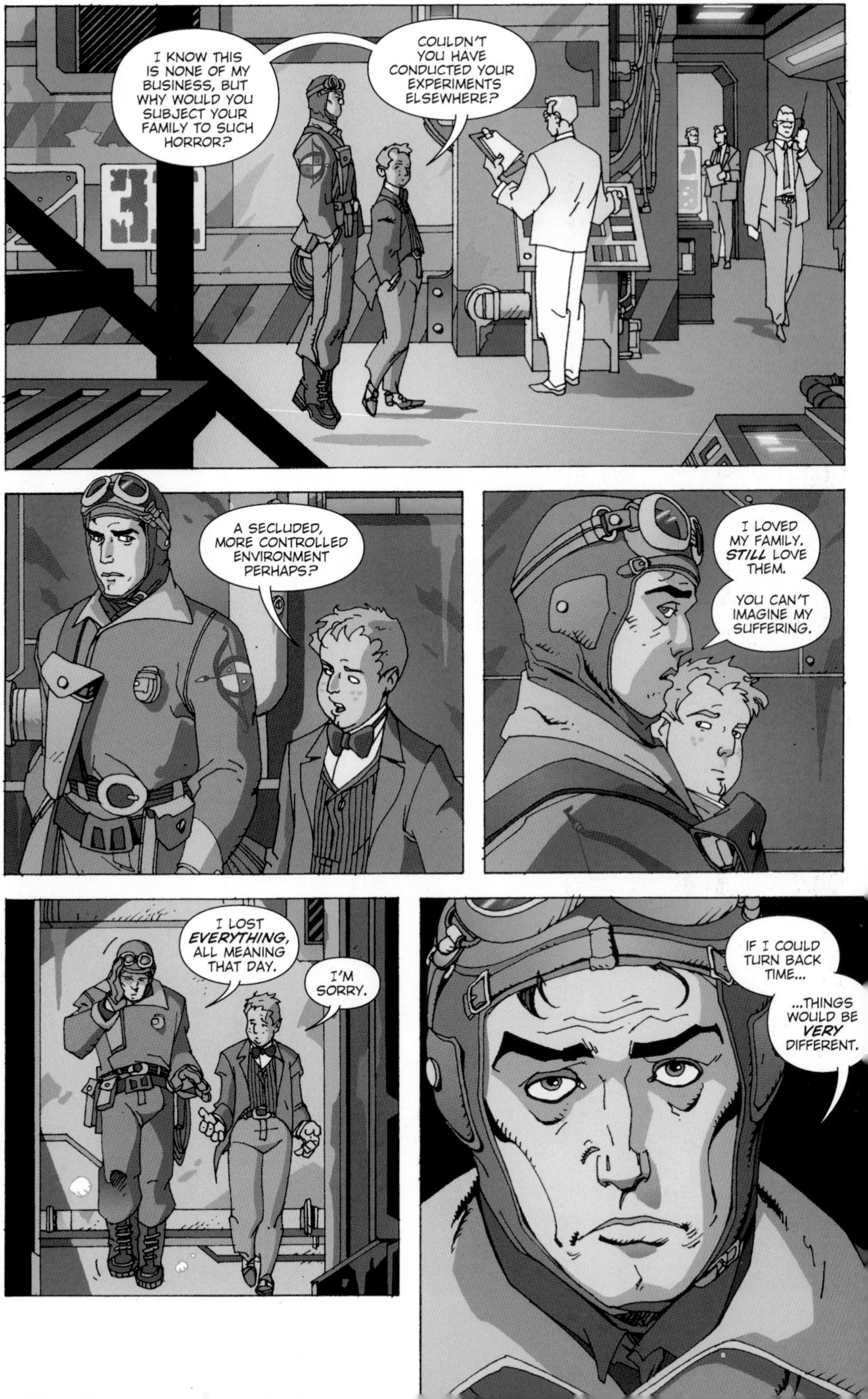
I KNOW THIS IS NONE OF MY BUSINESS, BUT WHY WOULD YOU SUBJECT YOUR FAMILY TO SUCH HORROR?
COULDN'T YOU HAVE CONDUCTED YOUR EXPERIMENTS ELSEWHERE?
A SECLUDED, MORE CONTROLLED ENVIRONMENT PERHAPS?
I LOVED MY FAMILY. STILL LOVE THEM.
YOU CAN'T IMAGINE MY SUFFERING.
I LOST EVERYTHING, ALL MEANING THAT DAY.
I'M SORRY.
IF I COULD TURN BACK TIME...
...THINGS WOULD BE VERY DIFFERENT.

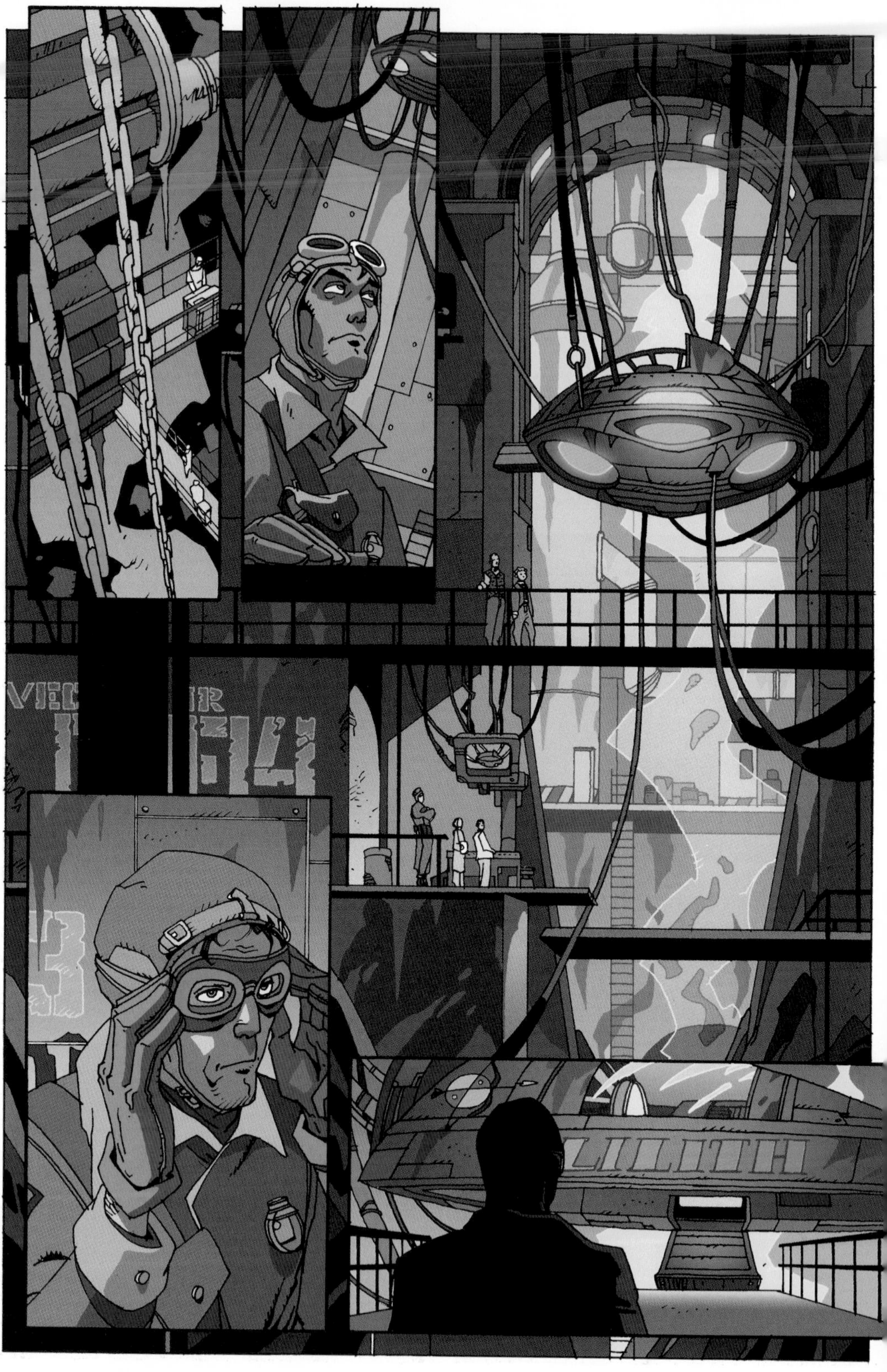
LILITH

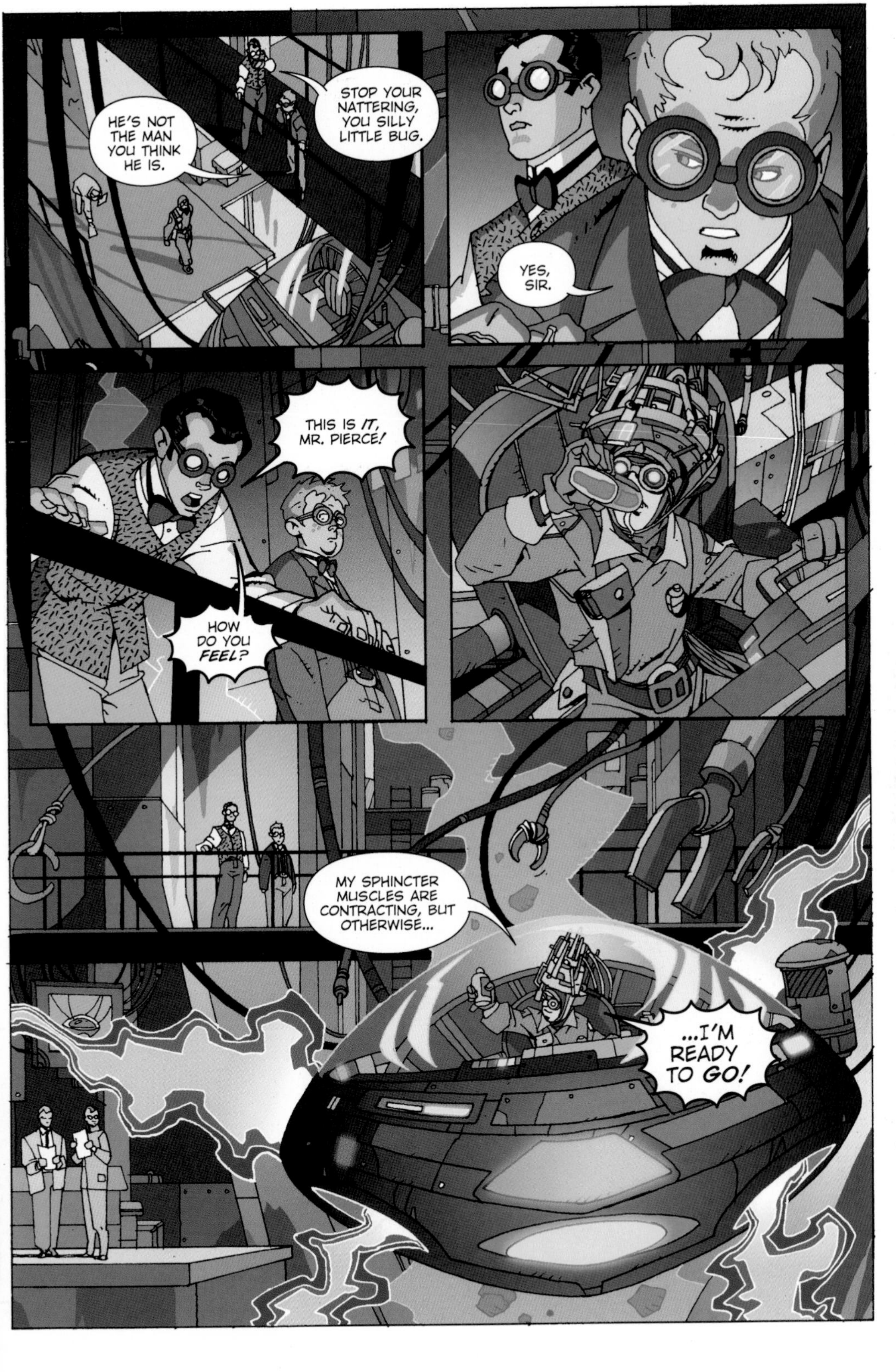
HE'S NOT THE MAN YOU THINK HE IS.
STOP YOUR NATTERING, YOU SILLY LITTLE BUG.
YES, SIR.
THIS IS *IT*, MR. PIERCE!
HOW DO YOU *FEEL*?
MY SPHINCTER MUSCLES ARE CONTRACTING, BUT OTHERWISE...
...I'M READY TO *GO*!

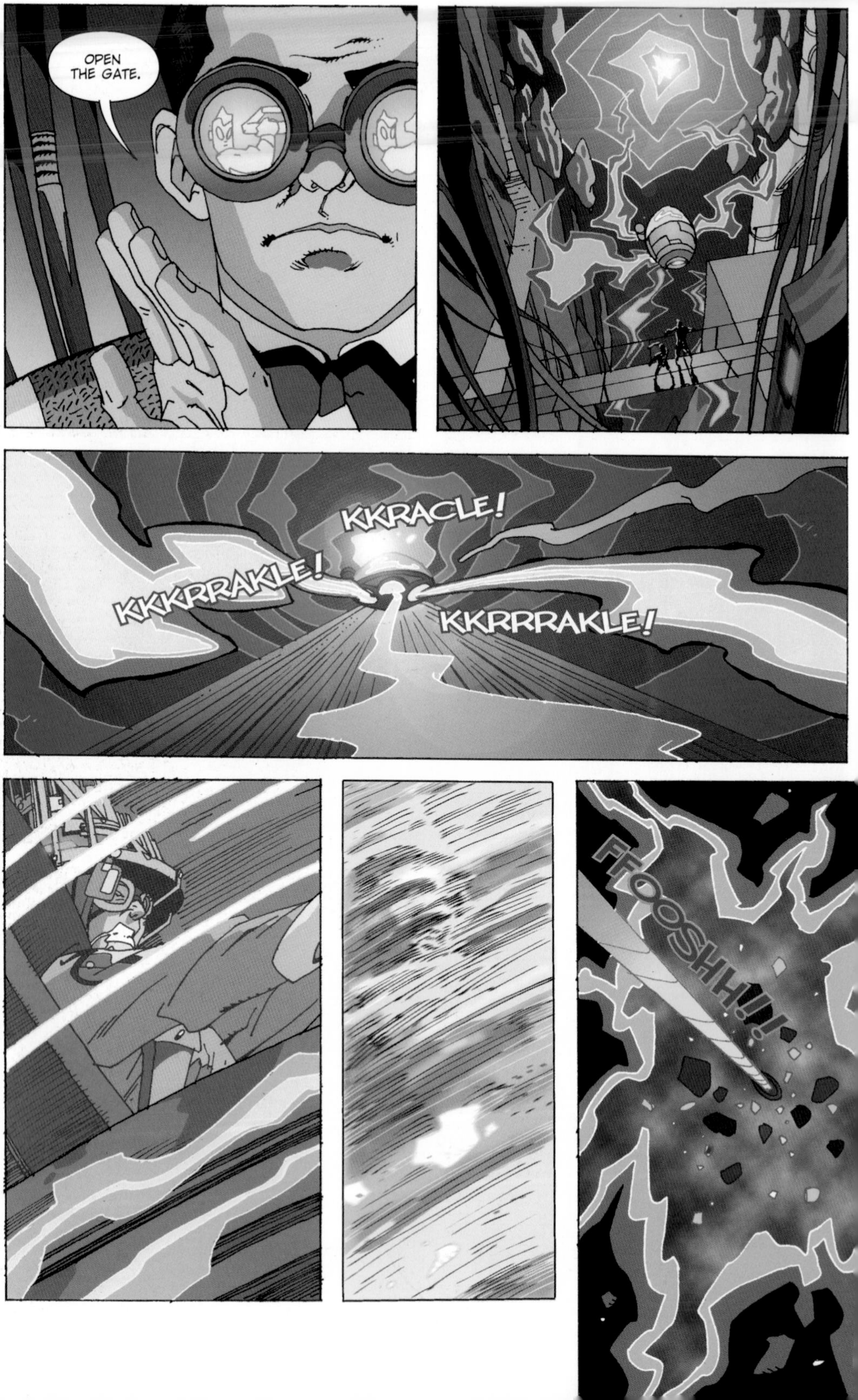
OPEN THE GATE.
KKRACLE!
KKKRRAKLE!
KKRRRAKLE!
FFOOSHH!!!!

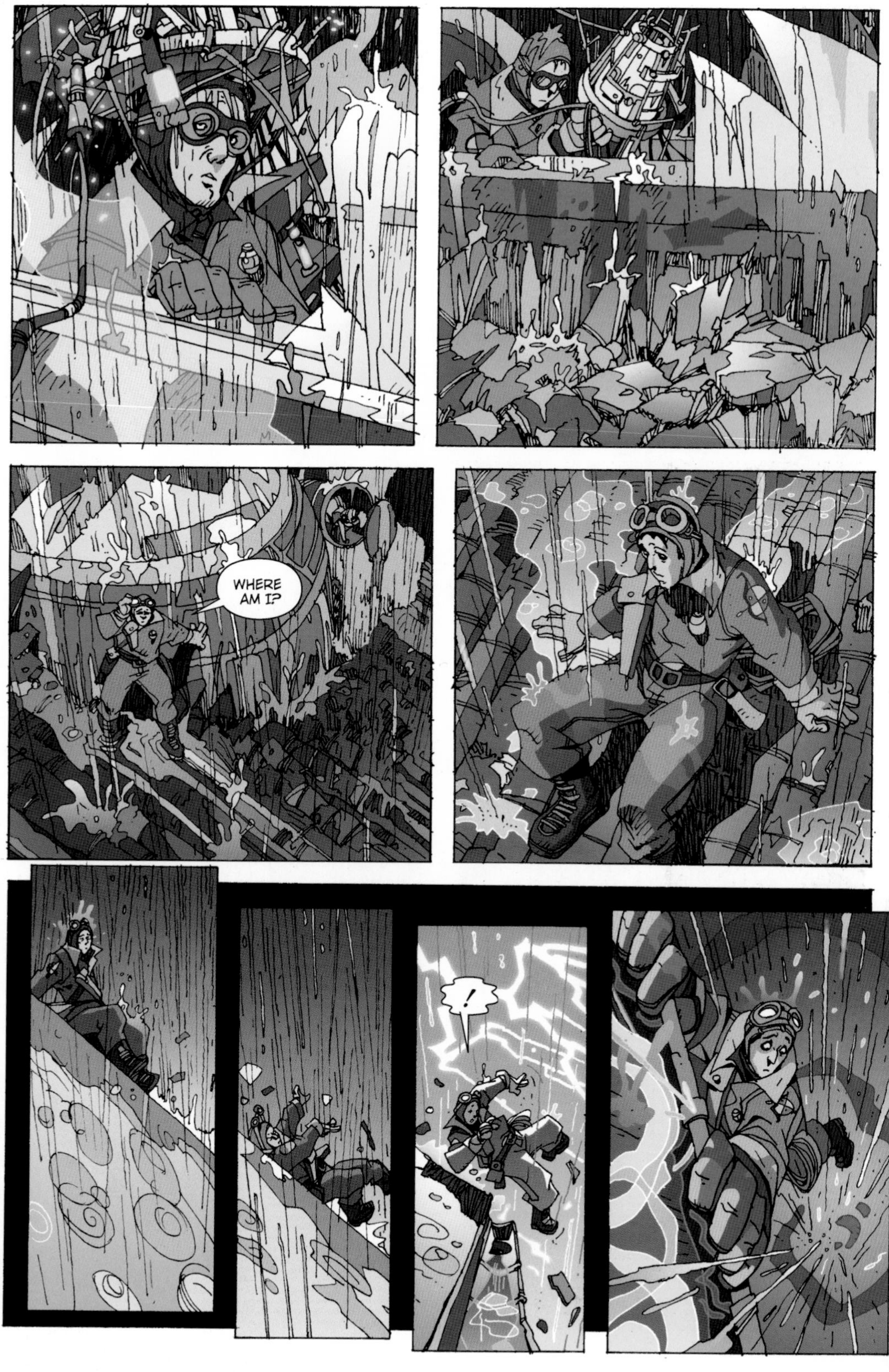
WHERE AM I?
!

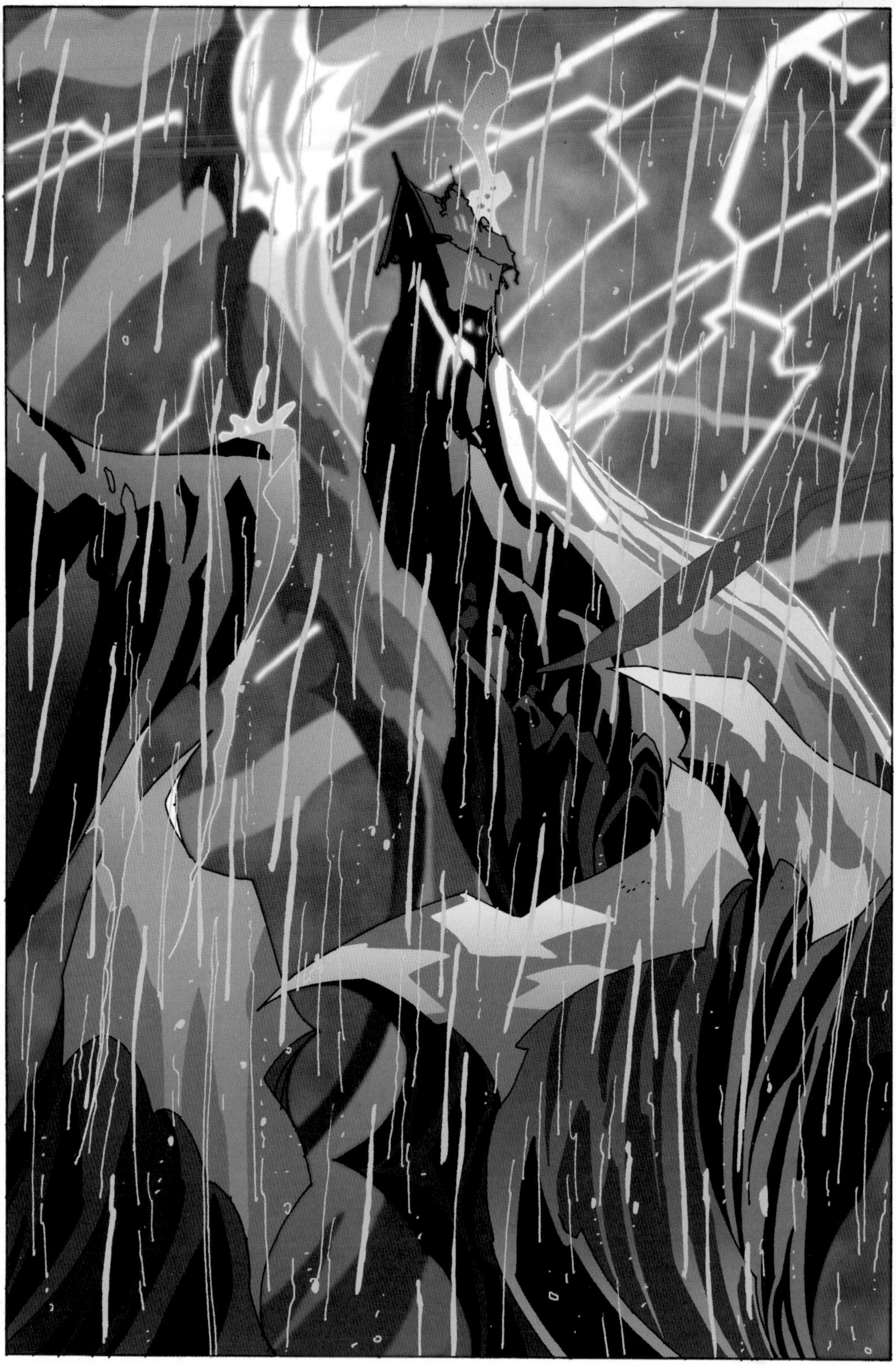

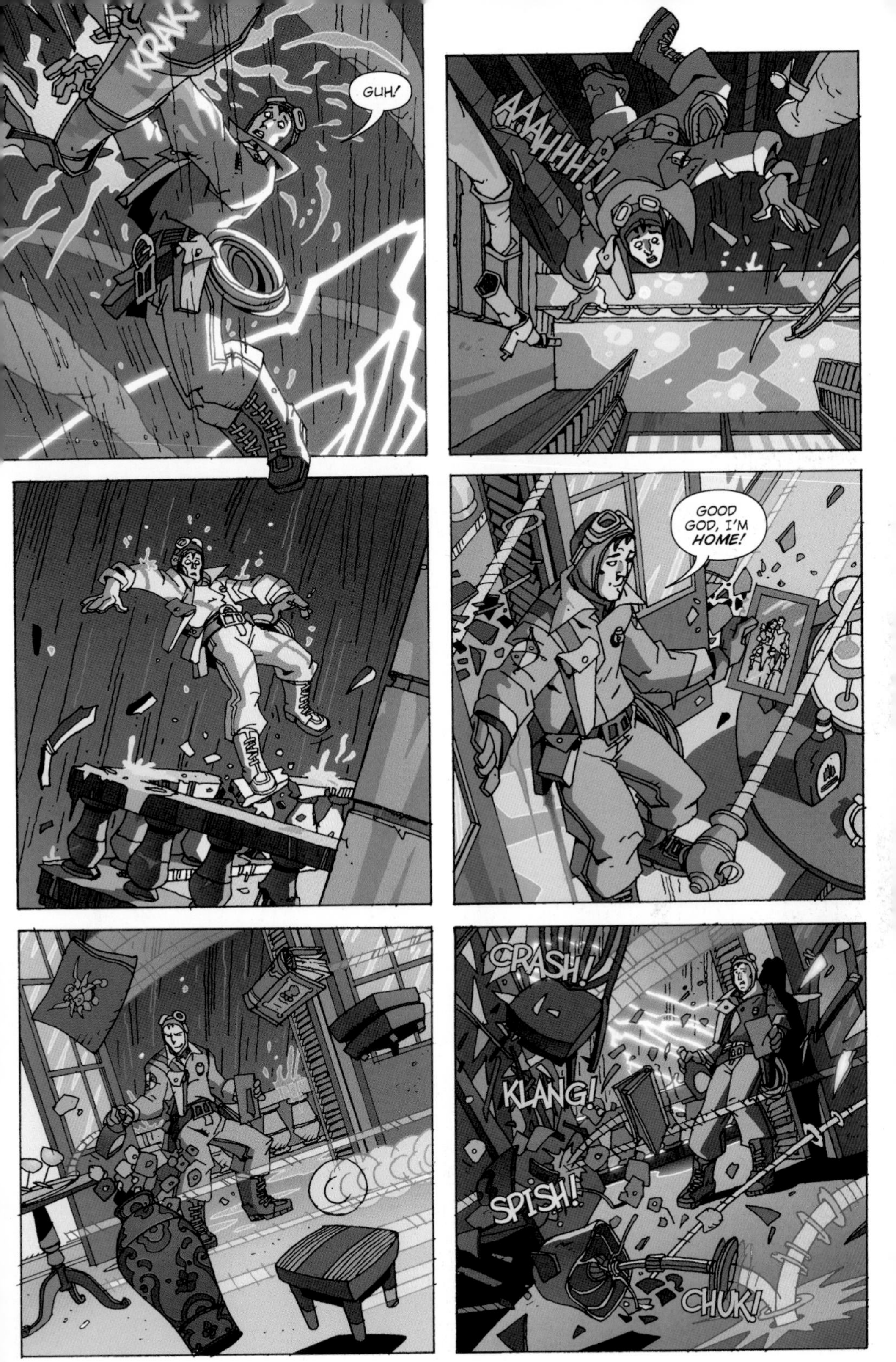
KRAK!
GUH!
AAAHHH!!
GOOD GOD, I'M *HOME!*
CRASH!
KLANG!
SPISH!
CHUK!

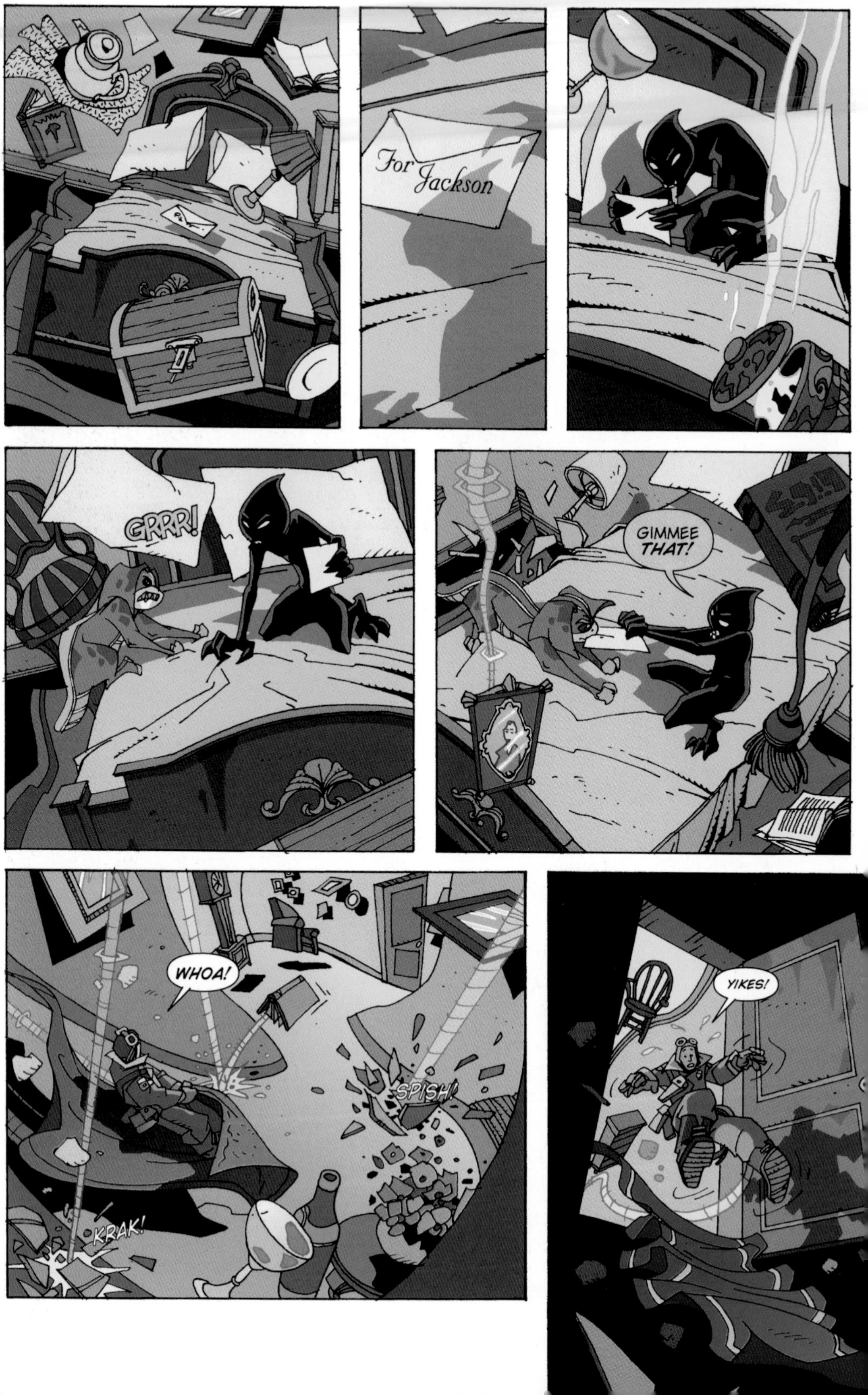
For Jackson
GRRR!
GIMMEE THAT!
WHOA!
SPISH!
KRAK!
YIKES!

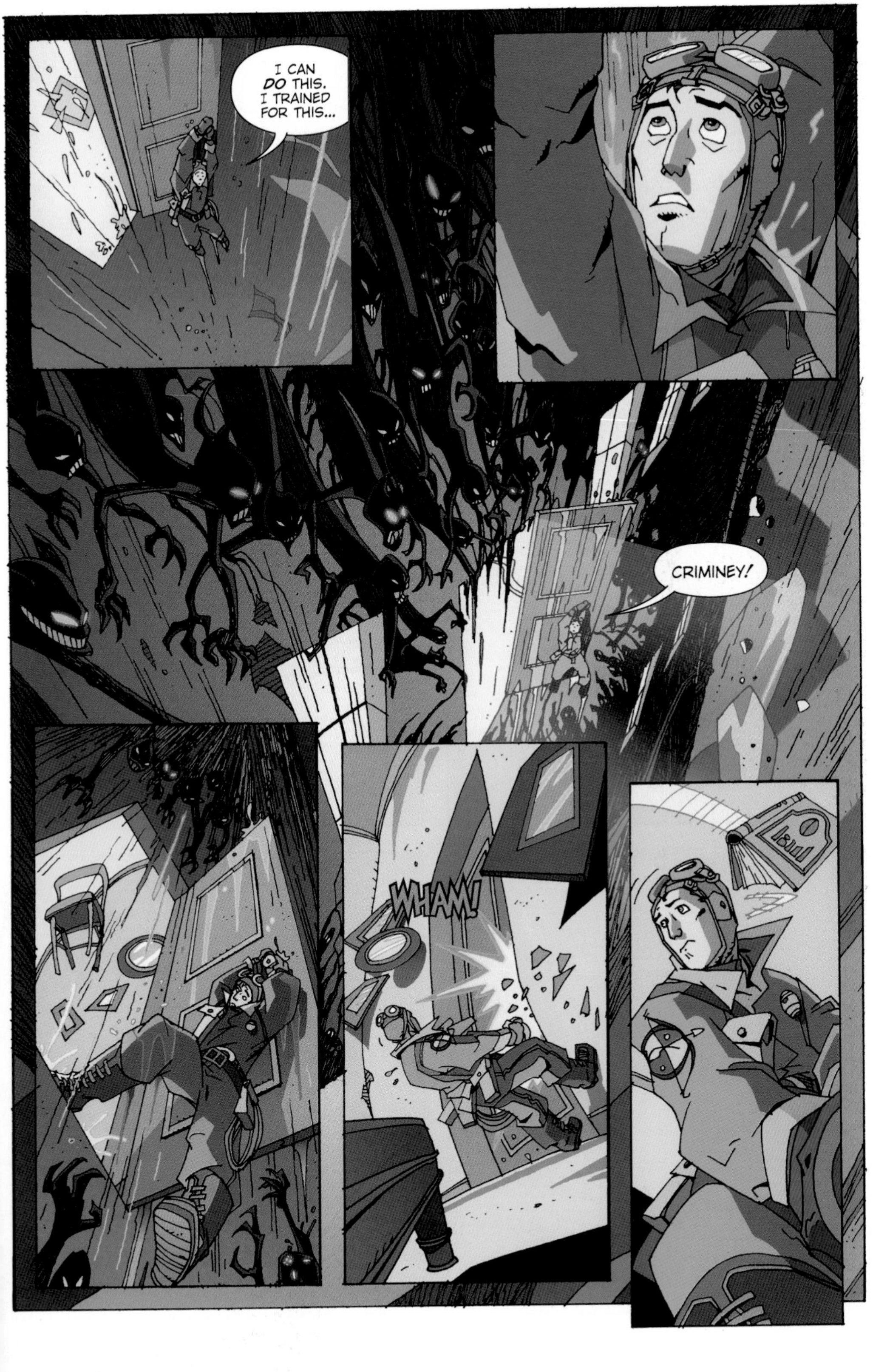
I CAN DO THIS. I TRAINED FOR THIS...
CRIMINEY!
WHAM!

IS THAT YOU, HARRY?
GLUB!
HARRY!!

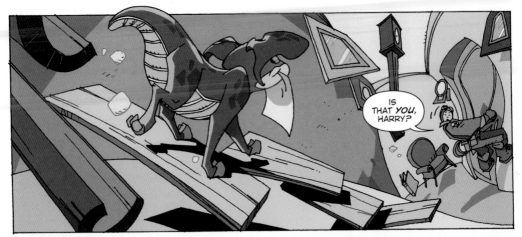

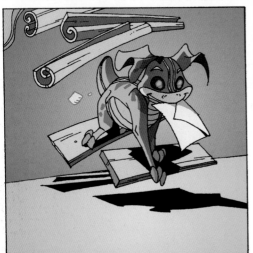

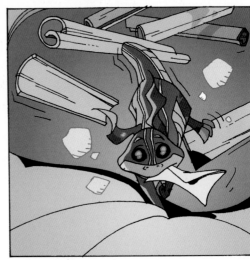

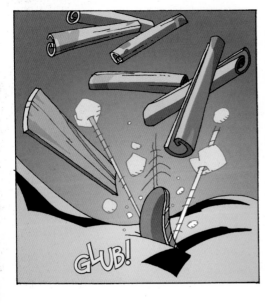

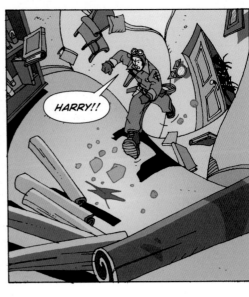

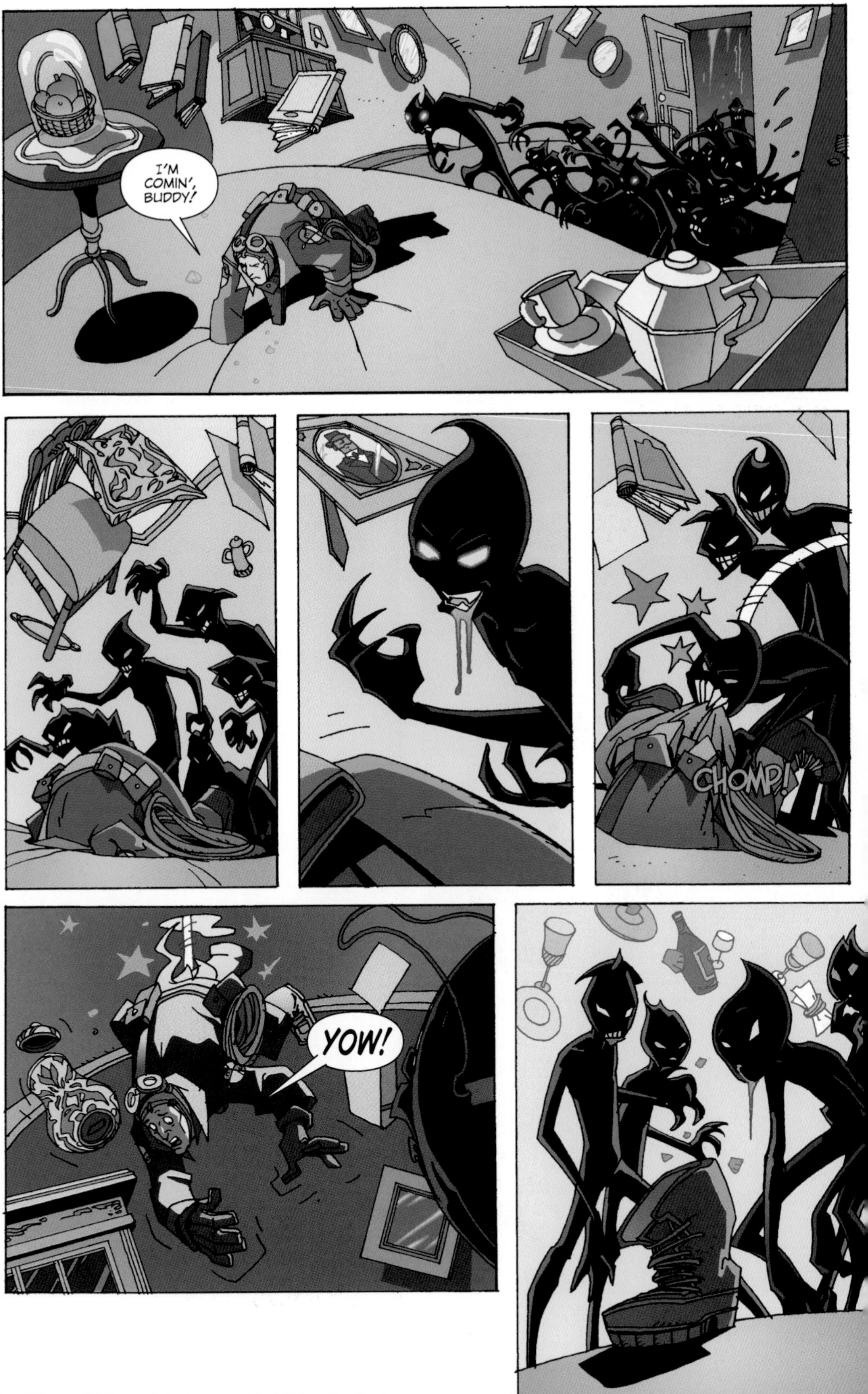
I'M COMIN', BUDDY!
CHOMP!
YOW!

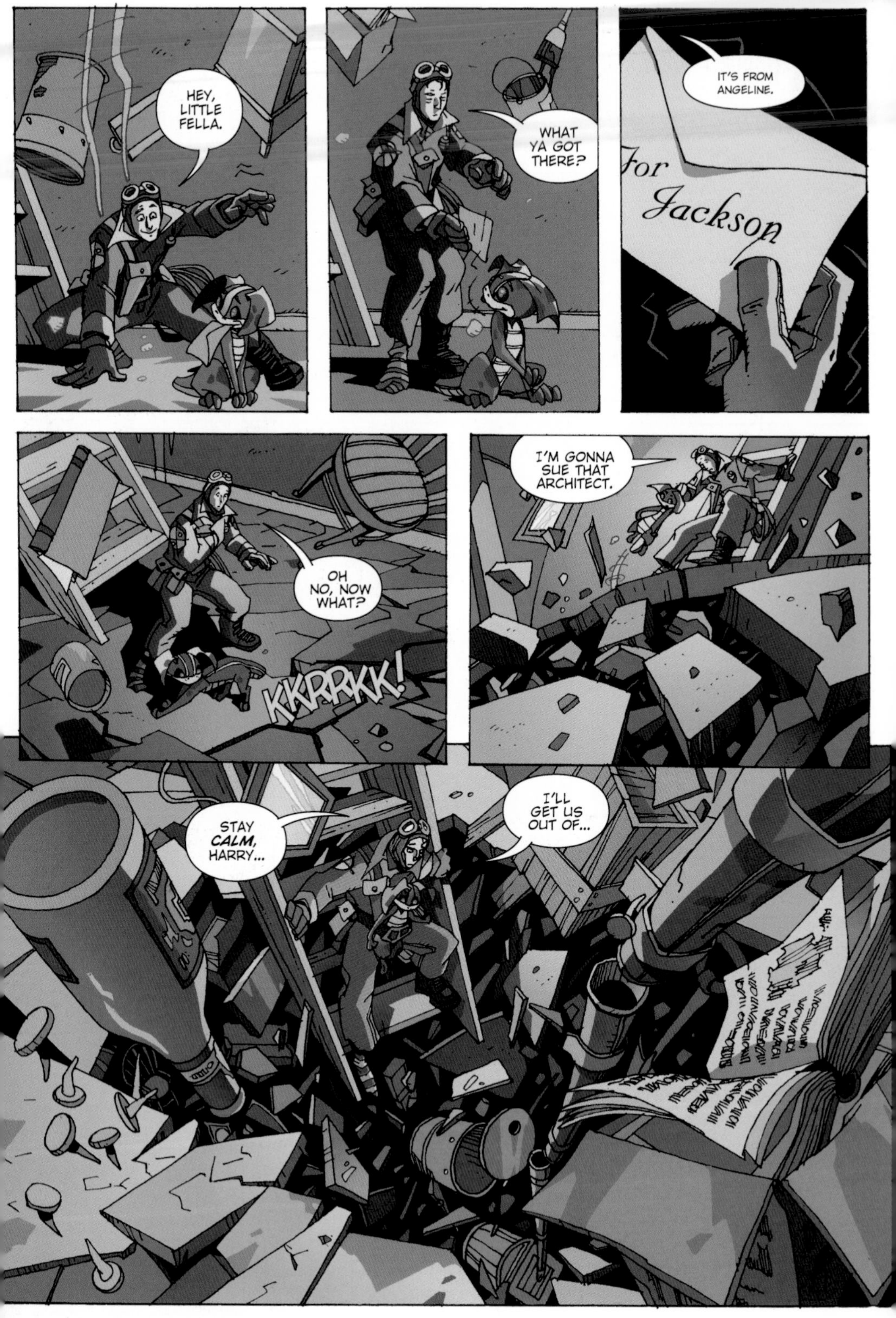
HEY, LITTLE FELLA.
WHAT YA GOT THERE?
IT'S FROM ANGELINE.
For Jackson
OH NO, NOW WHAT?
KKRRKK!
I'M GONNA SUE THAT ARCHITECT.
STAY CALM, HARRY...
I'LL GET US OUT OF...

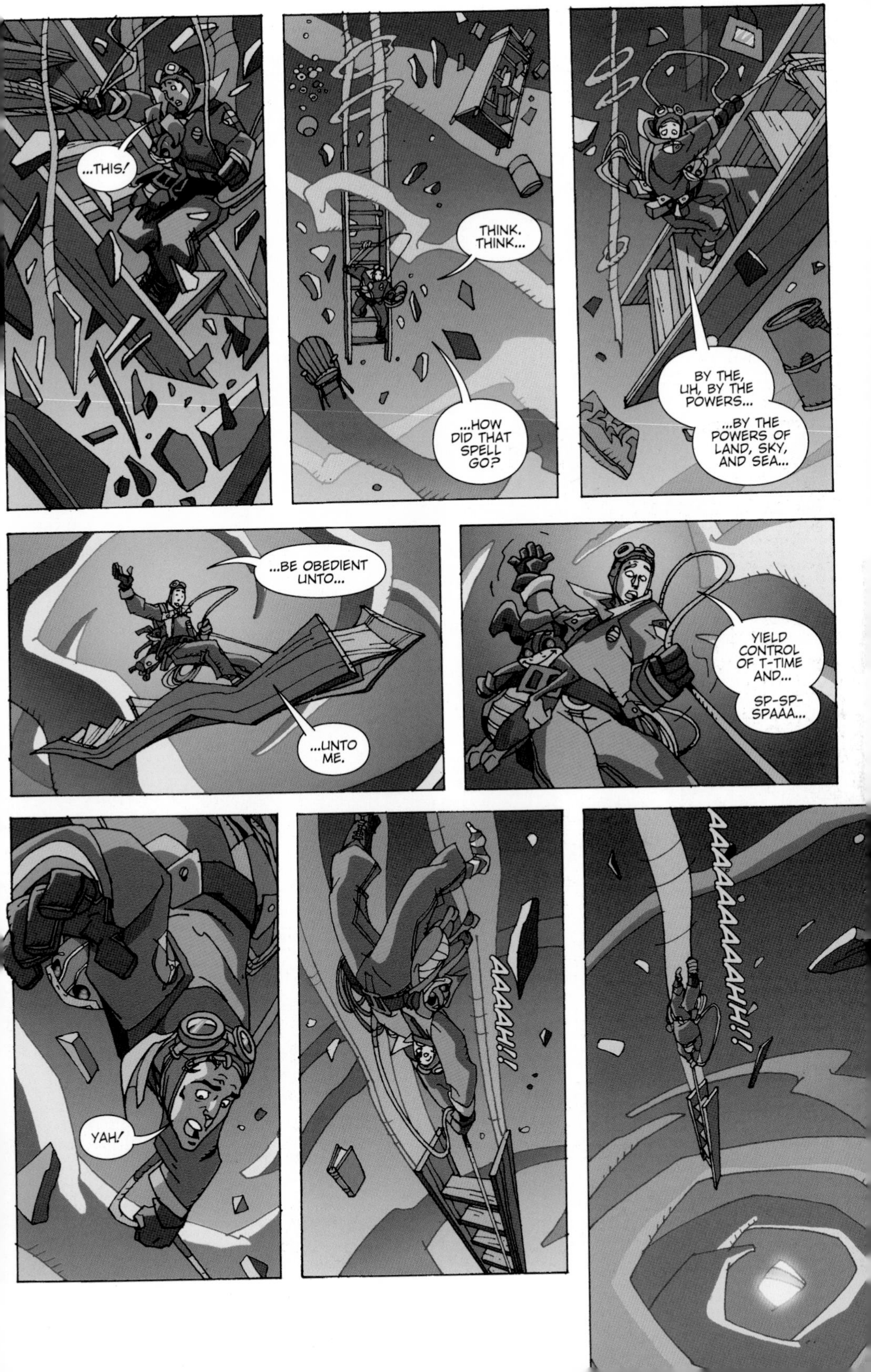
...THIS!
THINK. THINK...
...HOW DID THAT SPELL GO?
BY THE, UH, BY THE POWERS...
...BY THE POWERS OF LAND, SKY, AND SEA...
...BE OBEDIENT UNTO...
...UNTO ME.
YIELD CONTROL OF T-TIME AND...
SP-SP-SPAAA...
YAH!
AAAAH!!
AAAAAAAAAAHH!!

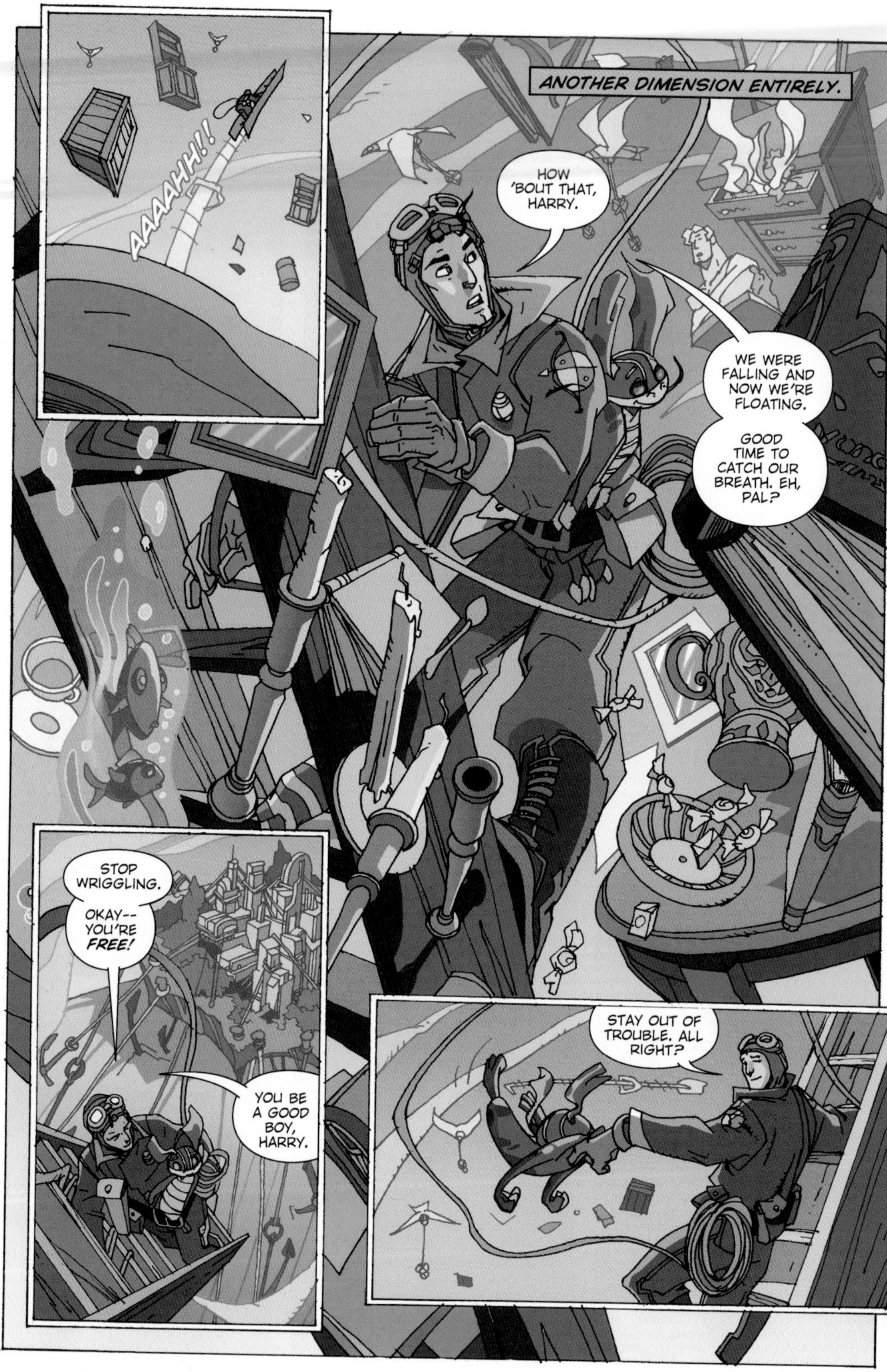
AAAAHH!!
ANOTHER DIMENSION ENTIRELY.
HOW 'BOUT THAT, HARRY.
WE WERE FALLING AND NOW WE'RE FLOATING.
GOOD TIME TO CATCH OUR BREATH. EH, PAL?
STOP WRIGGLING.
OKAY-- YOU'RE *FREE!*
YOU BE A GOOD BOY, HARRY.
STAY OUT OF TROUBLE. ALL RIGHT?

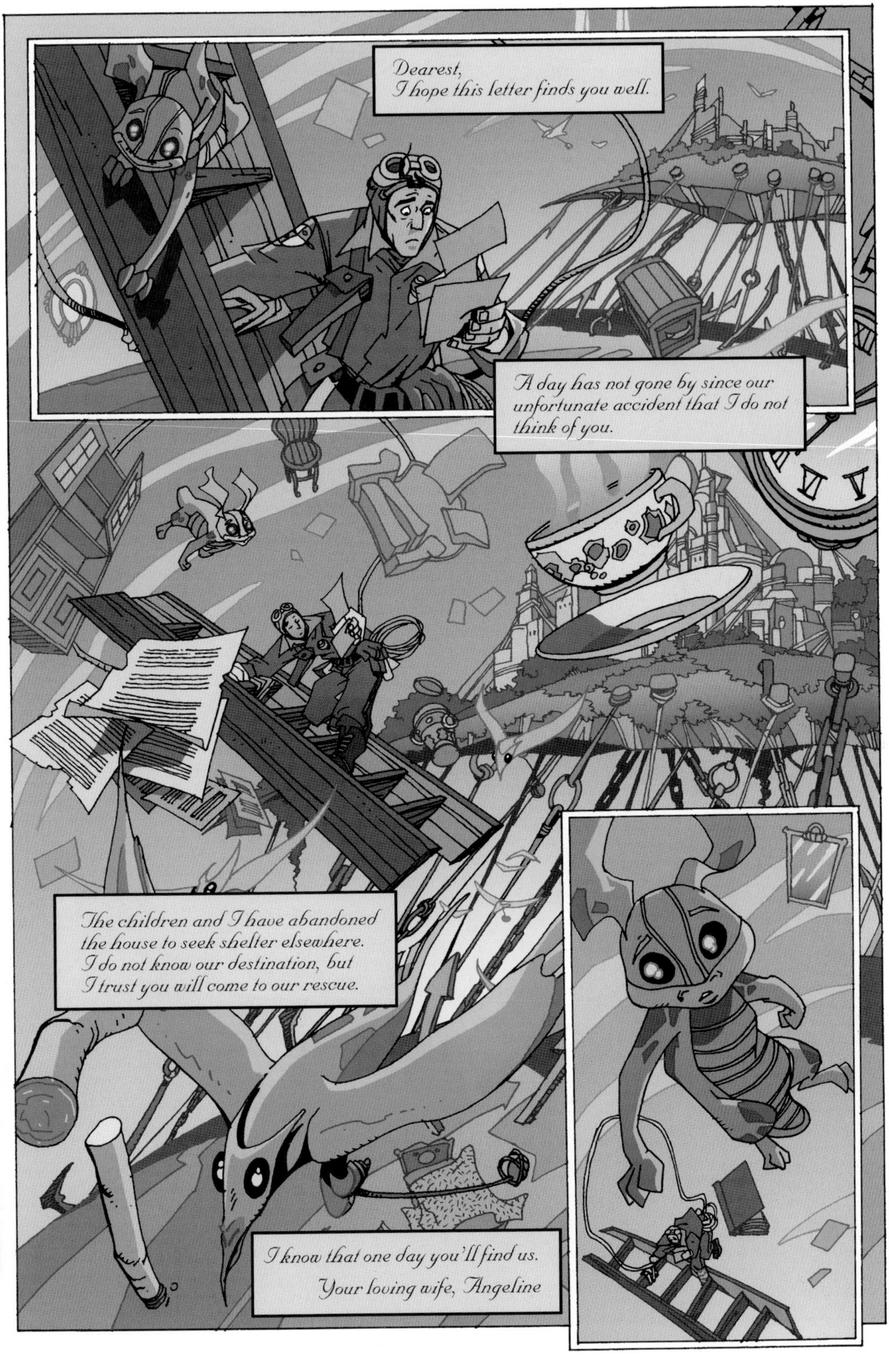
Dearest,
I hope this letter finds you well.
A day has not gone by since our unfortunate accident that I do not think of you.
The children and I have abandoned the house to seek shelter elsewhere. I do not know our destination, but I trust you will come to our rescue.
I know that one day you'll find us.
Your loving wife, Angeline

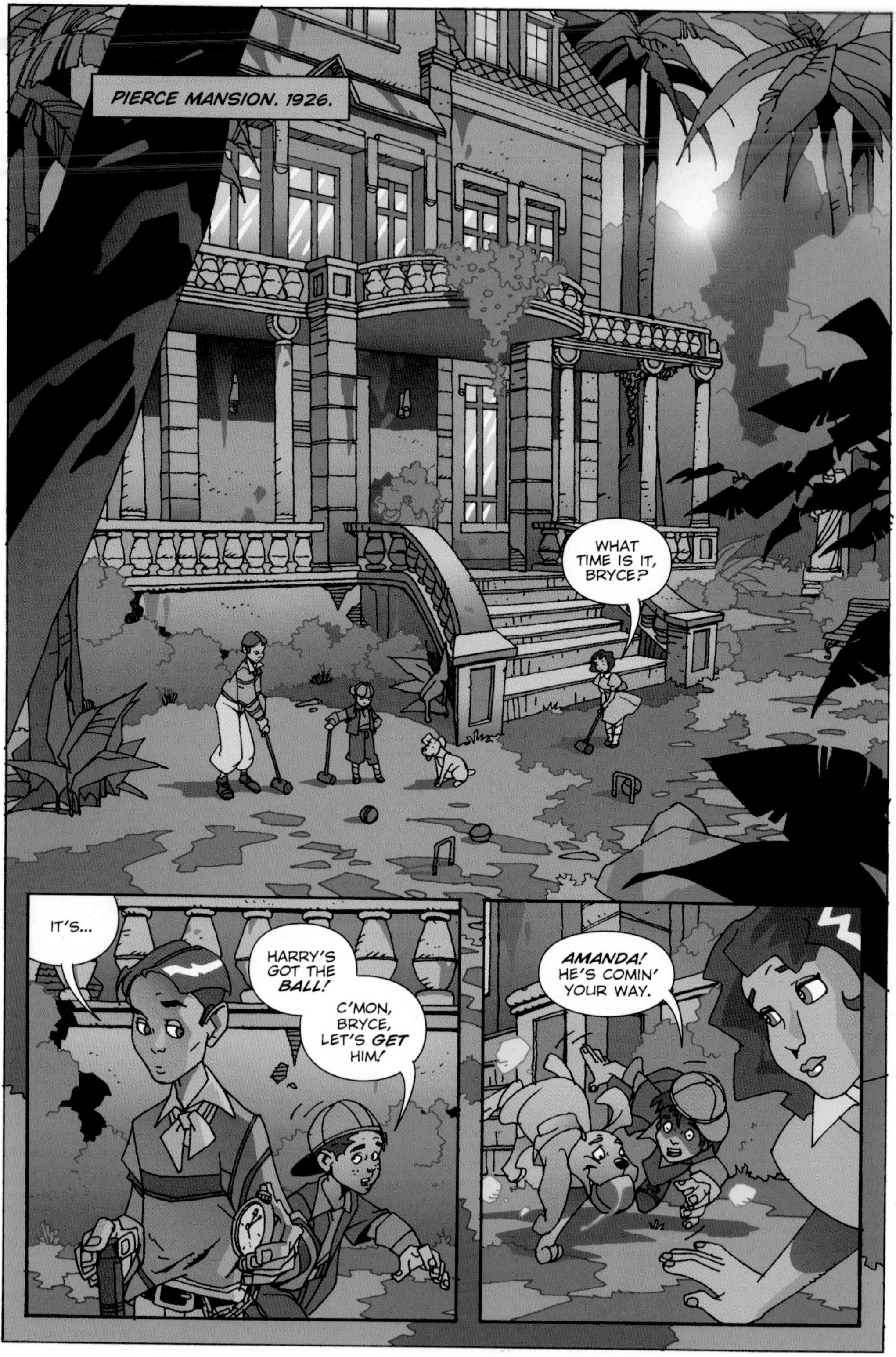
PIERCE MANSION. 1926.
WHAT TIME IS IT, BRYCE?
IT'S...
HARRY'S GOT THE BALL!
C'MON, BRYCE, LET'S GET HIM!
AMANDA! HE'S COMIN' YOUR WAY.

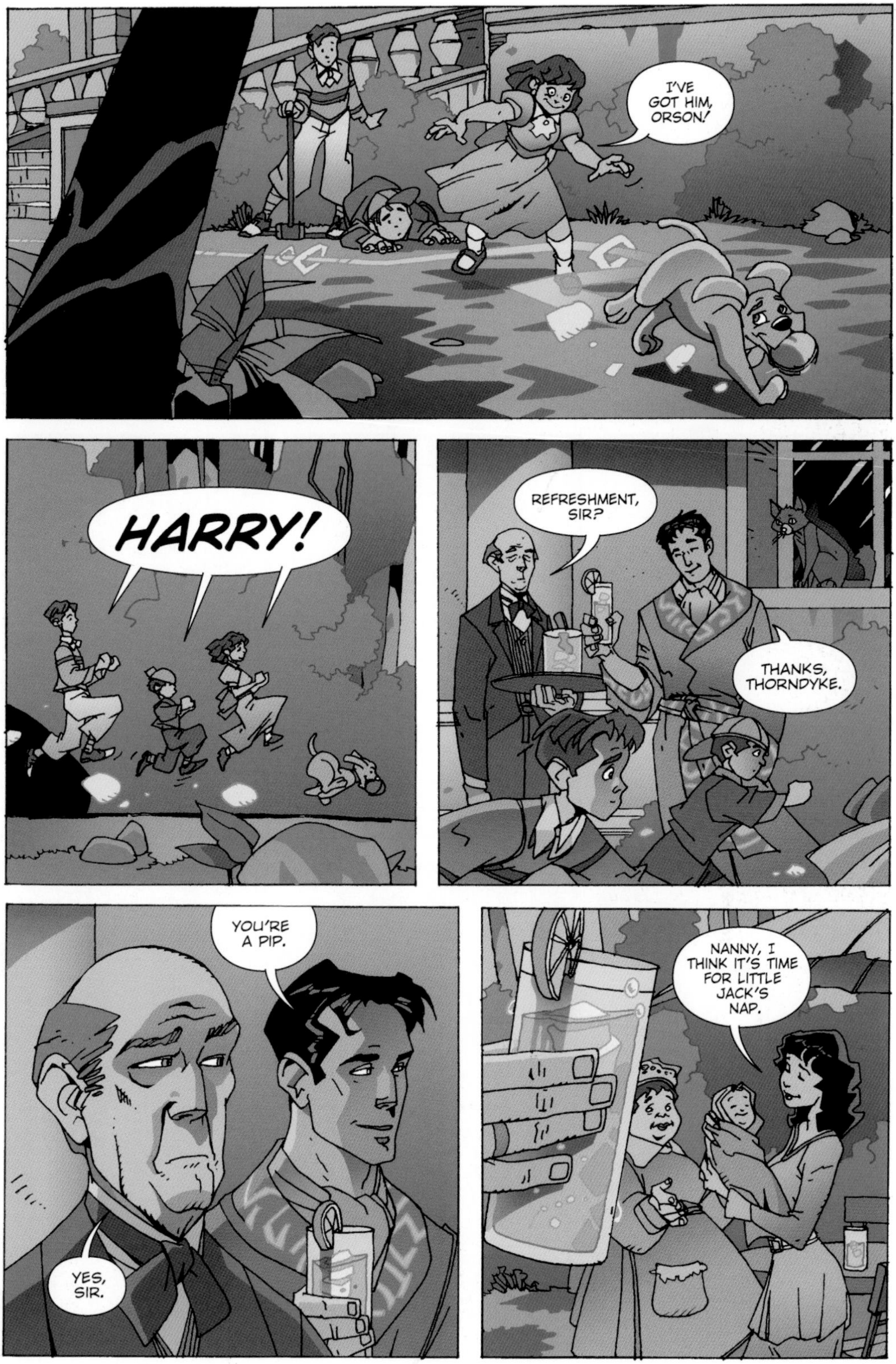
I'VE GOT HIM, ORSON!
HARRY!
REFRESHMENT, SIR?
THANKS, THORNDYKE.
YOU'RE A PIP.
YES, SIR.
NANNY, I THINK IT'S TIME FOR LITTLE JACK'S NAP.

IT'S DEFINITELY QUIET TIME FOR MOMMY.

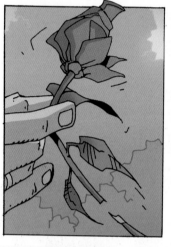

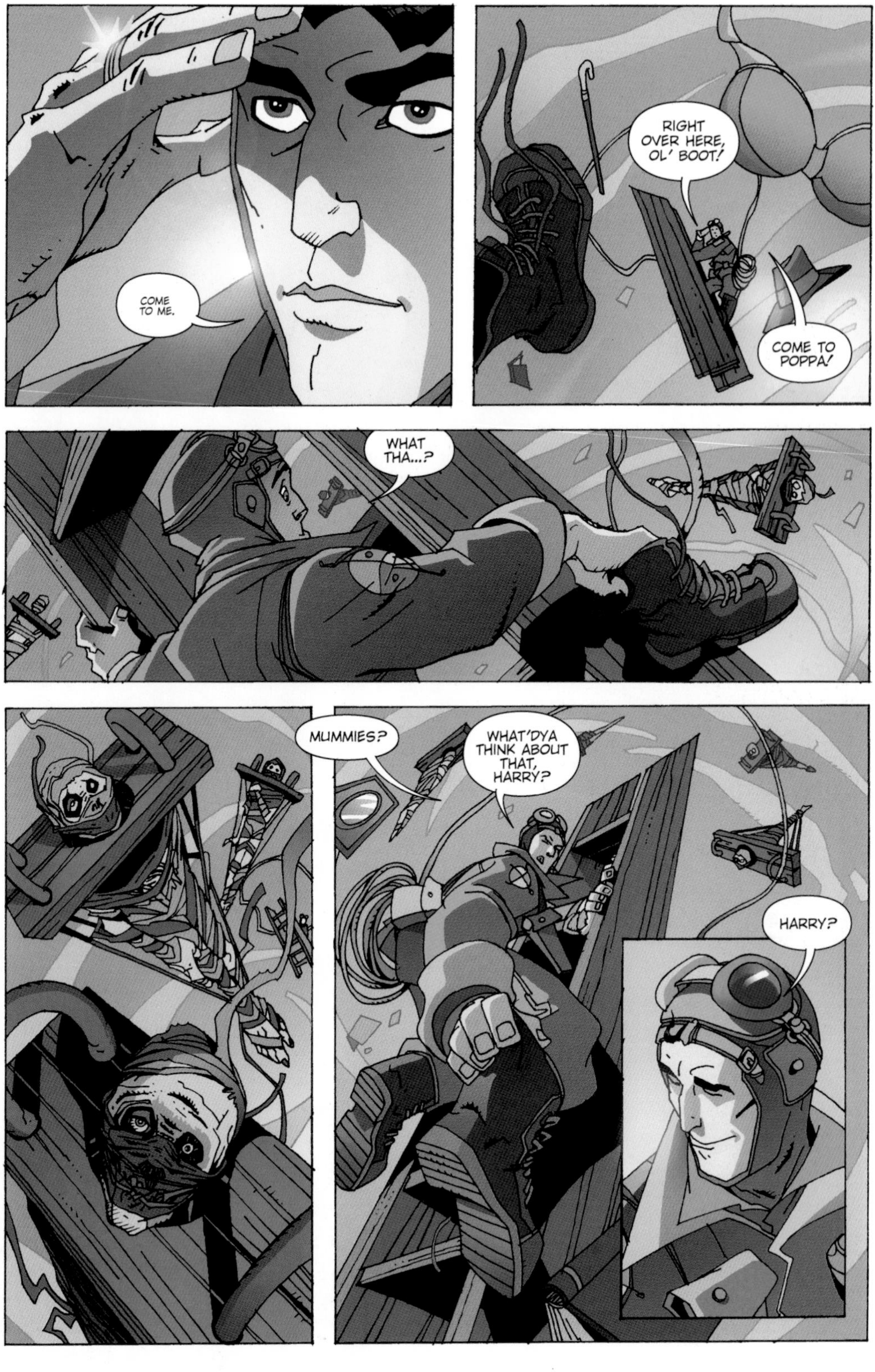
COME TO ME.
RIGHT OVER HERE, OL' BOOT!
COME TO POPPA!
WHAT THA...?
MUMMIES?
WHAT'DYA THINK ABOUT THAT, HARRY?
HARRY?

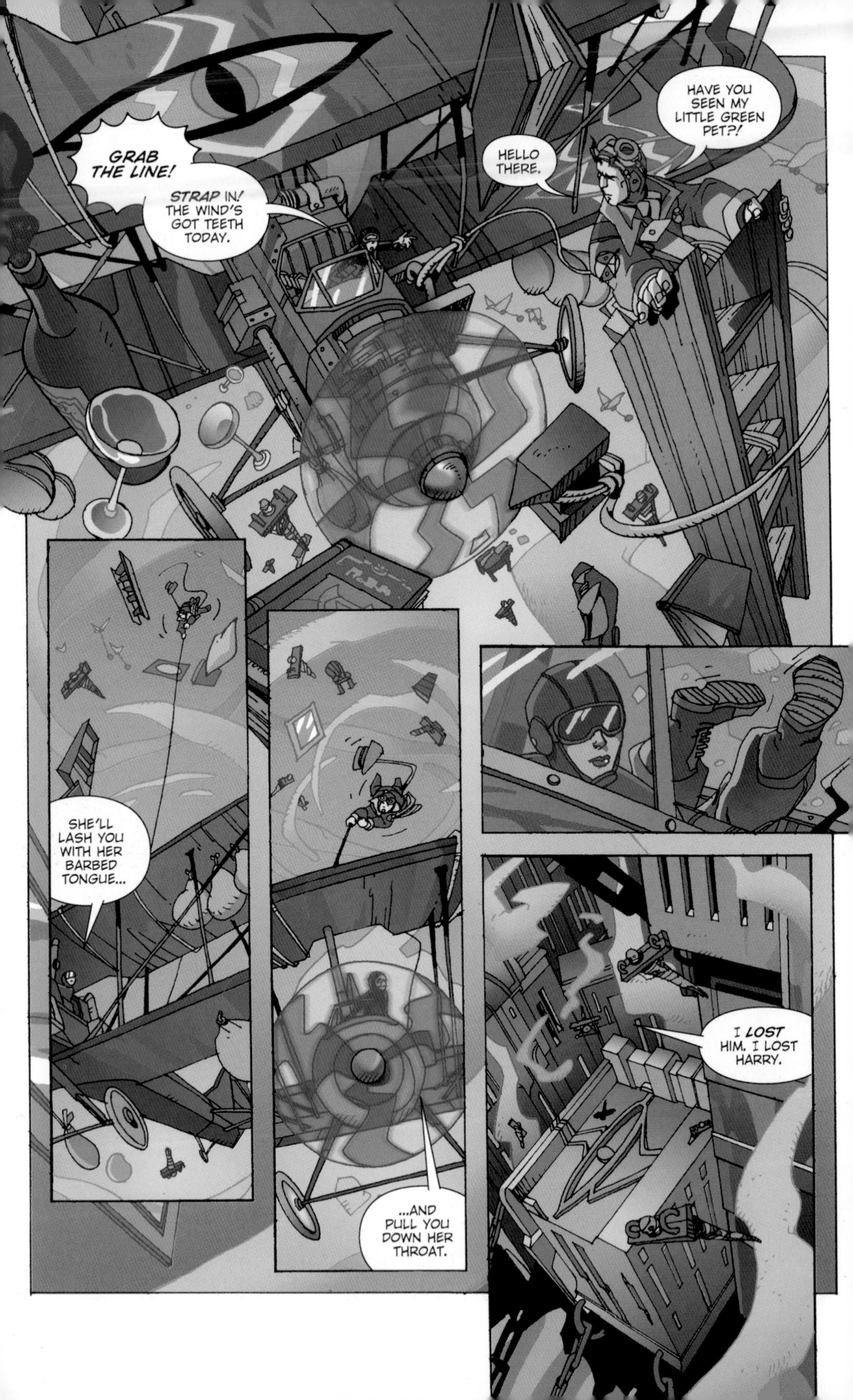
GRAB THE LINE!
STRAP IN! THE WIND'S GOT TEETH TODAY.
HELLO THERE.
HAVE YOU SEEN MY LITTLE GREEN PET?!
SHE'LL LASH YOU WITH HER BARBED TONGUE...
...AND PULL YOU DOWN HER THROAT.
I LOST HIM. I LOST HARRY.

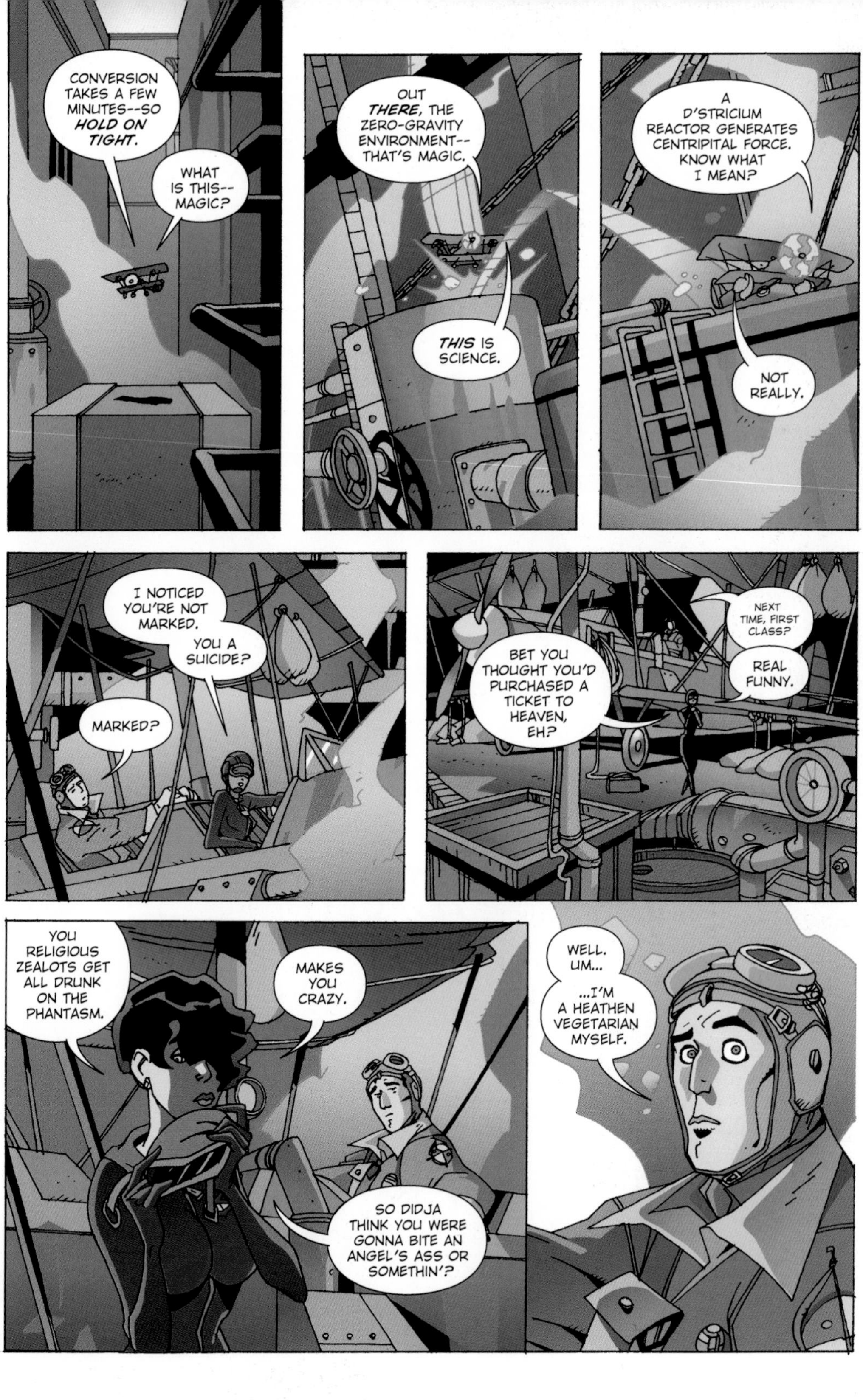
CONVERSION TAKES A FEW MINUTES--SO HOLD ON TIGHT.
WHAT IS THIS--MAGIC?
OUT THERE, THE ZERO-GRAVITY ENVIRONMENT--THAT'S MAGIC.
THIS IS SCIENCE.
A D'STRICIUM REACTOR GENERATES CENTRIPITAL FORCE. KNOW WHAT I MEAN?
NOT REALLY.
I NOTICED YOU'RE NOT MARKED.
YOU A SUICIDE?
MARKED?
NEXT TIME, FIRST CLASS?
REAL FUNNY.
BET YOU THOUGHT YOU'D PURCHASED A TICKET TO HEAVEN, EH?
YOU RELIGIOUS ZEALOTS GET ALL DRUNK ON THE PHANTASM.
MAKES YOU CRAZY.
SO DIDJA THINK YOU WERE GONNA BITE AN ANGEL'S ASS OR SOMETHIN'?
WELL. UM...
...I'M A HEATHEN VEGETARIAN MYSELF.

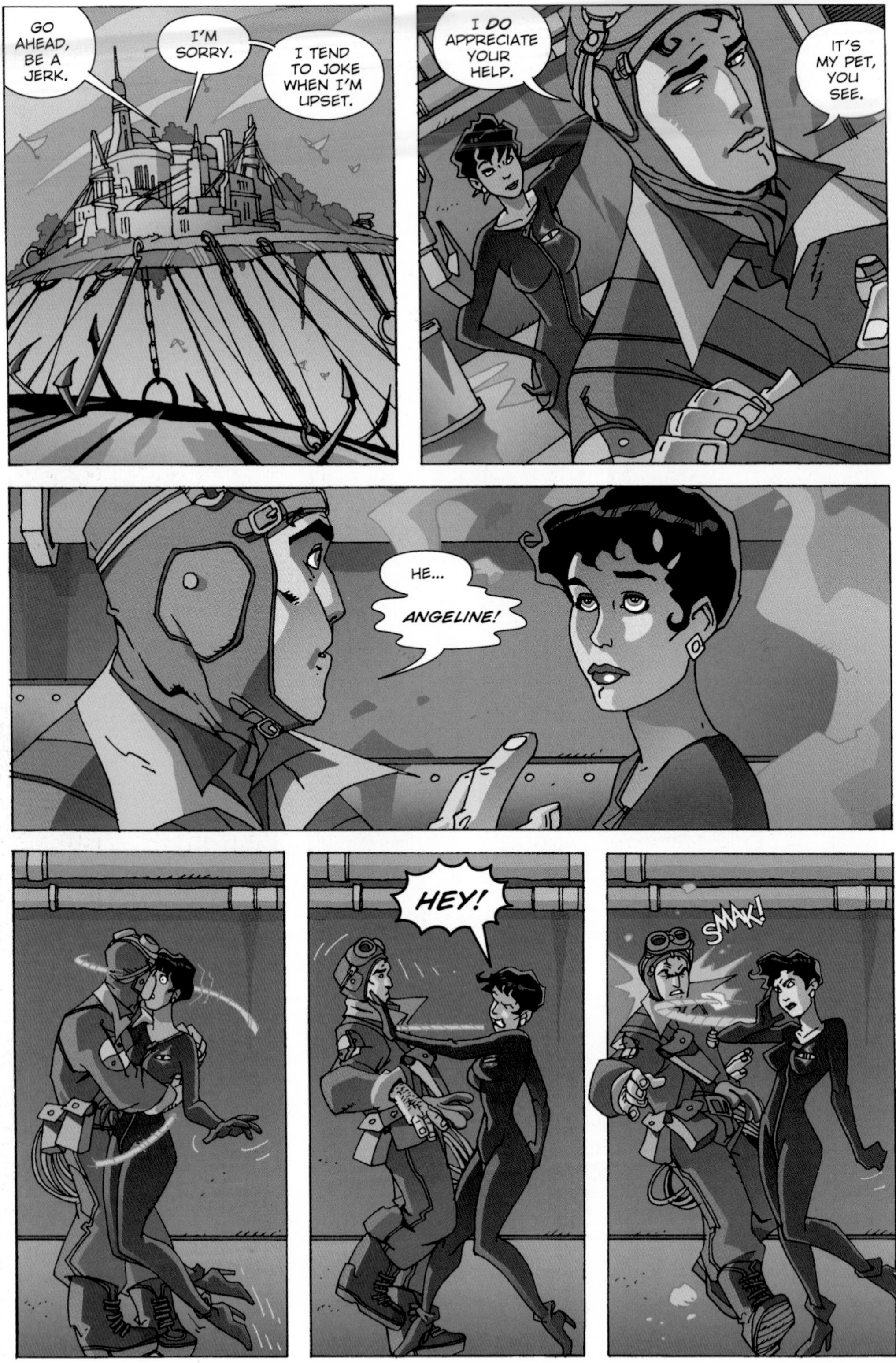
GO AHEAD, BE A JERK.
I'M SORRY.
I TEND TO JOKE WHEN I'M UPSET.
I *DO* APPRECIATE YOUR HELP.
IT'S MY PET, YOU SEE.
HE...
ANGELINE!
HEY!
SMAK!

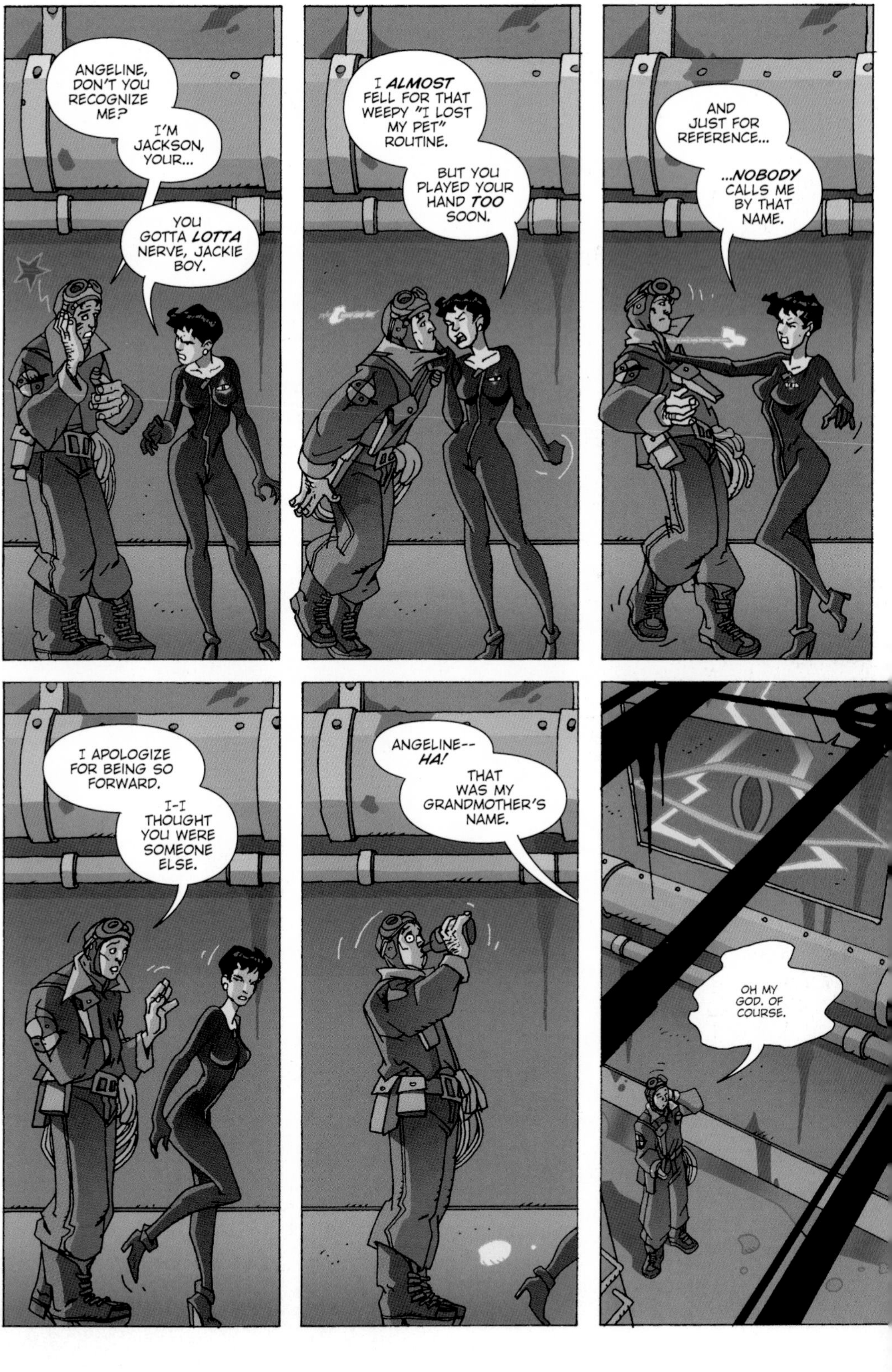

ANGELINE, DON'T YOU RECOGNIZE ME?
I'M JACKSON, YOUR...
YOU GOTTA LOTTA NERVE, JACKIE BOY.
I ALMOST FELL FOR THAT WEEPY "I LOST MY PET" ROUTINE.
BUT YOU PLAYED YOUR HAND TOO SOON.
AND JUST FOR REFERENCE...
...NOBODY CALLS ME BY THAT NAME.
I APOLOGIZE FOR BEING SO FORWARD.
I-I THOUGHT YOU WERE SOMEONE ELSE.
ANGELINE-- HA!
THAT WAS MY GRANDMOTHER'S NAME.
OH MY GOD. OF COURSE.

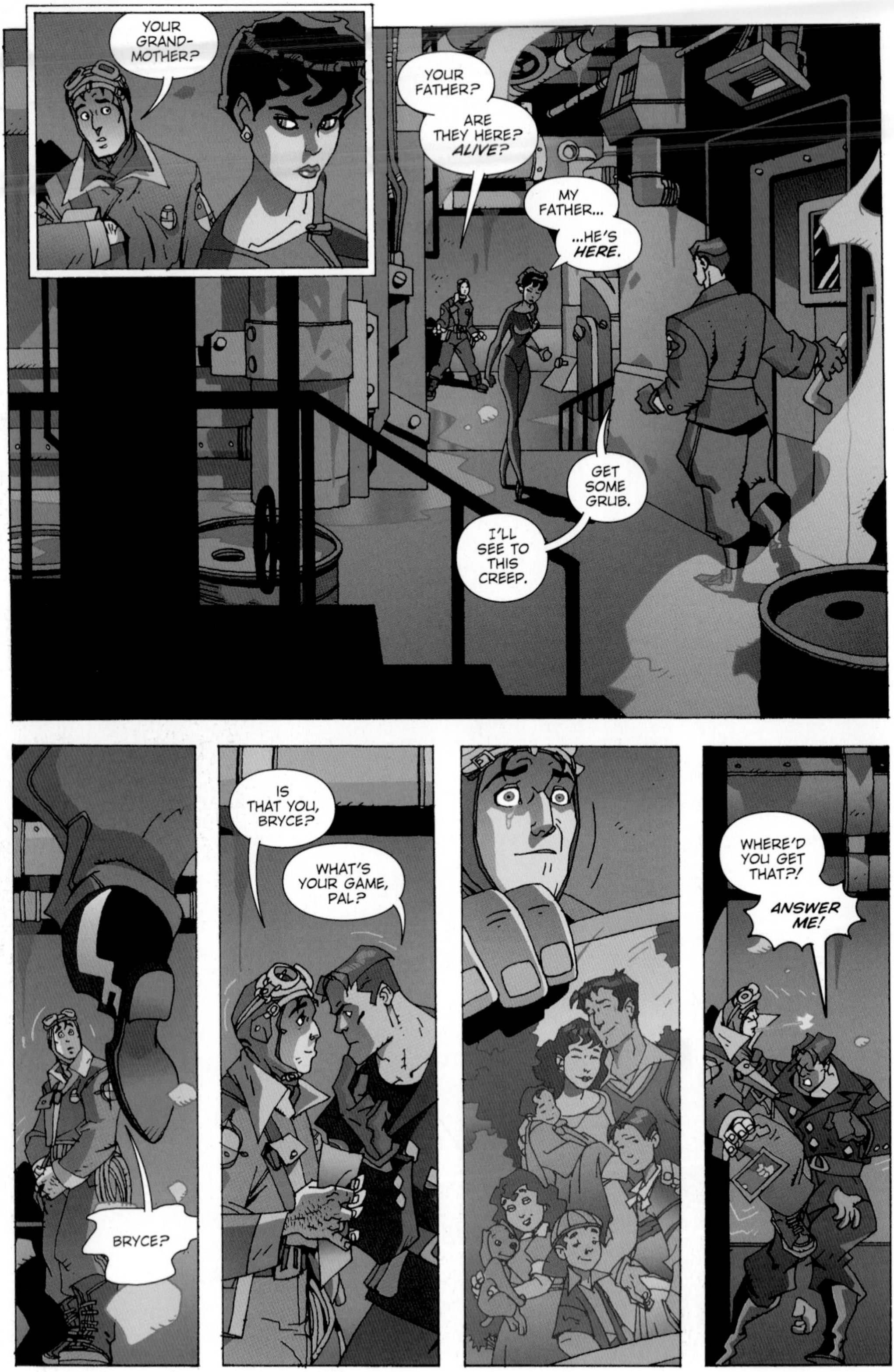
YOUR GRAND-MOTHER?
YOUR FATHER?
ARE THEY HERE? ALIVE?
MY FATHER...
...HE'S HERE.
GET SOME GRUB.
I'LL SEE TO THIS CREEP.
BRYCE?
IS THAT YOU, BRYCE?
WHAT'S YOUR GAME, PAL?
WHERE'D YOU GET THAT?!
ANSWER ME!

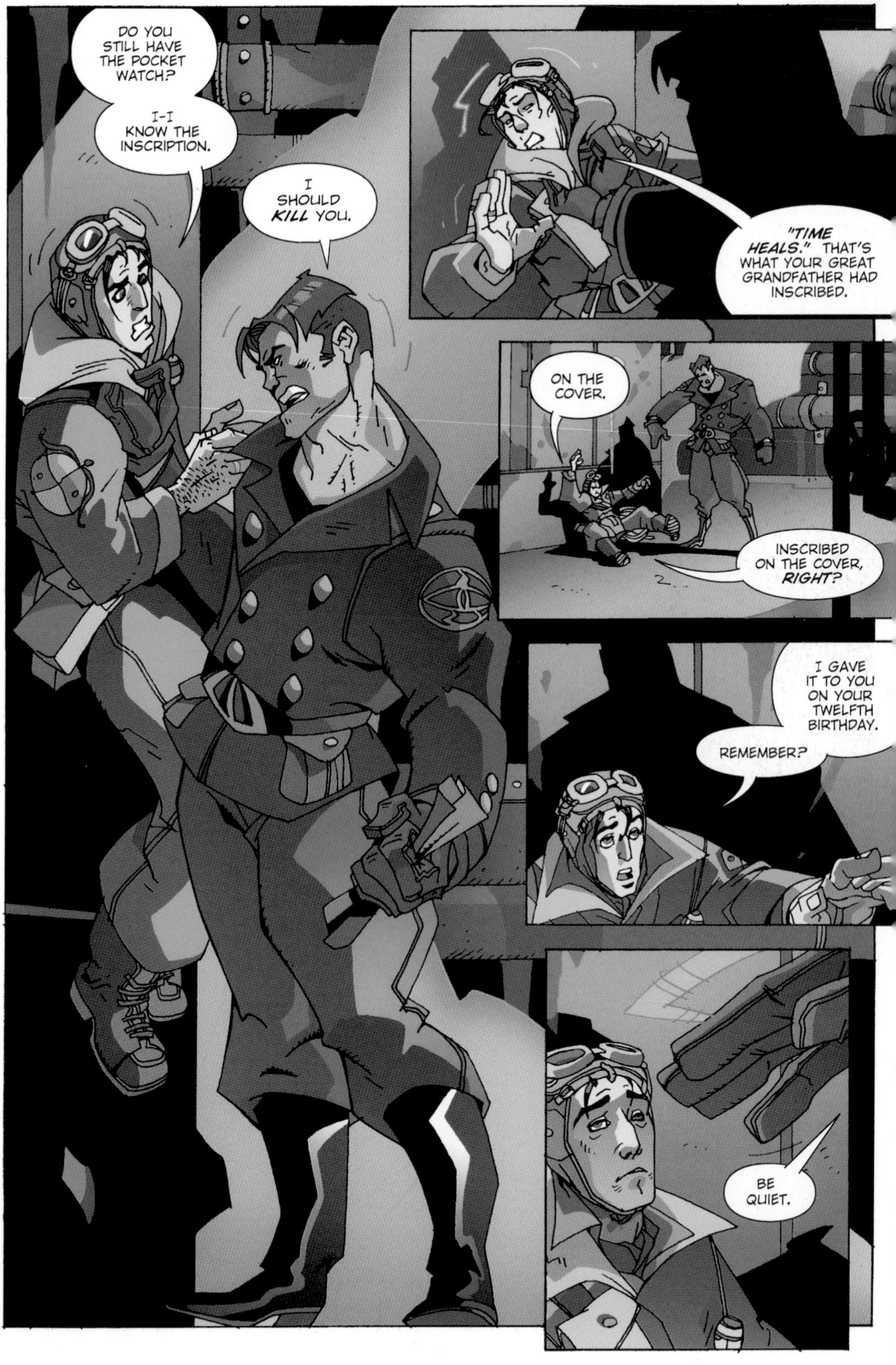
DO YOU STILL HAVE THE POCKET WATCH?
I-I KNOW THE INSCRIPTION.
I SHOULD KILL YOU.
"TIME HEALS." THAT'S WHAT YOUR GREAT GRANDFATHER HAD INSCRIBED.
ON THE COVER.
INSCRIBED ON THE COVER, RIGHT?
I GAVE IT TO YOU ON YOUR TWELFTH BIRTHDAY.
REMEMBER?
BE QUIET.

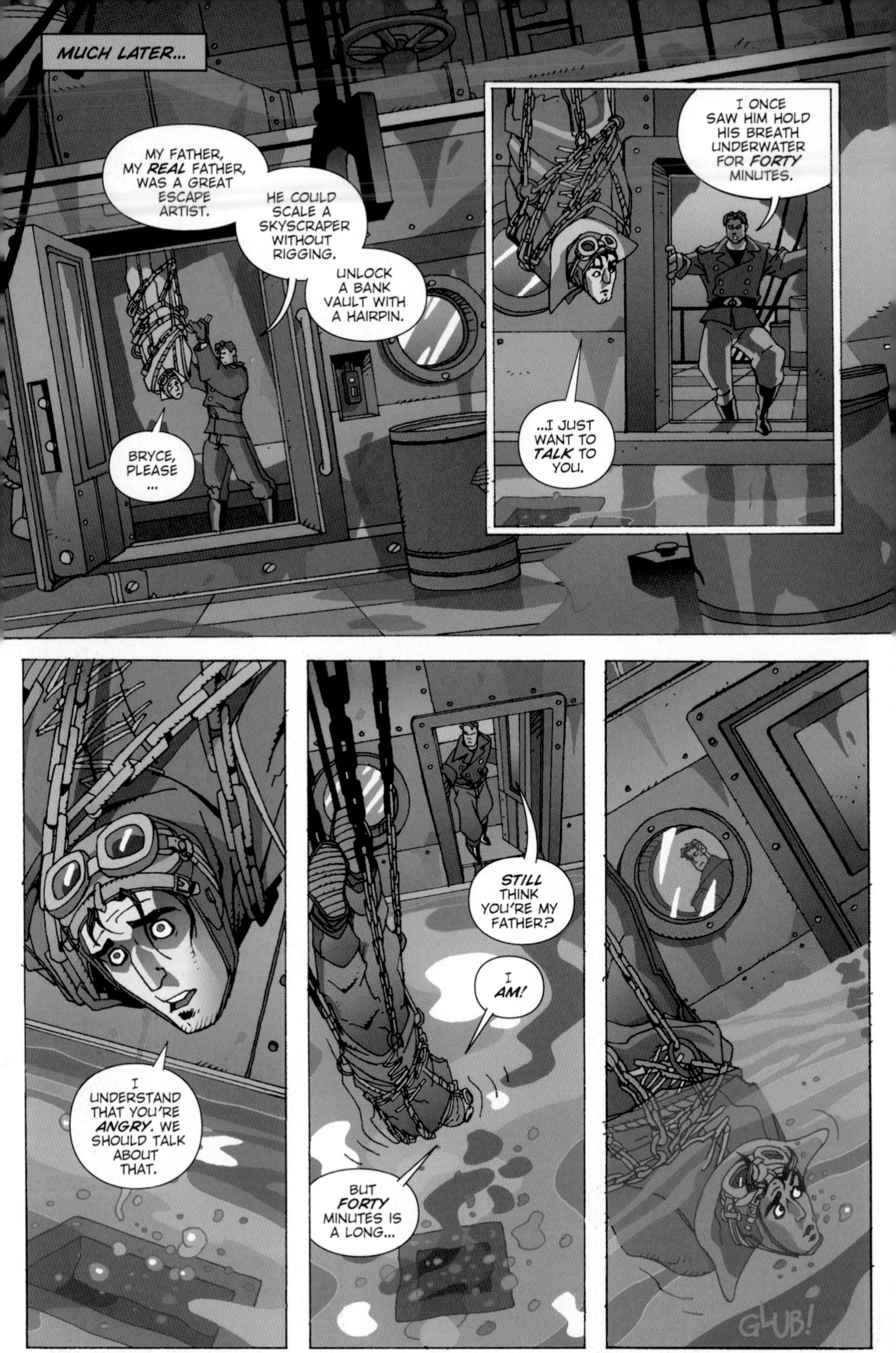
MUCH LATER...
MY FATHER, MY REAL FATHER, WAS A GREAT ESCAPE ARTIST.
HE COULD SCALE A SKYSCRAPER WITHOUT RIGGING.
UNLOCK A BANK VAULT WITH A HAIRPIN.
BRYCE, PLEASE ...
...I JUST WANT TO TALK TO YOU.
I ONCE SAW HIM HOLD HIS BREATH UNDERWATER FOR FORTY MINUTES.
I UNDERSTAND THAT YOU'RE ANGRY. WE SHOULD TALK ABOUT THAT.
STILL THINK YOU'RE MY FATHER?
I AM!
BUT FORTY MINUTES IS A LONG...
GLUB!

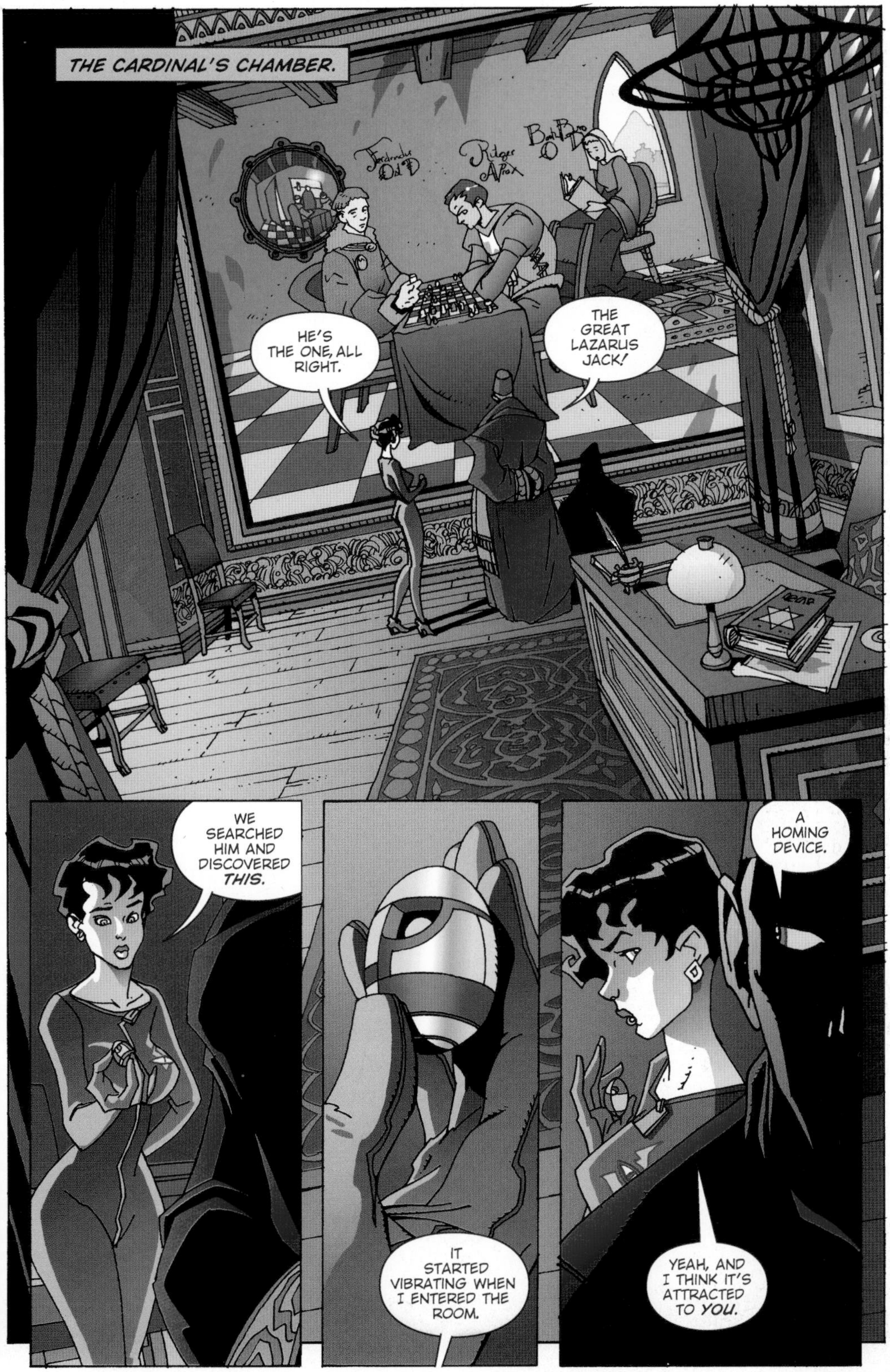

THE CARDINAL'S CHAMBER.
HE'S THE ONE, ALL RIGHT.
THE GREAT LAZARUS JACK!
WE SEARCHED HIM AND DISCOVERED THIS.
IT STARTED VIBRATING WHEN I ENTERED THE ROOM.
A HOMING DEVICE.
YEAH, AND I THINK IT'S ATTRACTED TO YOU.

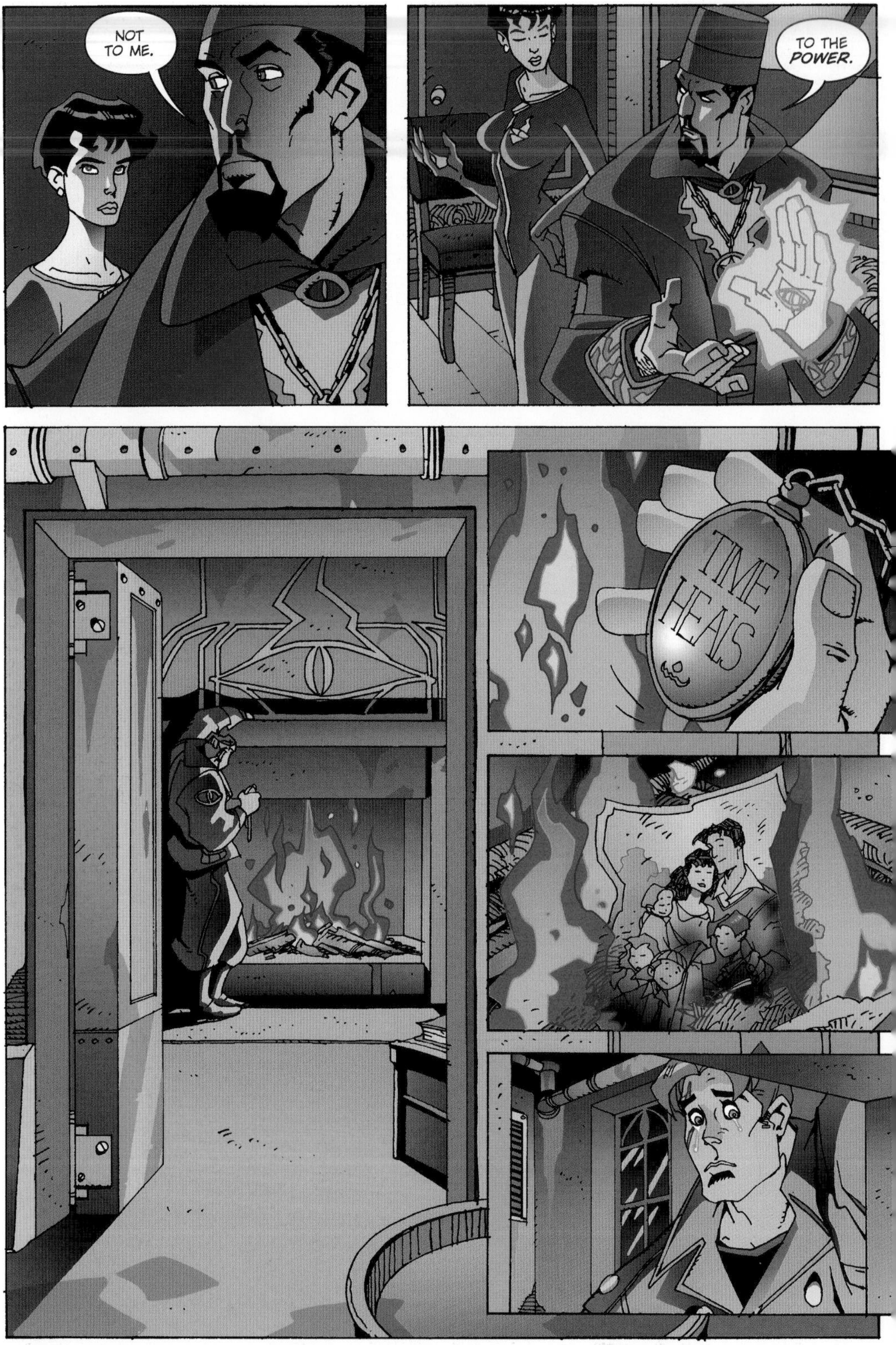
NOT TO ME.
TO THE POWER.
TIME HEALS

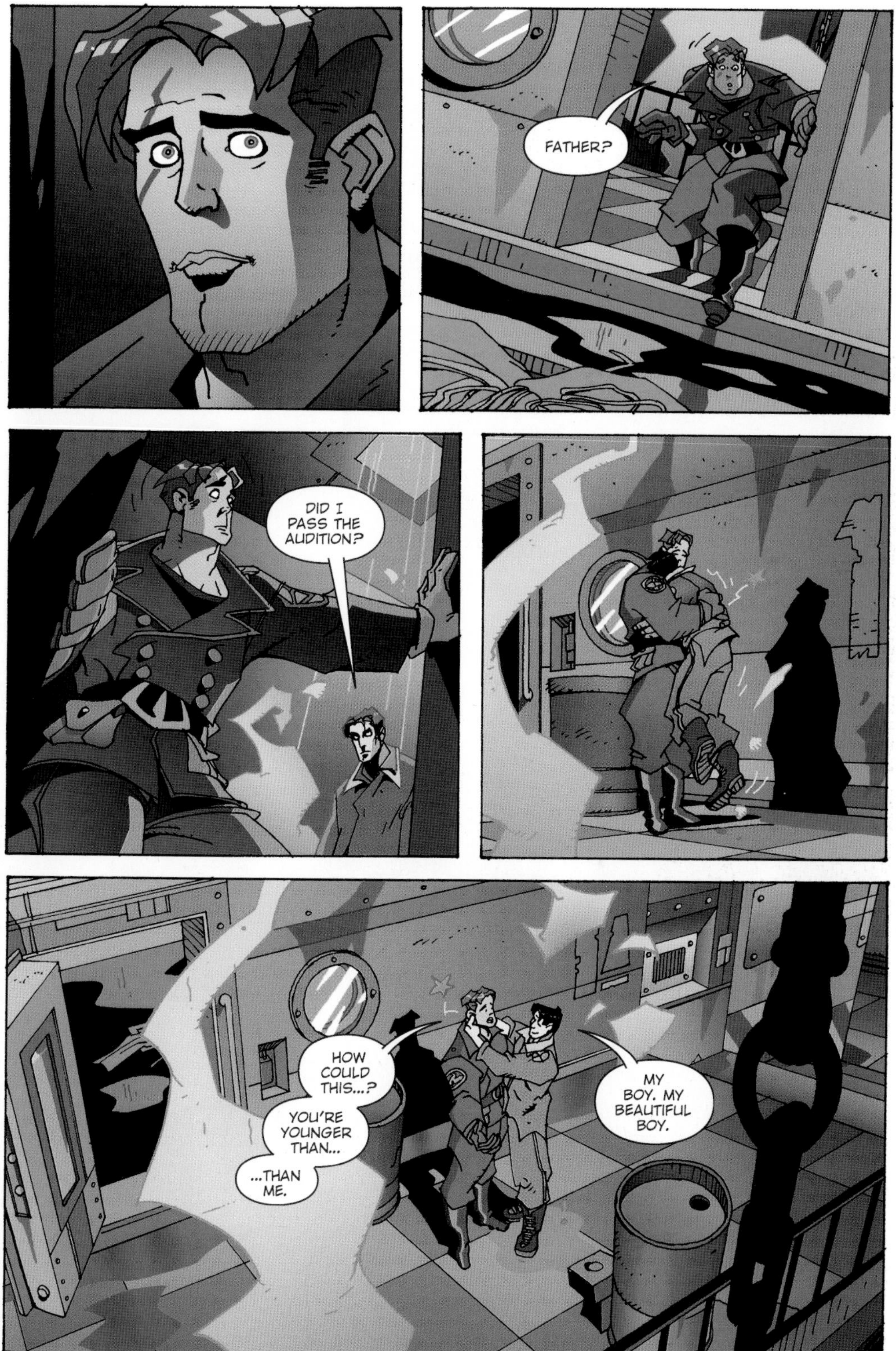
FATHER?
DID I PASS THE AUDITION?
HOW COULD THIS...?
YOU'RE YOUNGER THAN...
...THAN ME.
MY BOY. MY BEAUTIFUL BOY.

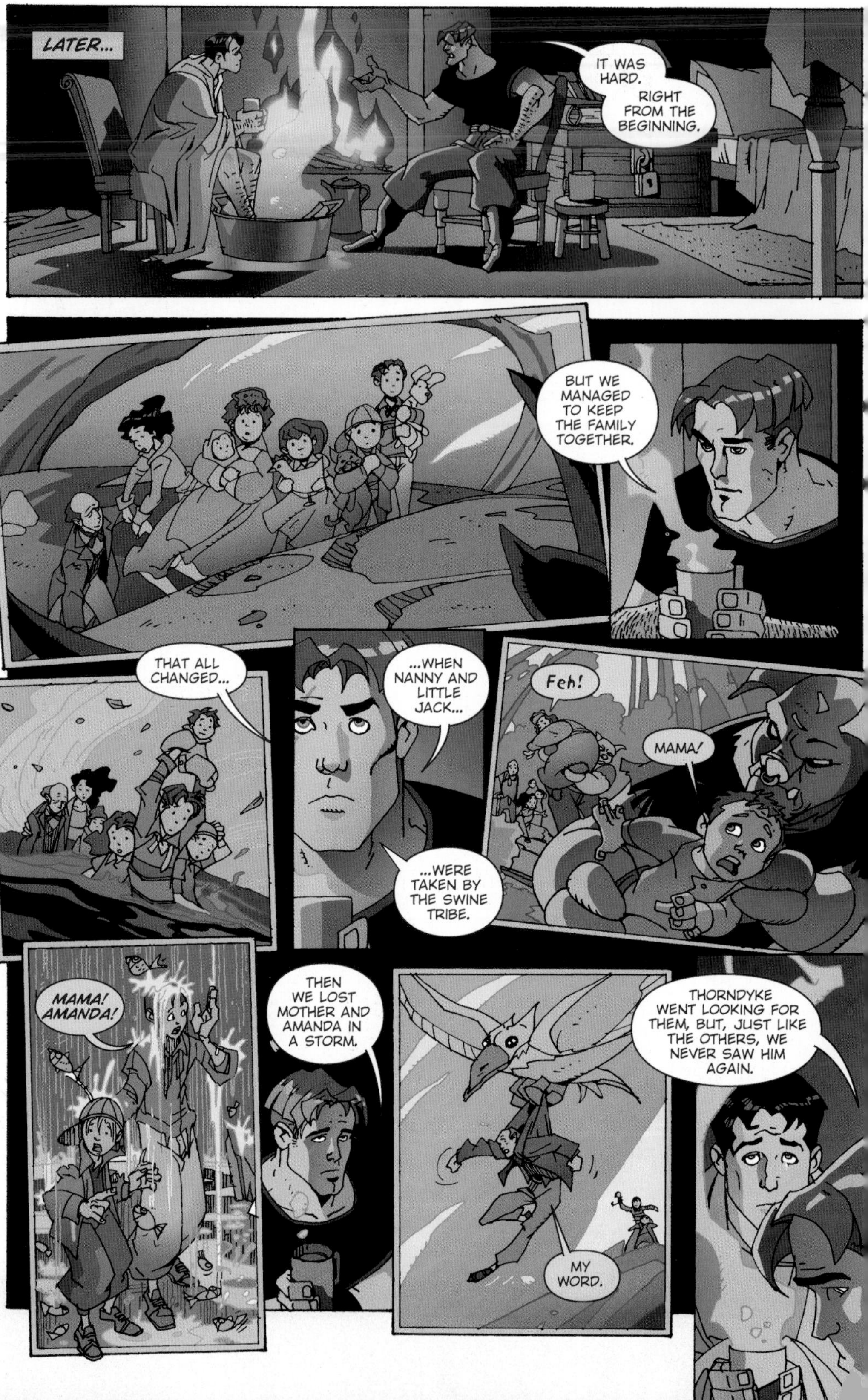
LATER...
IT WAS HARD.
RIGHT FROM THE BEGINNING.
BUT WE MANAGED TO KEEP THE FAMILY TOGETHER.
THAT ALL CHANGED...
...WHEN NANNY AND LITTLE JACK...
...WERE TAKEN BY THE SWINE TRIBE.
Feh!
MAMA!
MAMA! AMANDA!
THEN WE LOST MOTHER AND AMANDA IN A STORM.
MY WORD.
THORNDYKE WENT LOOKING FOR THEM, BUT, JUST LIKE THE OTHERS, WE NEVER SAW HIM AGAIN.

SO ORSON AND I MADE A LIFE FOR OURSELVES HERE.

WE EVEN JOINED THE REPRESSIONIST ARMY TO FIGHT THE MAGIC.

ORSON, IS HE...?

HE WAS A *HERO*.

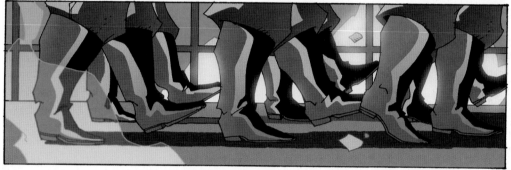

WHENEVER ORSON AND I WERE IN A JAM, WE DIDN'T FRET IT.

WE WERE THE SONS OF LAZARUS JACK.

WE WERE INVINCIBLE.

I DON'T DESERVE A SON LIKE YOU.

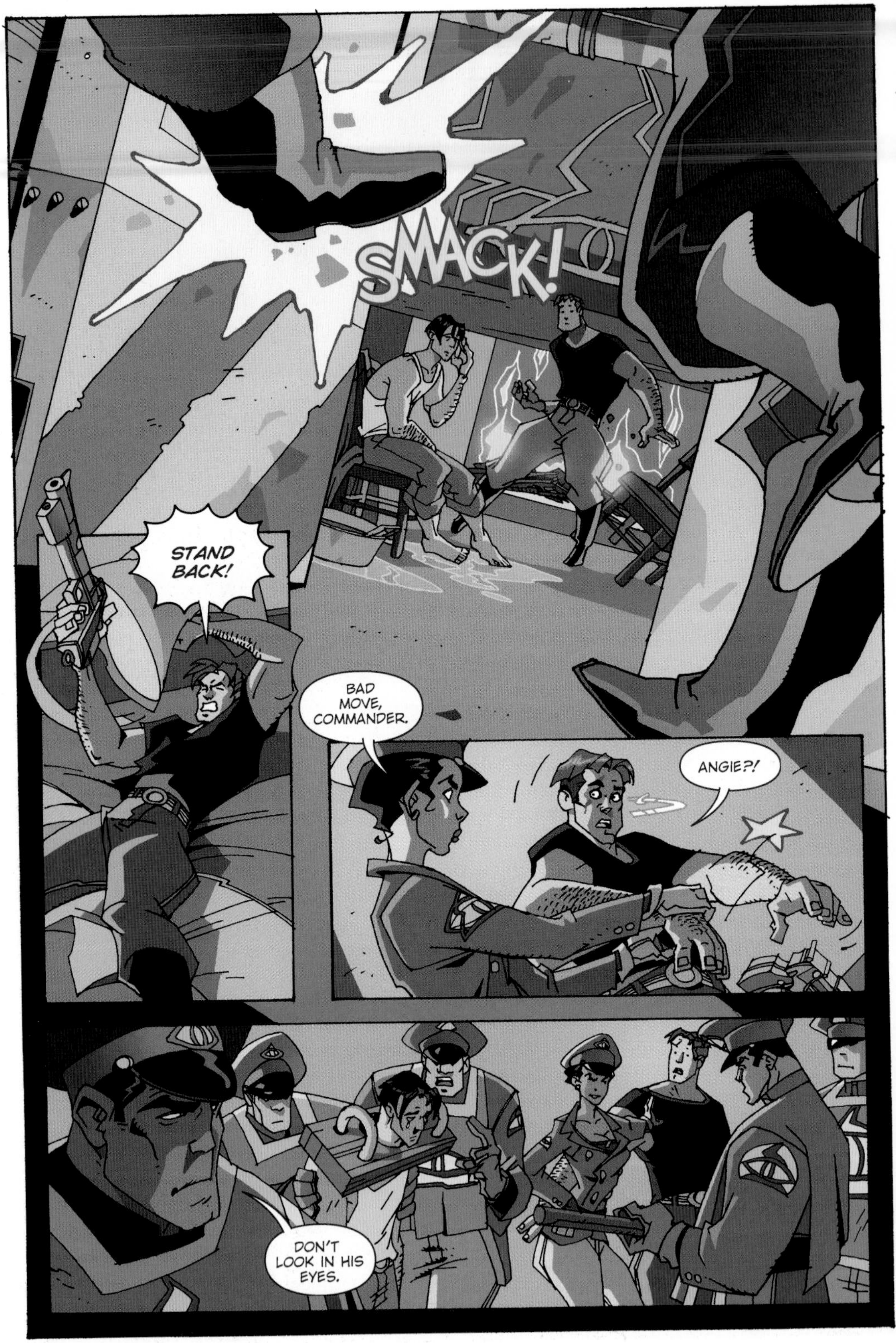
SMACK!
STAND BACK!
BAD MOVE, COMMANDER.
ANGIE?!
DON'T LOOK IN HIS EYES.

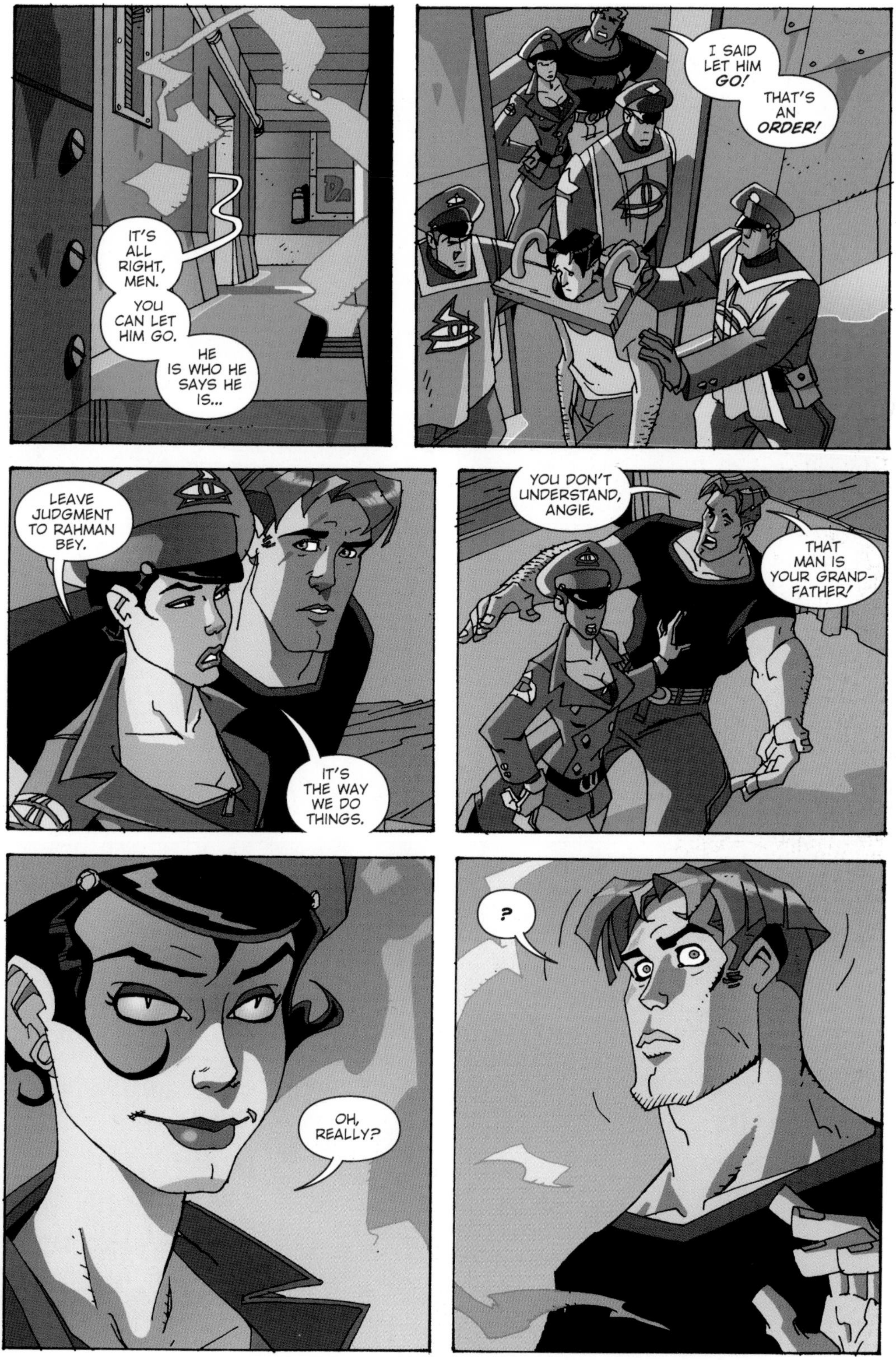
IT'S ALL RIGHT, MEN.
YOU CAN LET HIM GO.
HE IS WHO HE SAYS HE IS...
I SAID LET HIM GO!
THAT'S AN ORDER!
LEAVE JUDGMENT TO RAHMAN BEY.
IT'S THE WAY WE DO THINGS.
YOU DON'T UNDERSTAND, ANGIE.
THAT MAN IS YOUR GRAND-FATHER!
OH, REALLY?
?

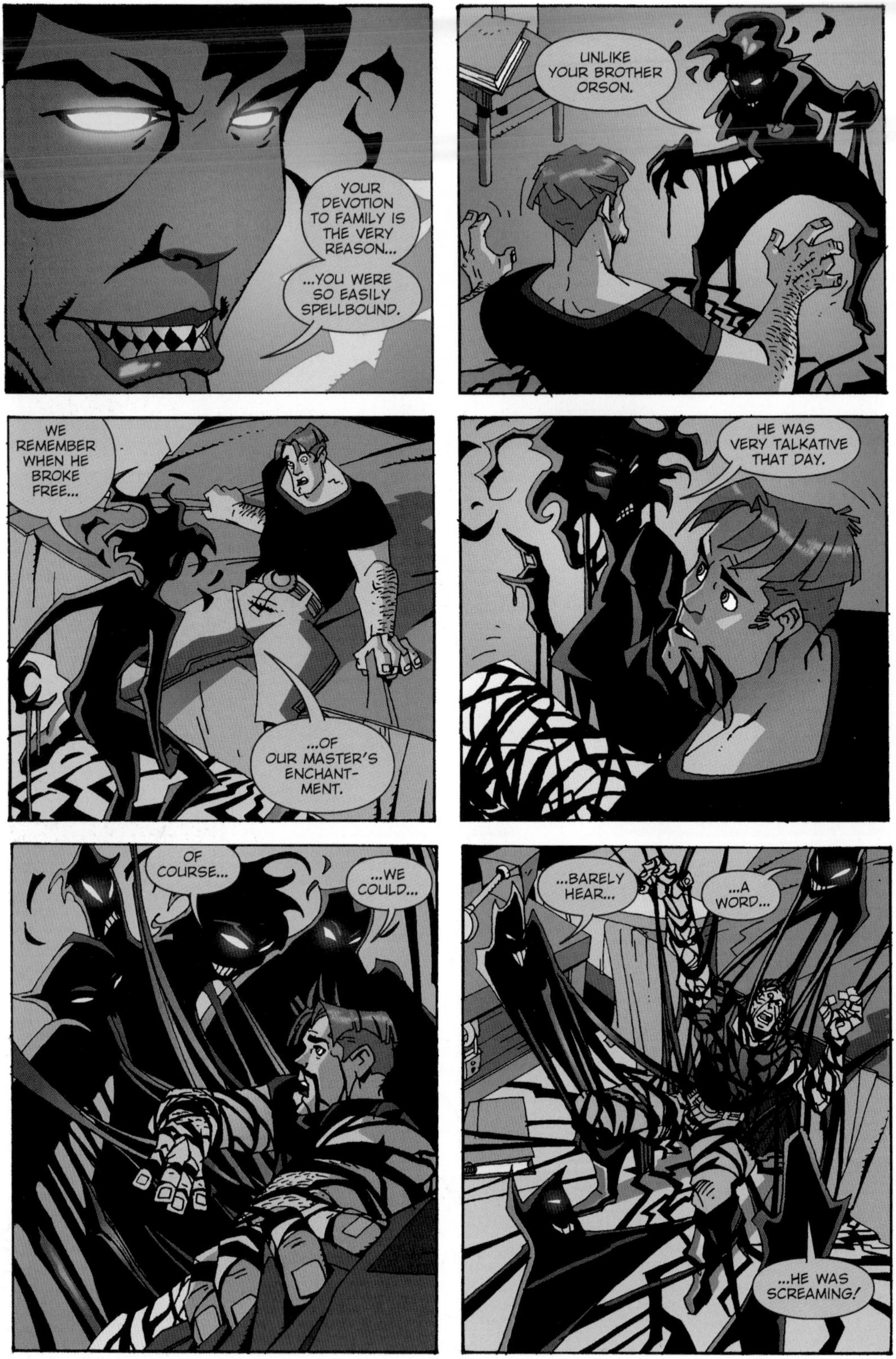
YOUR DEVOTION TO FAMILY IS THE VERY REASON...
...YOU WERE SO EASILY SPELLBOUND.
UNLIKE YOUR BROTHER ORSON.
WE REMEMBER WHEN HE BROKE FREE...
...OF OUR MASTER'S ENCHANT-MENT.
HE WAS VERY TALKATIVE THAT DAY.
OF COURSE...
...WE COULD...
...BARELY HEAR...
...A WORD...
...HE WAS SCREAMING!

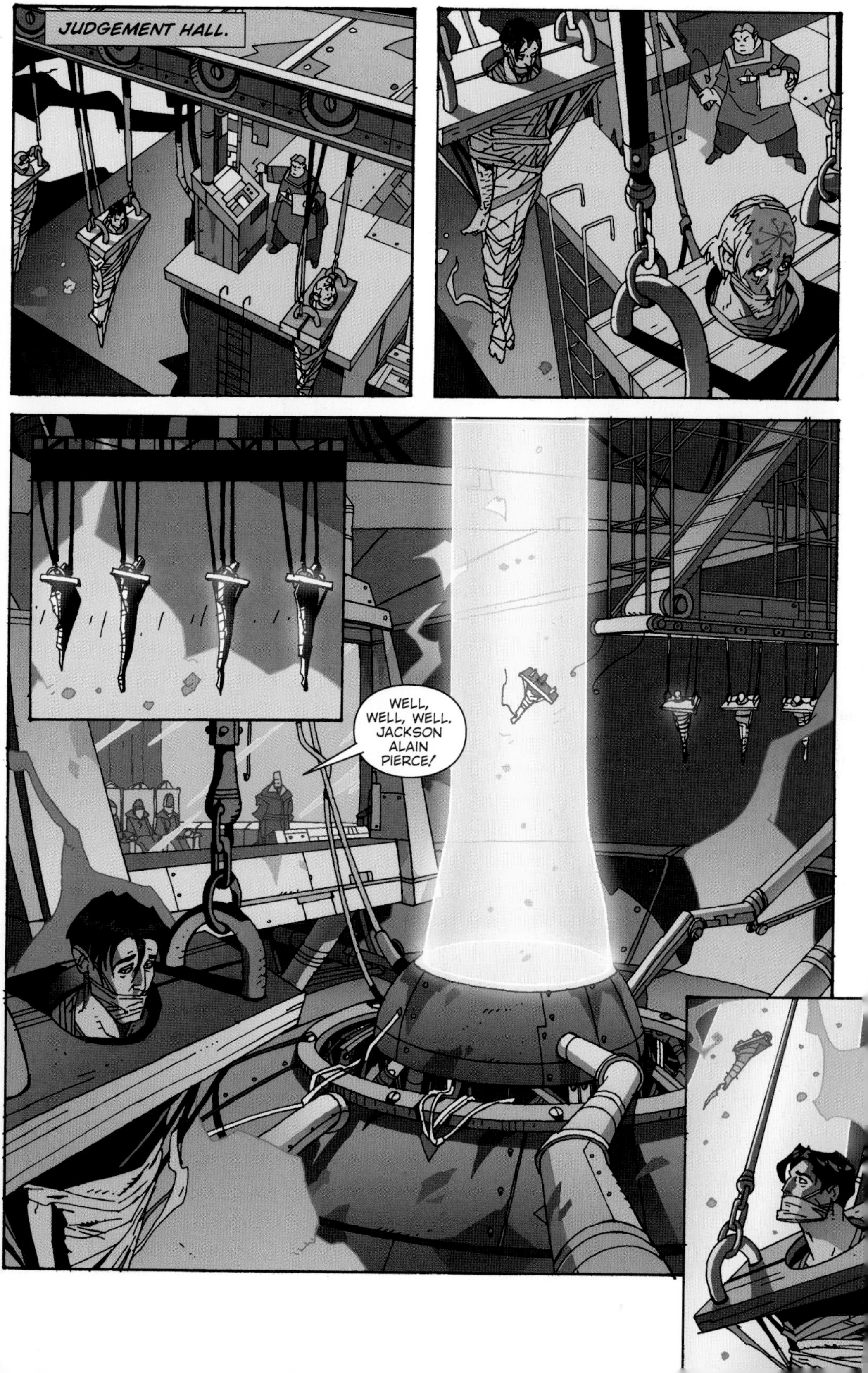
JUDGEMENT HALL.
WELL, WELL, WELL. JACKSON ALAIN PIERCE!

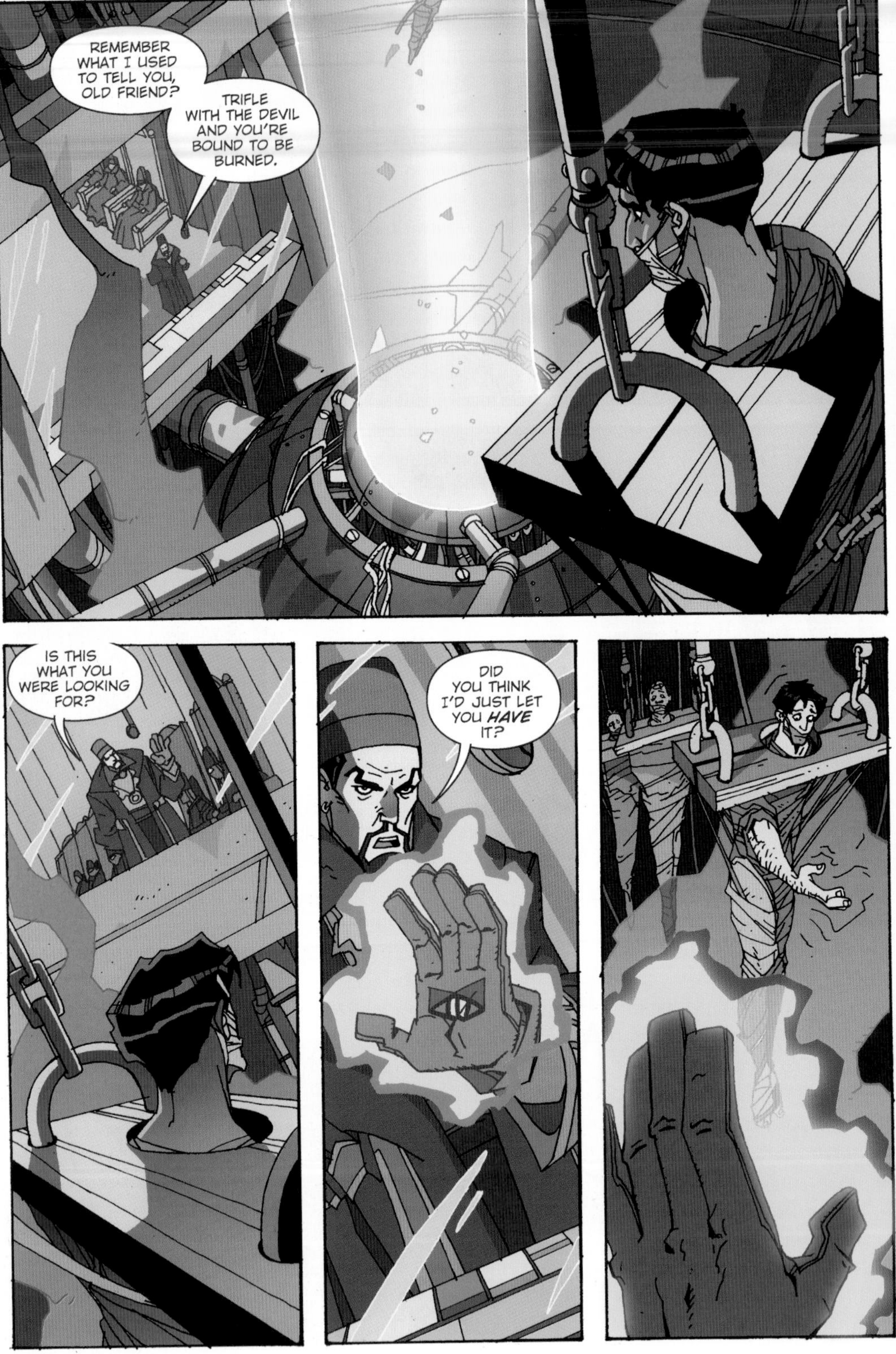
REMEMBER WHAT I USED TO TELL YOU, OLD FRIEND?
TRIFLE WITH THE DEVIL AND YOU'RE BOUND TO BE BURNED.
IS THIS WHAT YOU WERE LOOKING FOR?
DID YOU THINK I'D JUST LET YOU *HAVE* IT?

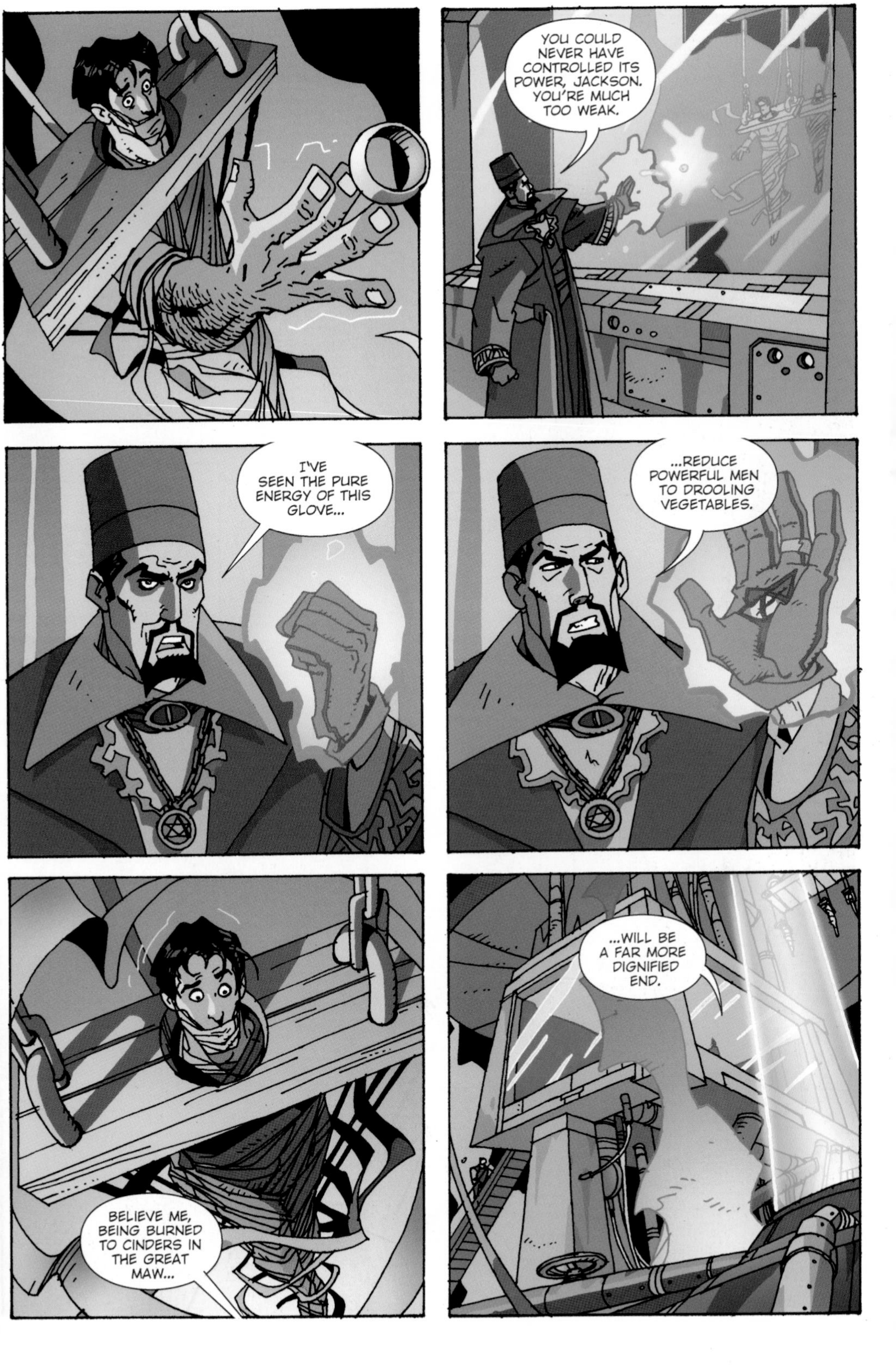
YOU COULD NEVER HAVE CONTROLLED ITS POWER, JACKSON. YOU'RE MUCH TOO WEAK.
I'VE SEEN THE PURE ENERGY OF THIS GLOVE...
...REDUCE POWERFUL MEN TO DROOLING VEGETABLES.
BELIEVE ME, BEING BURNED TO CINDERS IN THE GREAT MAW...
...WILL BE A FAR MORE DIGNIFIED END.

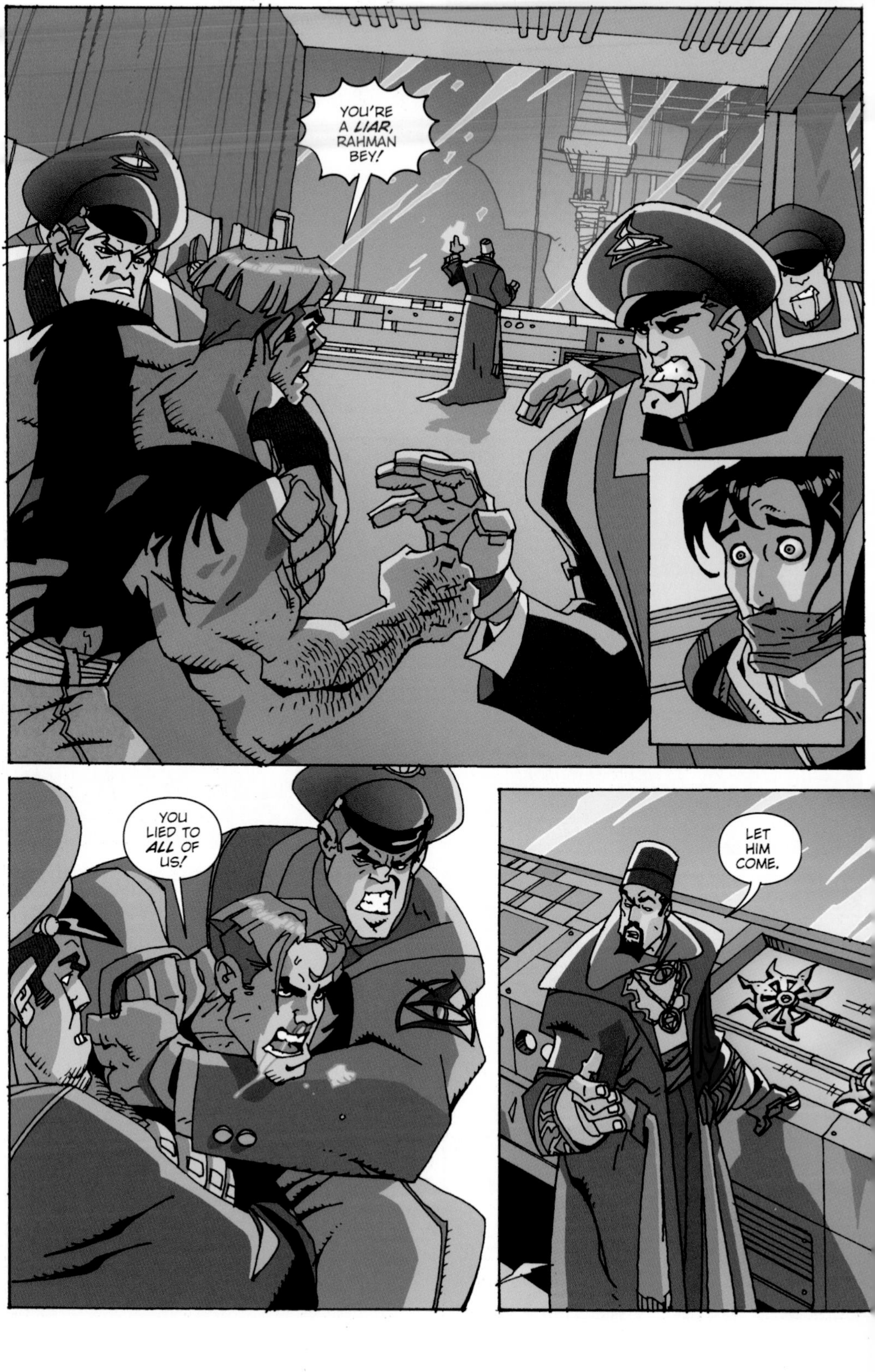
YOU'RE A *LIAR*, RAHMAN BEY!
YOU LIED TO *ALL* OF US!
LET HIM COME.

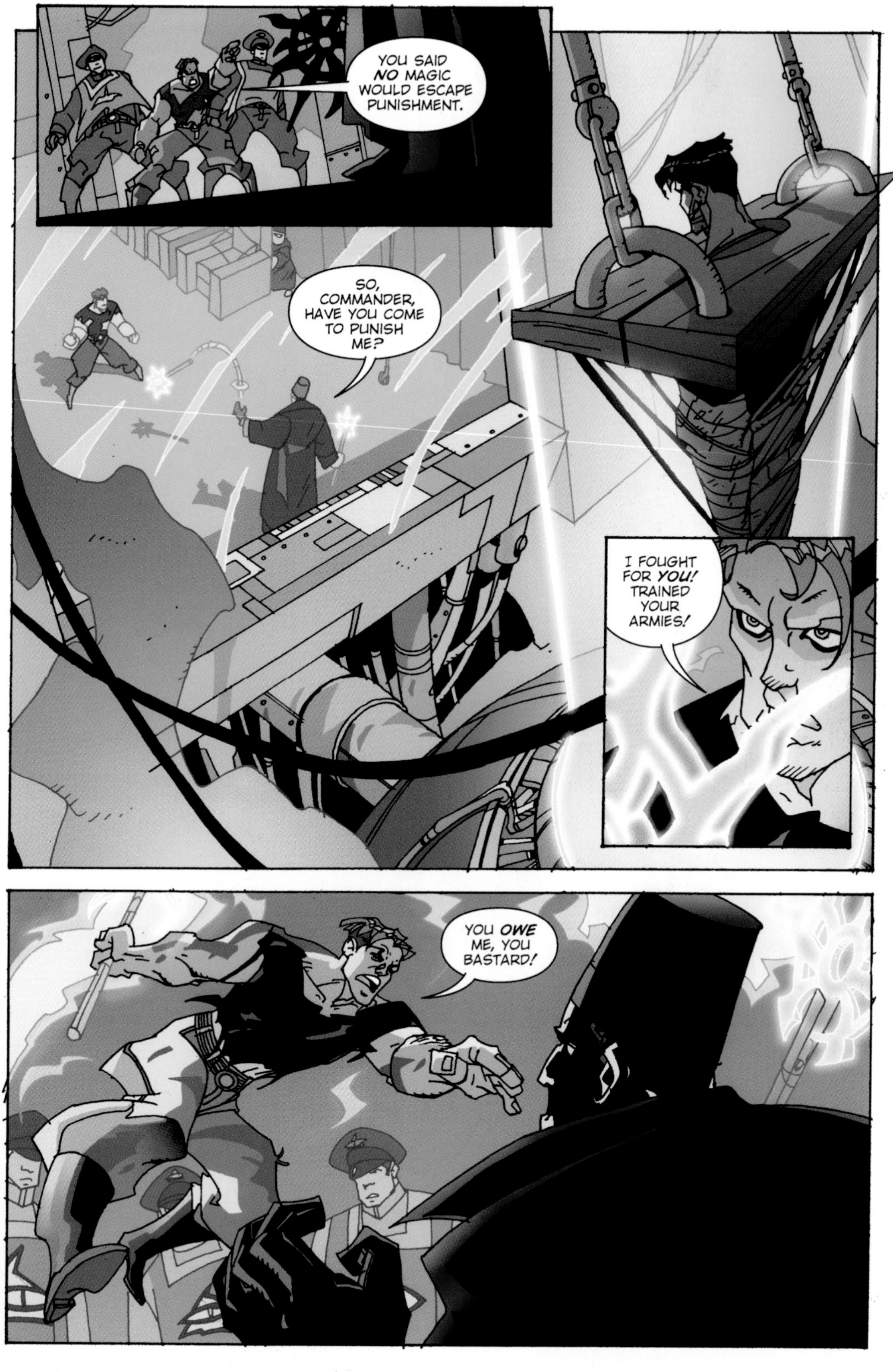
YOU SAID NO MAGIC WOULD ESCAPE PUNISHMENT.
SO, COMMANDER, HAVE YOU COME TO PUNISH ME?
I FOUGHT FOR YOU! TRAINED YOUR ARMIES!
YOU OWE ME, YOU BASTARD!

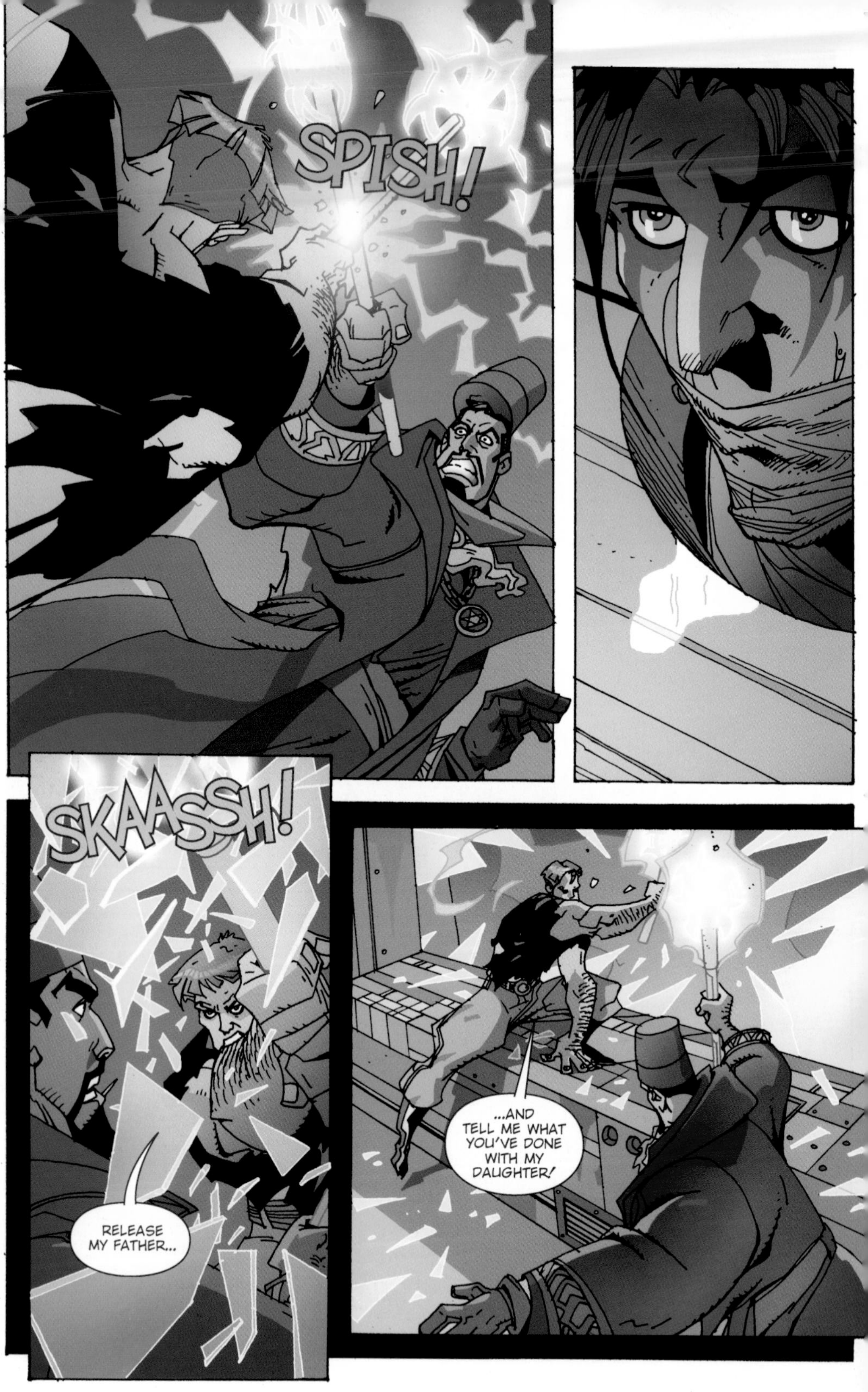
SPISH!
SKAASSH!
RELEASE MY FATHER...
...AND TELL ME WHAT YOU'VE DONE WITH MY DAUGHTER!

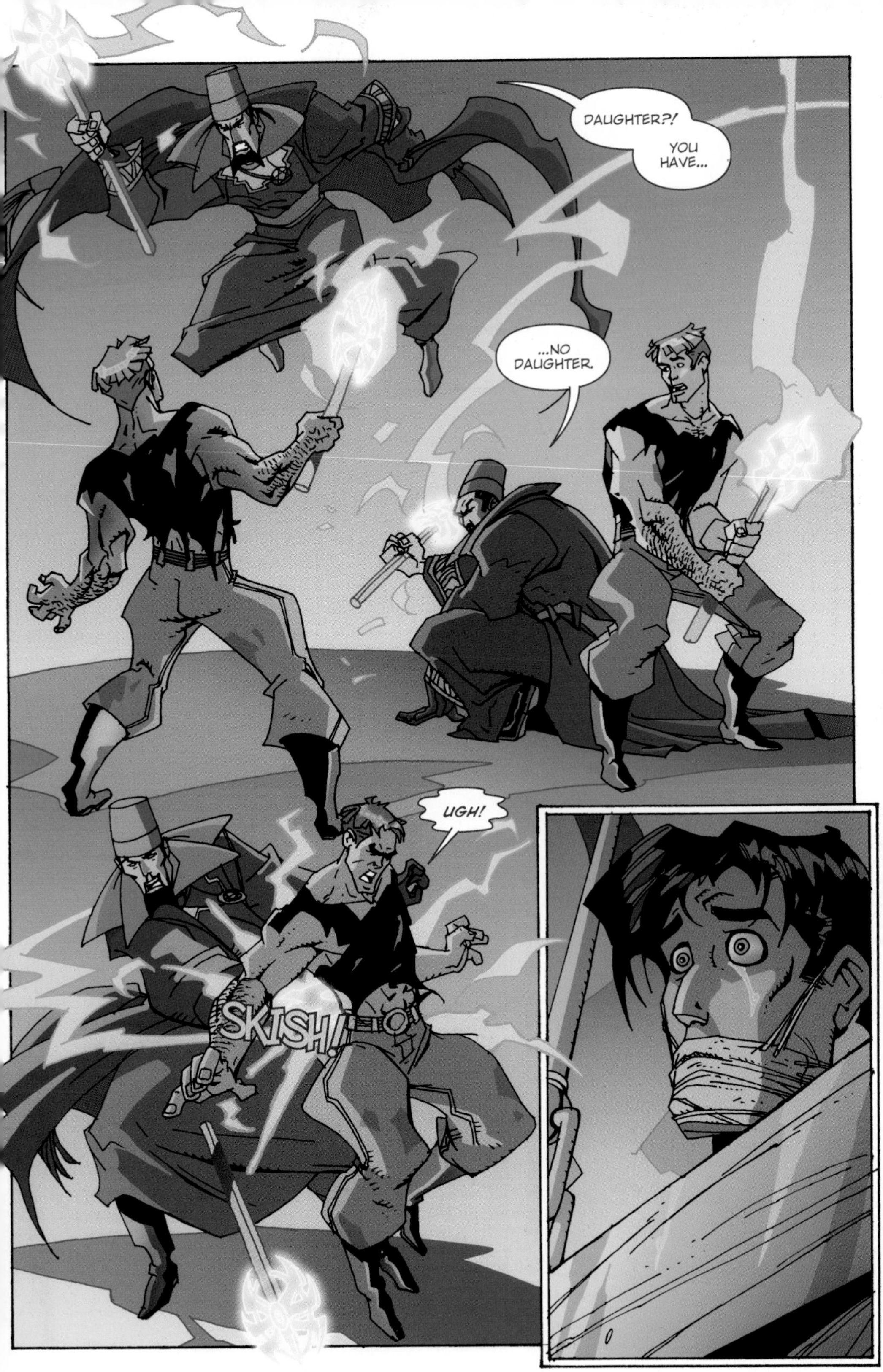
DAUGHTER?! YOU HAVE...
...NO DAUGHTER.
UGH!
SKISH!

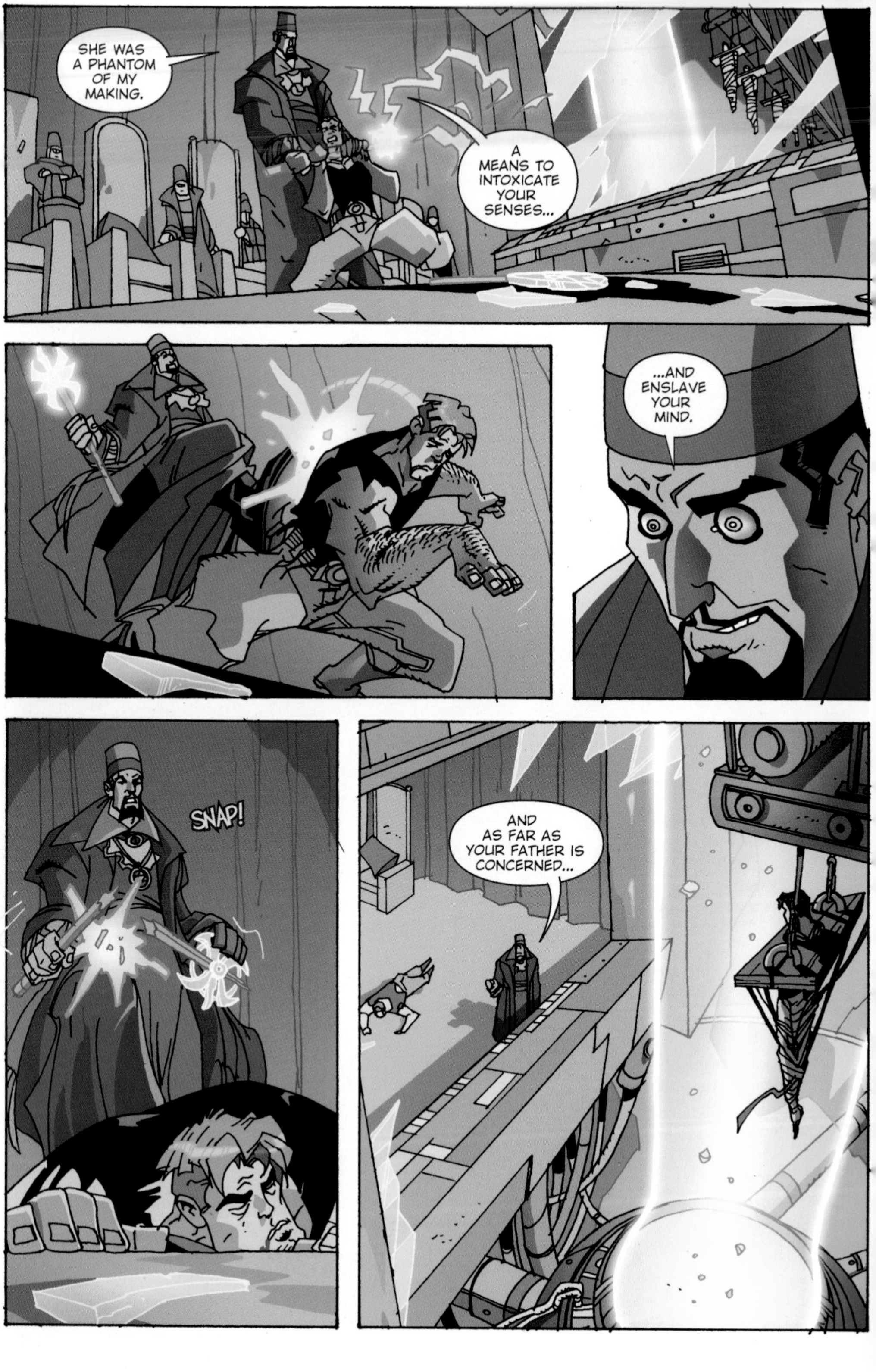
SHE WAS A PHANTOM OF MY MAKING.
A MEANS TO INTOXICATE YOUR SENSES...
...AND ENSLAVE YOUR MIND.
SNAP!
AND AS FAR AS YOUR FATHER IS CONCERNED...

...I'LL WIPE OUT YOUR MEMORY OF HIM FOREVER.

YOU'LL BE PURGED OF HIS INFLUENCE ONCE AND FOR ALL.

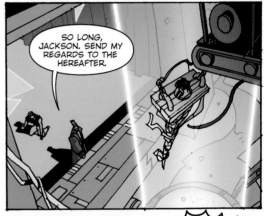

SO LONG, JACKSON. SEND MY REGARDS TO THE HEREAFTER.

RAAHHH!!

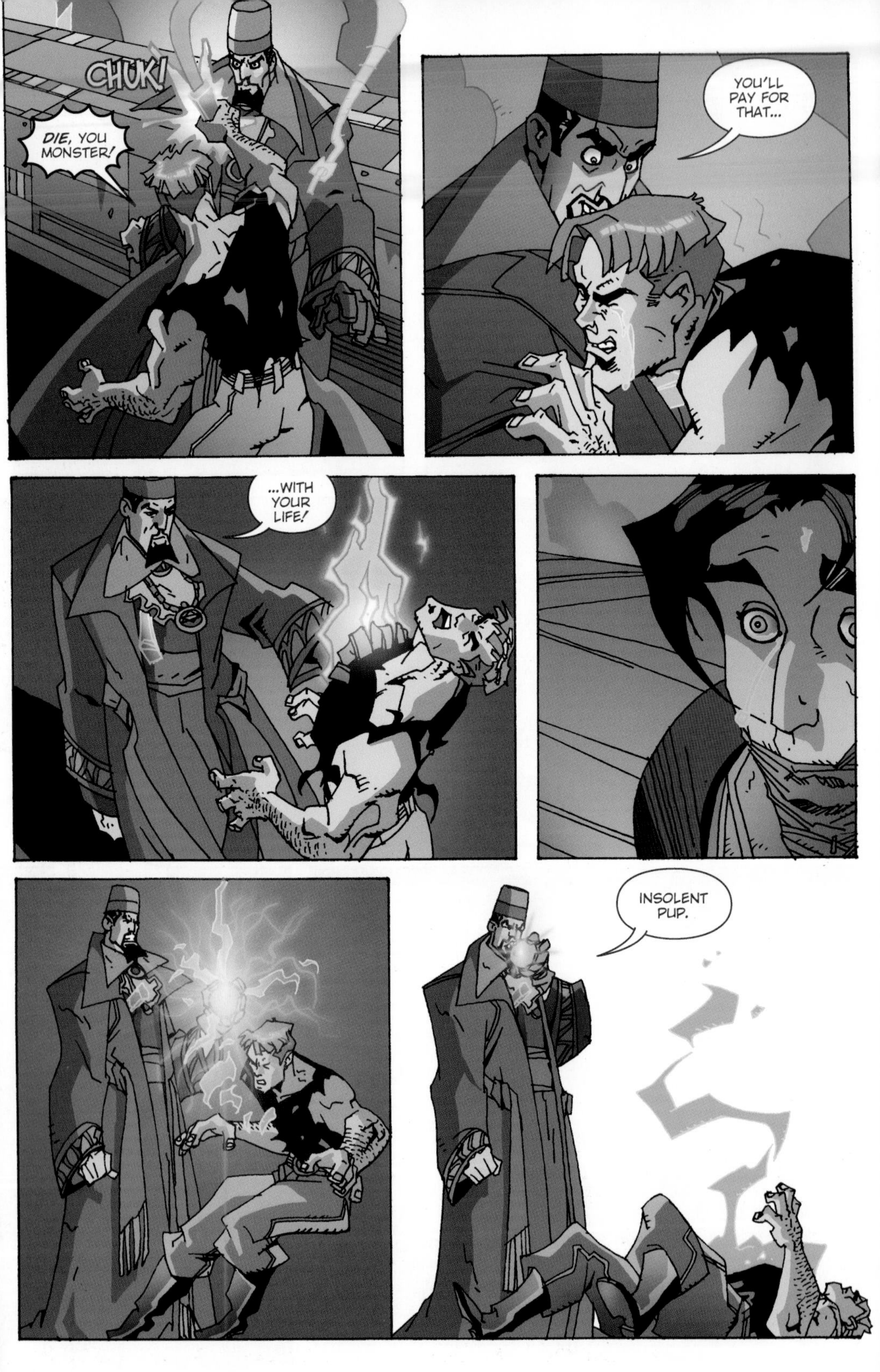
CHUK!
DIE, YOU MONSTER!
YOU'LL PAY FOR THAT...
...WITH YOUR LIFE!
INSOLENT PUP.

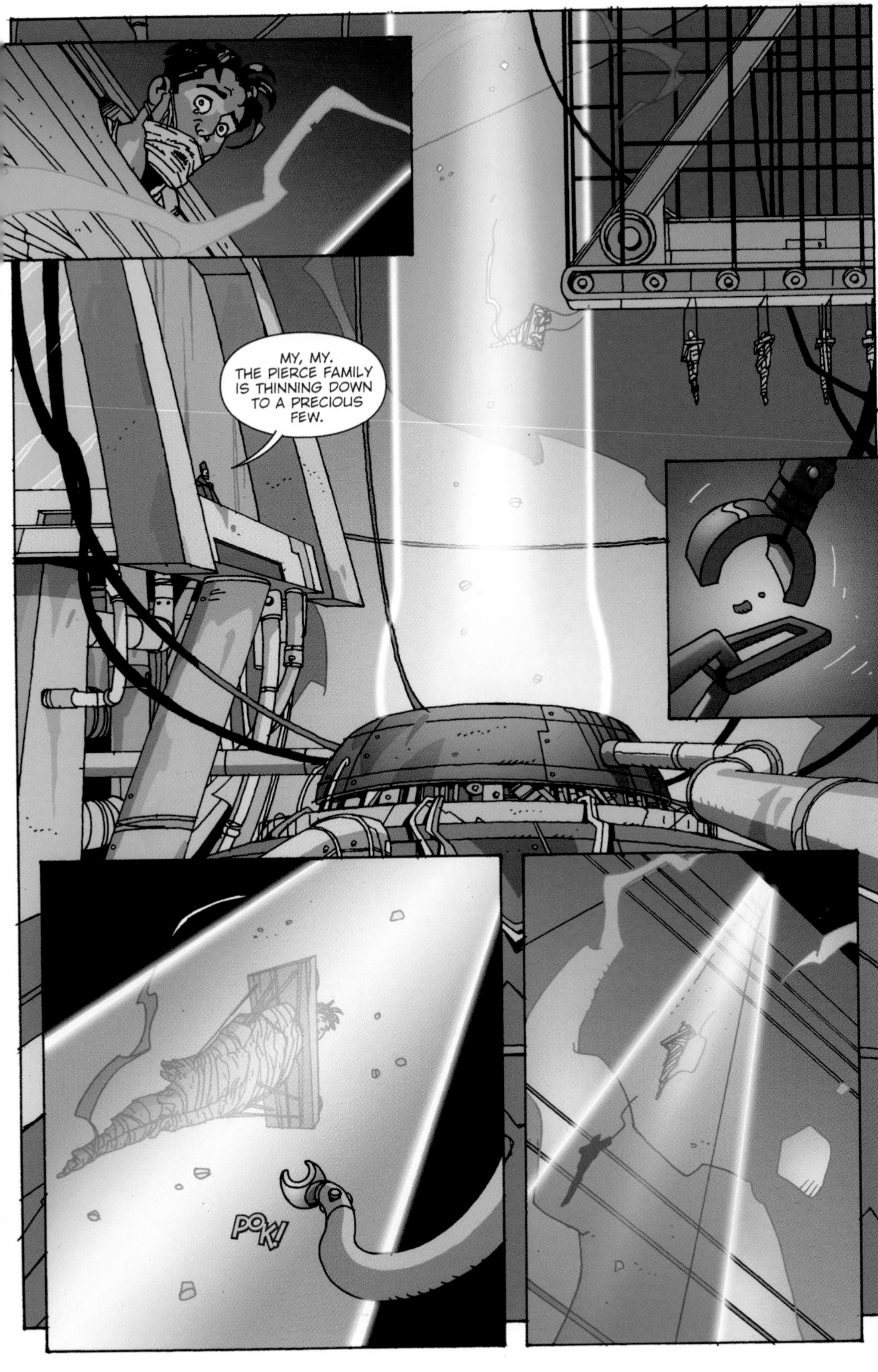
MY, MY. THE PIERCE FAMILY IS THINNING DOWN TO A PRECIOUS FEW.
POK!

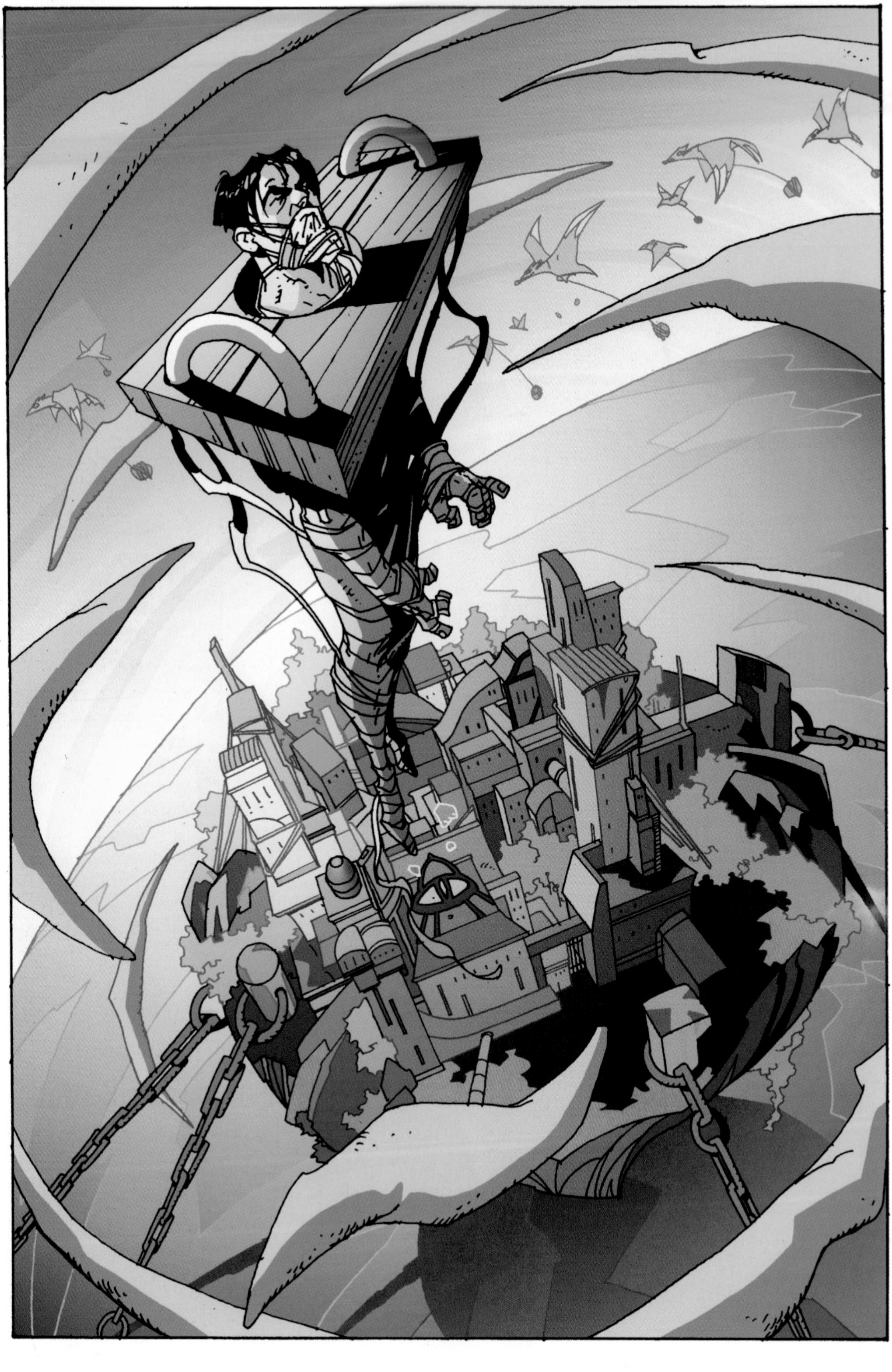

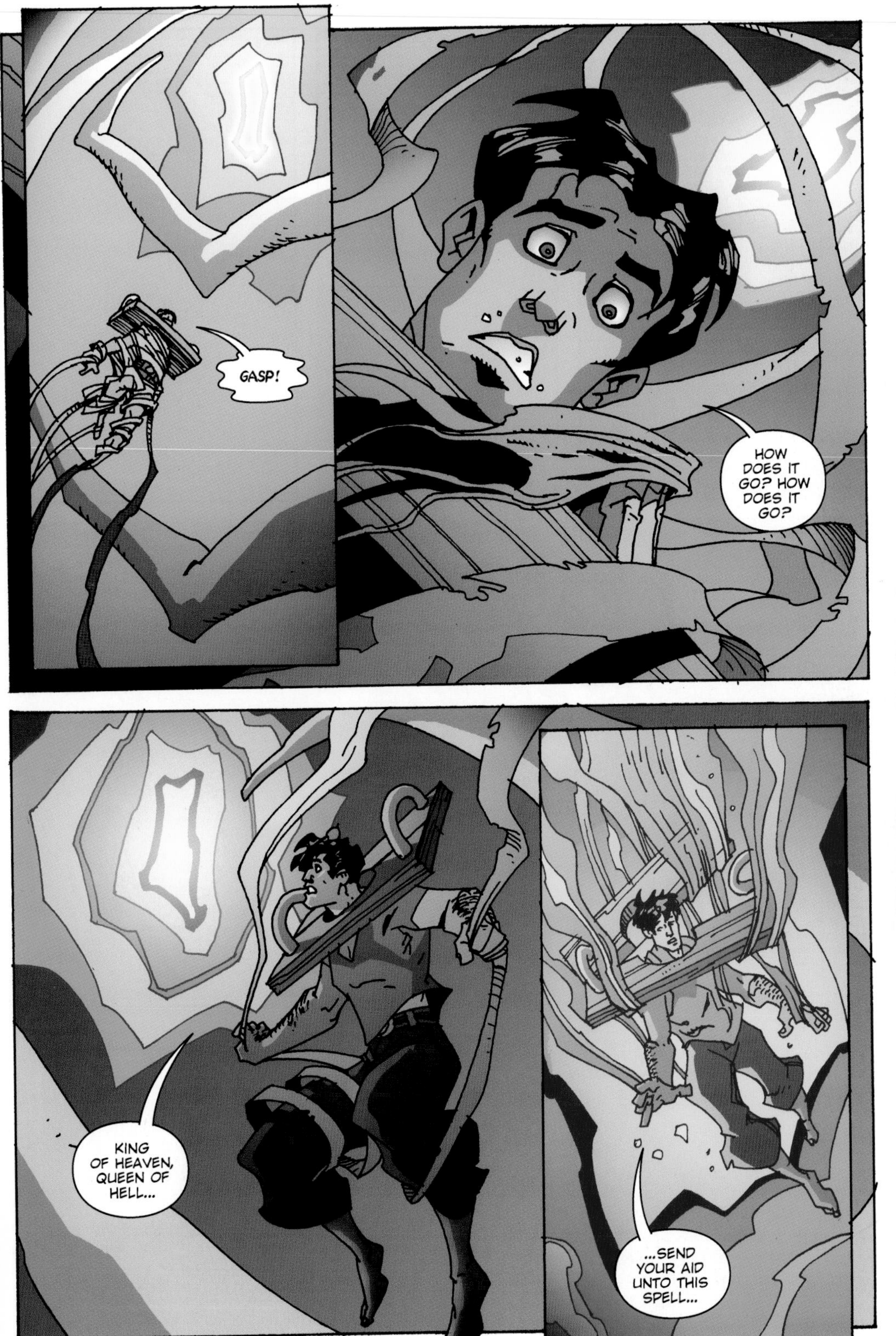
GASP!
HOW DOES IT GO? HOW DOES IT GO?
KING OF HEAVEN, QUEEN OF HELL...
...SEND YOUR AID UNTO THIS SPELL...

...WORK MY WILL BY MAGIC RITE...

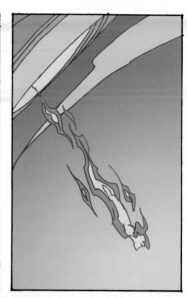

YET ANOTHER DIMENSION.

SPLOOSH!

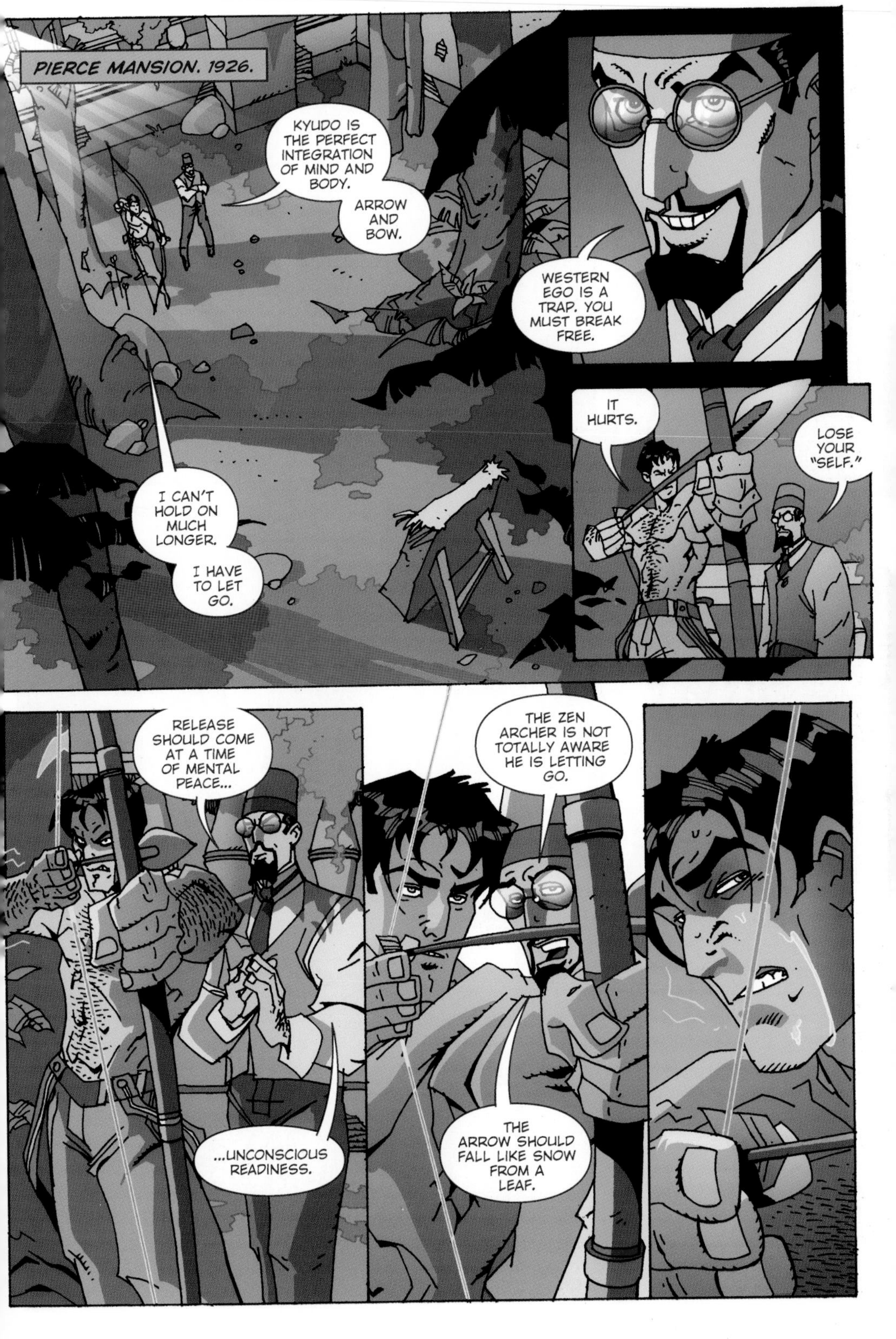
PIERCE MANSION. 1926.
KYUDO IS THE PERFECT INTEGRATION OF MIND AND BODY.
ARROW AND BOW.
WESTERN EGO IS A TRAP. YOU MUST BREAK FREE.
I CAN'T HOLD ON MUCH LONGER.
I HAVE TO LET GO.
IT HURTS.
LOSE YOUR "SELF."
RELEASE SHOULD COME AT A TIME OF MENTAL PEACE...
...UNCONSCIOUS READINESS.
THE ZEN ARCHER IS NOT TOTALLY AWARE HE IS LETTING GO.
THE ARROW SHOULD FALL LIKE SNOW FROM A LEAF.

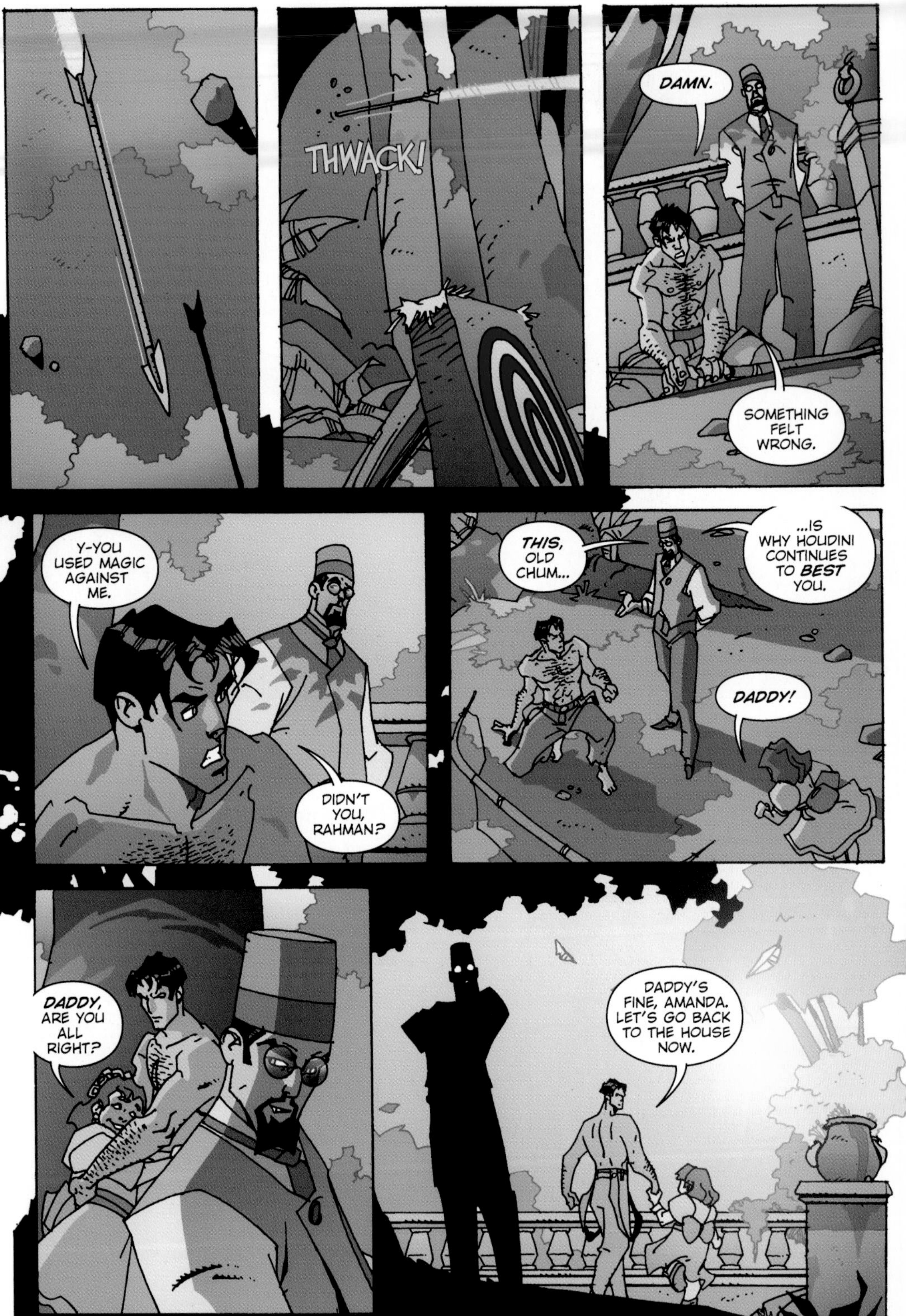
THWACK!
DAMN.
SOMETHING FELT WRONG.
Y-YOU USED MAGIC AGAINST ME.
DIDN'T YOU, RAHMAN?
THIS, OLD CHUM...
...IS WHY HOUDINI CONTINUES TO BEST YOU.
DADDY!
DADDY, ARE YOU ALL RIGHT?
DADDY'S FINE, AMANDA. LET'S GO BACK TO THE HOUSE NOW.

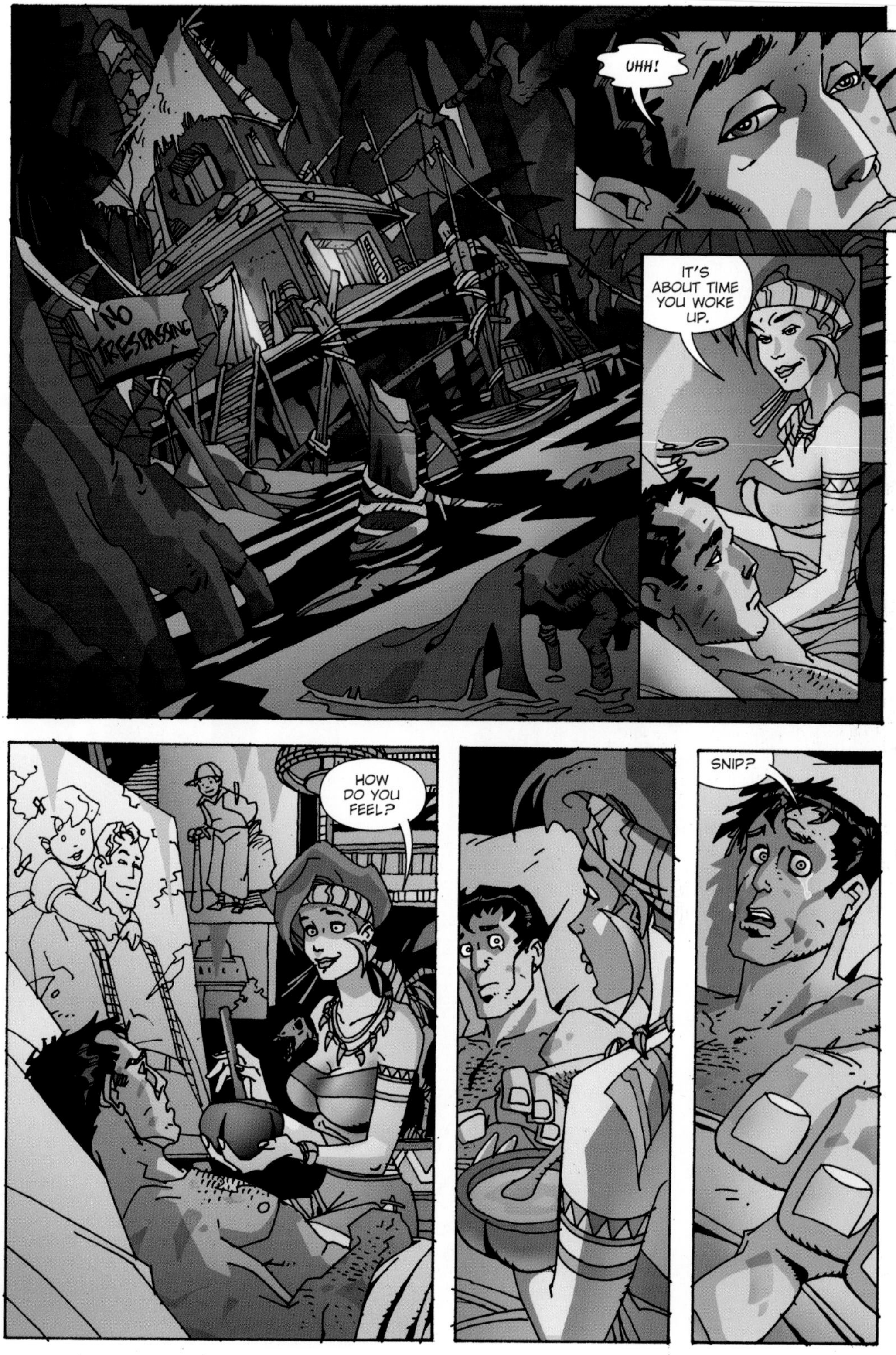
NO TRESPASSING
UHH!
IT'S ABOUT TIME YOU WOKE UP.
HOW DO YOU FEEL?
SNIP?

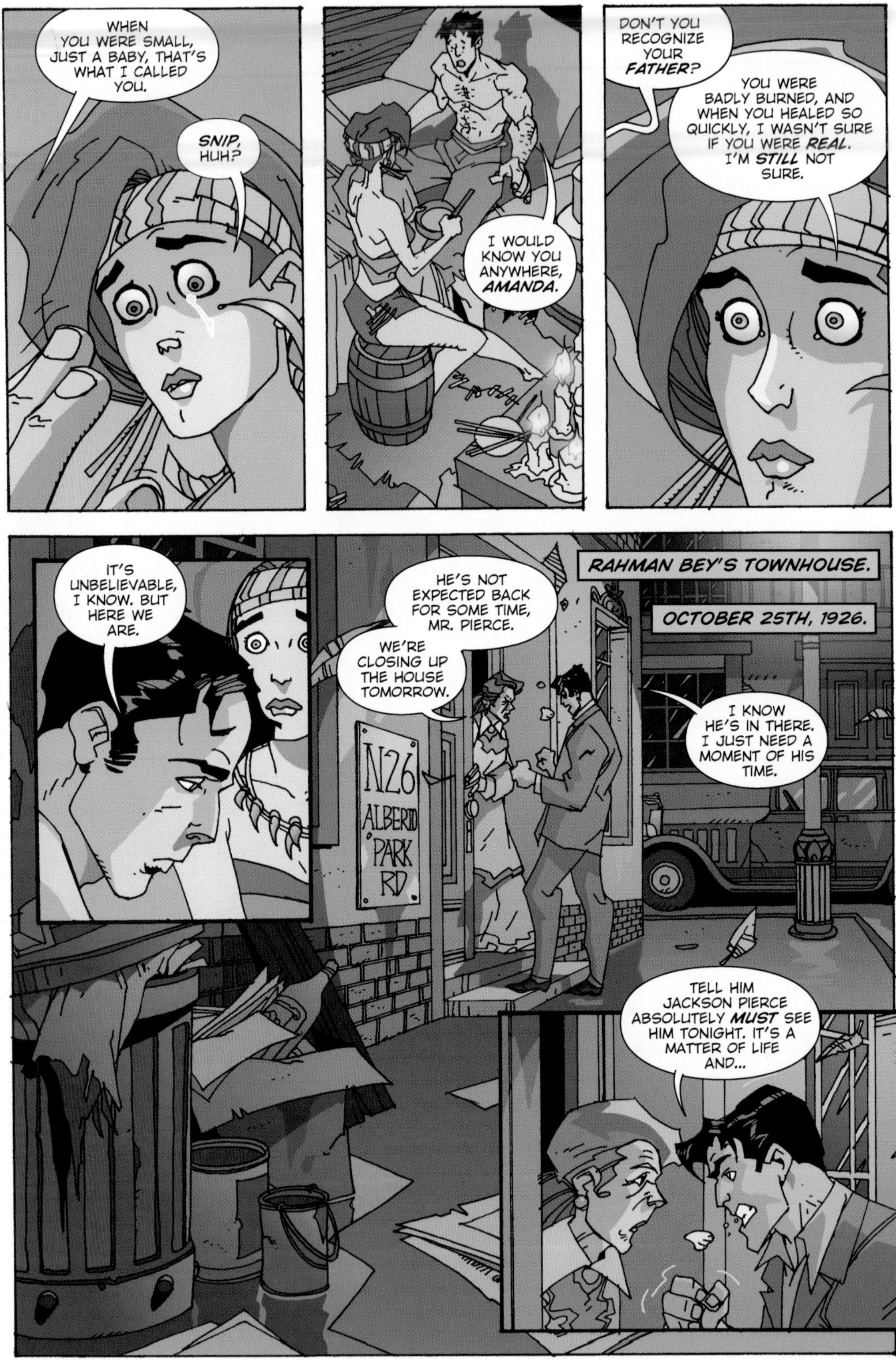
WHEN YOU WERE SMALL, JUST A BABY, THAT'S WHAT I CALLED YOU.
SNIP, HUH?
I WOULD KNOW YOU ANYWHERE, AMANDA.
DON'T YOU RECOGNIZE YOUR FATHER?
YOU WERE BADLY BURNED, AND WHEN YOU HEALED SO QUICKLY, I WASN'T SURE IF YOU WERE REAL. I'M STILL NOT SURE.
IT'S UNBELIEVABLE, I KNOW. BUT HERE WE ARE.
RAHMAN BEY'S TOWNHOUSE.
OCTOBER 25TH, 1926.
HE'S NOT EXPECTED BACK FOR SOME TIME, MR. PIERCE.
WE'RE CLOSING UP THE HOUSE TOMORROW.
N26 ALBERTO PARK RD
I KNOW HE'S IN THERE. I JUST NEED A MOMENT OF HIS TIME.
TELL HIM JACKSON PIERCE ABSOLUTELY MUST SEE HIM TONIGHT. IT'S A MATTER OF LIFE AND...

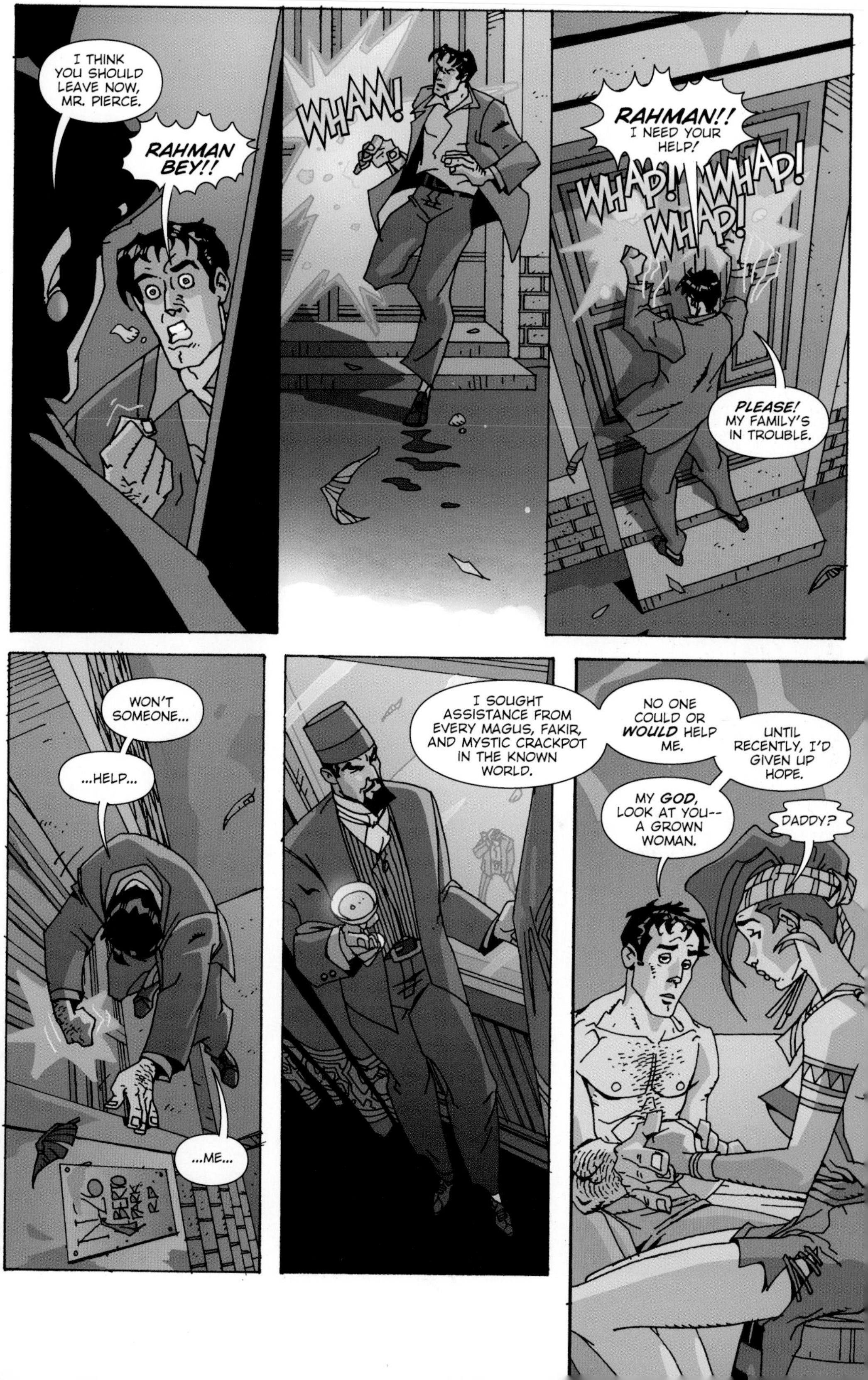
I THINK YOU SHOULD LEAVE NOW, MR. PIERCE.
RAHMAN BEY!!
WHAM!
RAHMAN!! I NEED YOUR HELP!
WHAP! WHAP! WHAP!
PLEASE! MY FAMILY'S IN TROUBLE.
WON'T SOMEONE...
...HELP...
...ME...
I SOUGHT ASSISTANCE FROM EVERY MAGUS, FAKIR, AND MYSTIC CRACKPOT IN THE KNOWN WORLD.
NO ONE COULD OR WOULD HELP ME.
UNTIL RECENTLY, I'D GIVEN UP HOPE.
MY GOD, LOOK AT YOU-- A GROWN WOMAN.
DADDY?

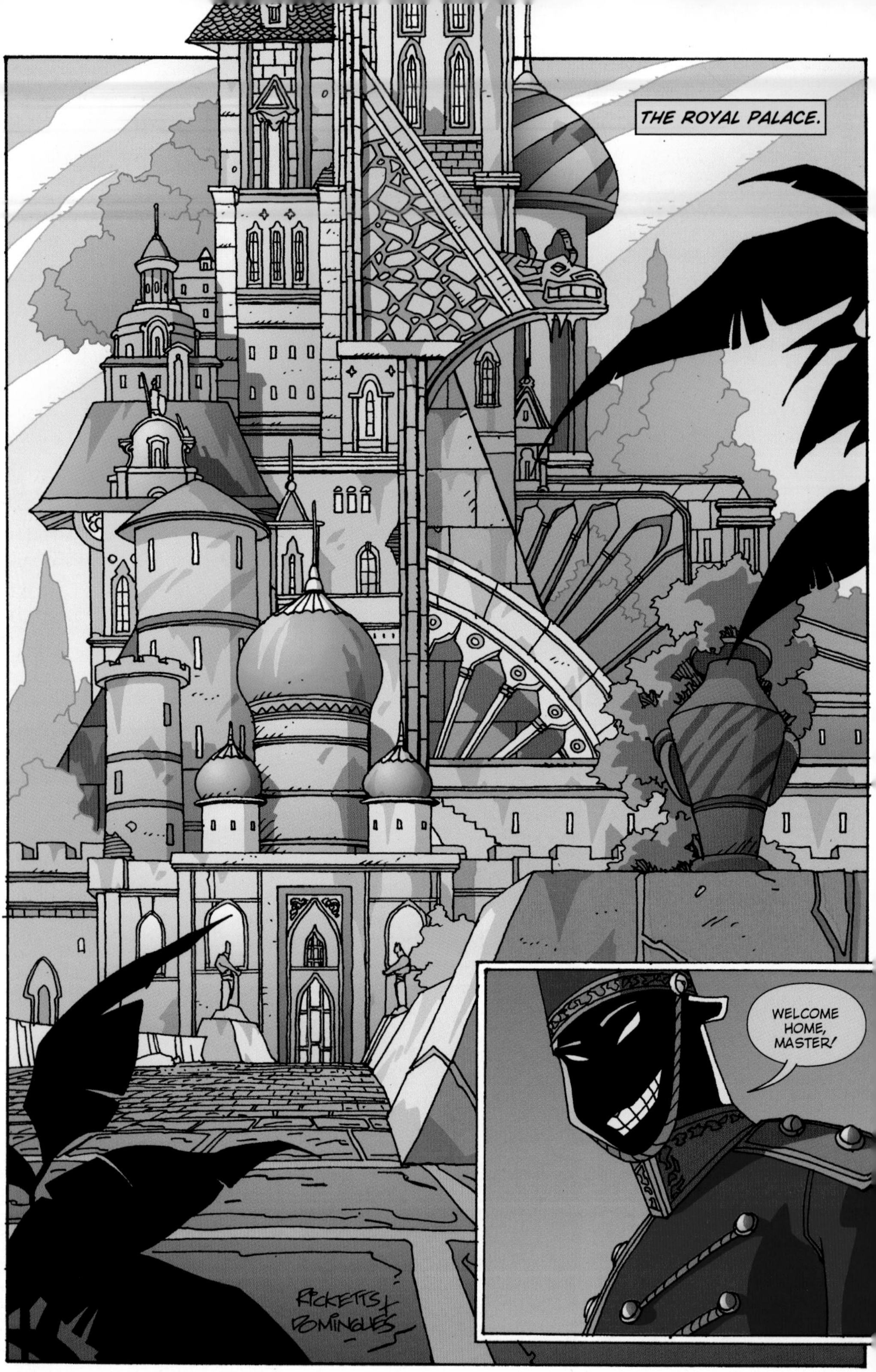
THE ROYAL PALACE.
WELCOME HOME, MASTER!
RICKETTS + DOMINGUES

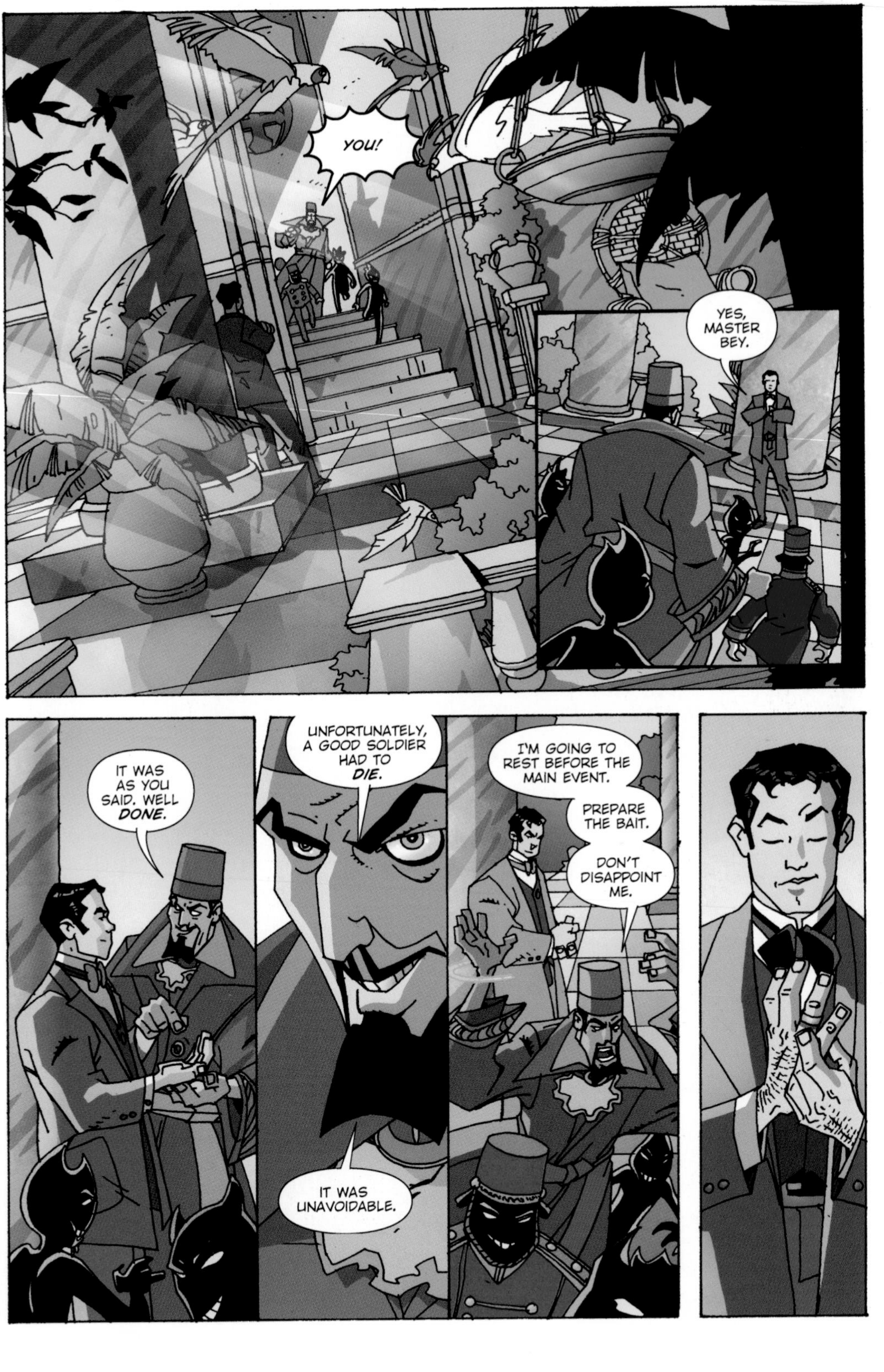
YOU!
YES, MASTER BEY.
IT WAS AS YOU SAID. WELL DONE.
UNFORTUNATELY, A GOOD SOLDIER HAD TO DIE.
IT WAS UNAVOIDABLE.
I'M GOING TO REST BEFORE THE MAIN EVENT.
PREPARE THE BAIT.
DON'T DISAPPOINT ME.

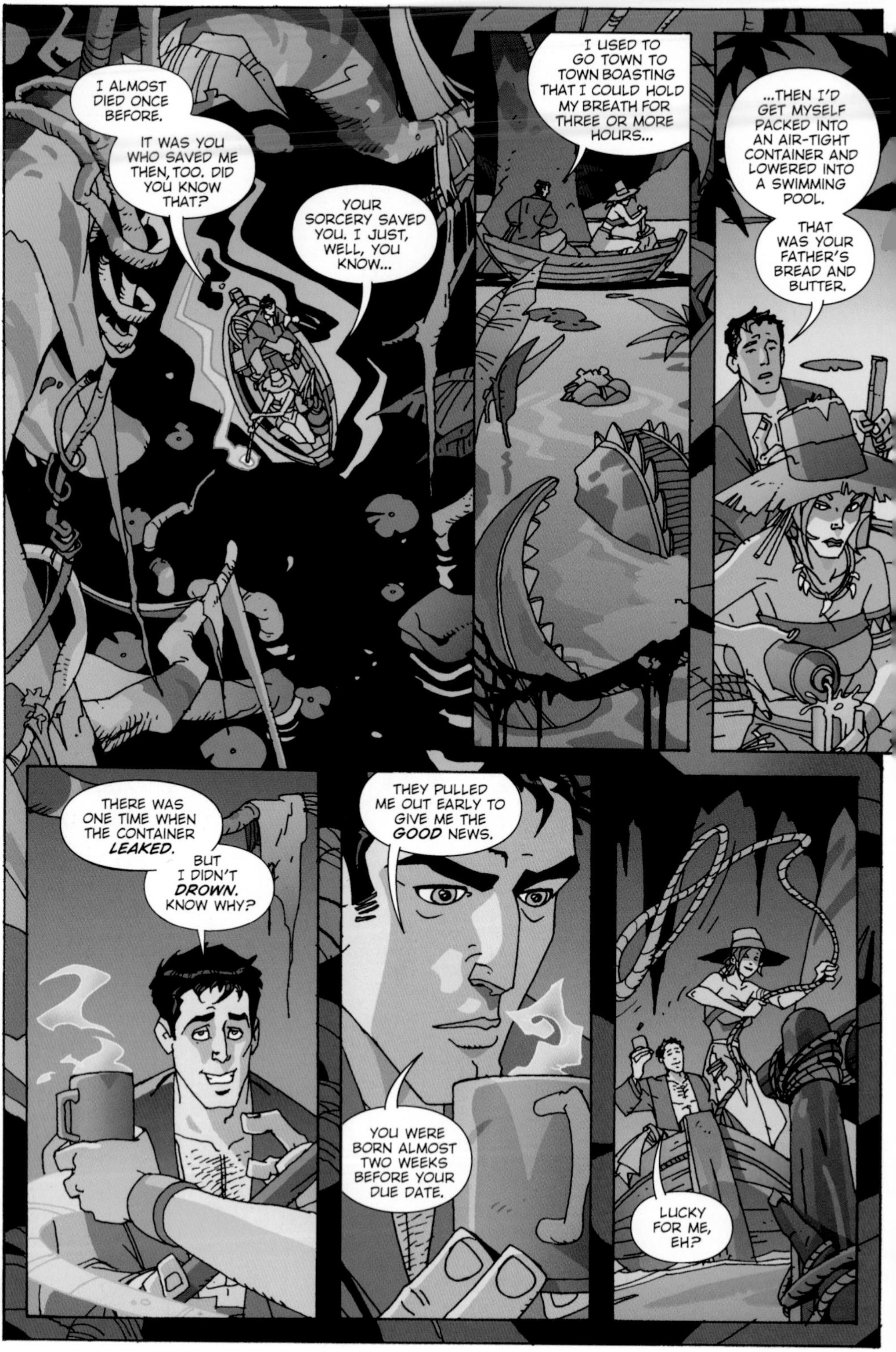
I ALMOST DIED ONCE BEFORE.
IT WAS YOU WHO SAVED ME THEN, TOO. DID YOU KNOW THAT?
YOUR SORCERY SAVED YOU. I JUST, WELL, YOU KNOW...
I USED TO GO TOWN TO TOWN BOASTING THAT I COULD HOLD MY BREATH FOR THREE OR MORE HOURS...
...THEN I'D GET MYSELF PACKED INTO AN AIR-TIGHT CONTAINER AND LOWERED INTO A SWIMMING POOL.
THAT WAS YOUR FATHER'S BREAD AND BUTTER.
THERE WAS ONE TIME WHEN THE CONTAINER LEAKED.
BUT I DIDN'T DROWN. KNOW WHY?
THEY PULLED ME OUT EARLY TO GIVE ME THE GOOD NEWS.
YOU WERE BORN ALMOST TWO WEEKS BEFORE YOUR DUE DATE.
LUCKY FOR ME, EH?

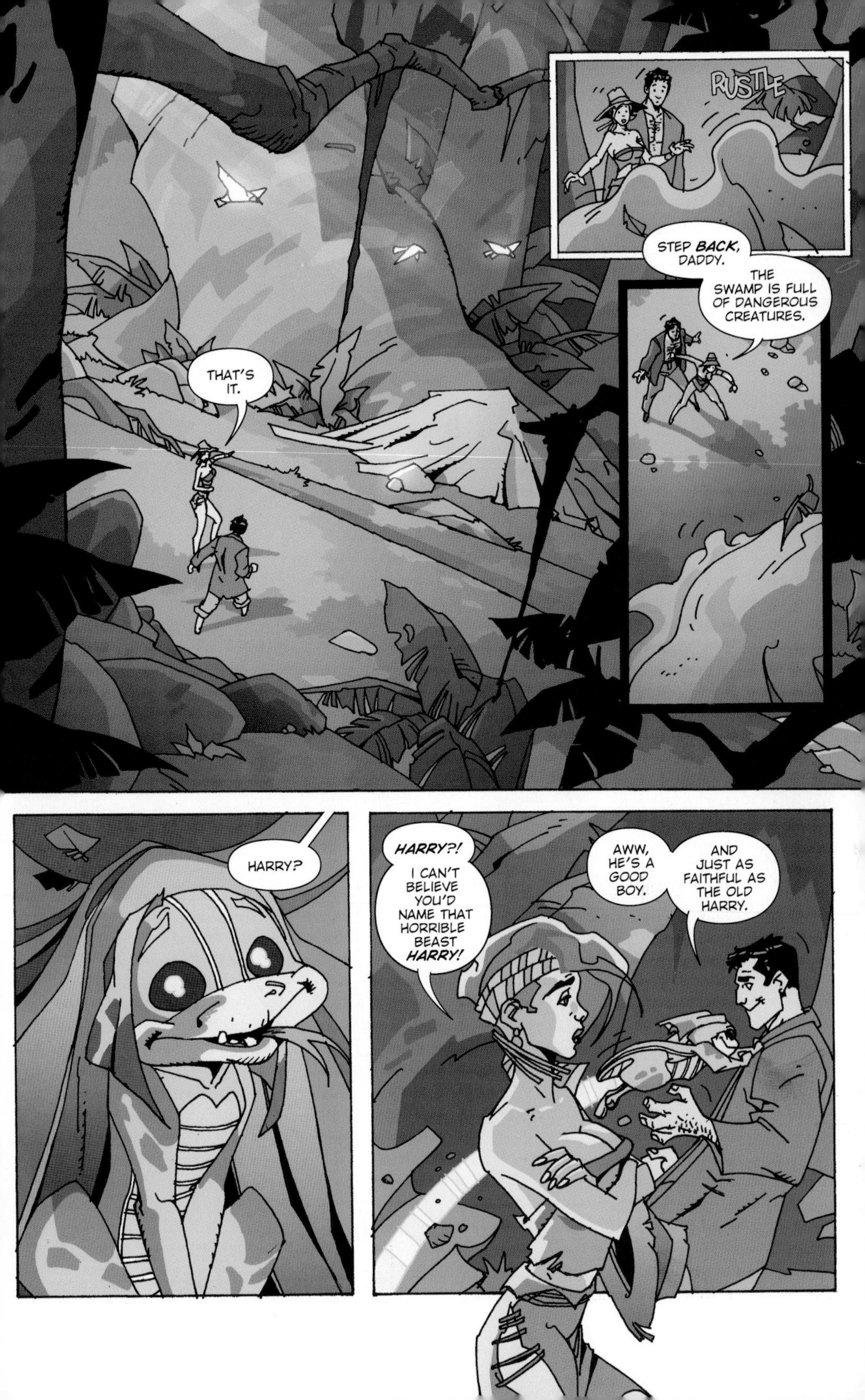
RUSTLE
STEP BACK, DADDY.
THE SWAMP IS FULL OF DANGEROUS CREATURES.
THAT'S IT.
HARRY?
HARRY?!
I CAN'T BELIEVE YOU'D NAME THAT HORRIBLE BEAST HARRY!
AWW, HE'S A GOOD BOY.
AND JUST AS FAITHFUL AS THE OLD HARRY.

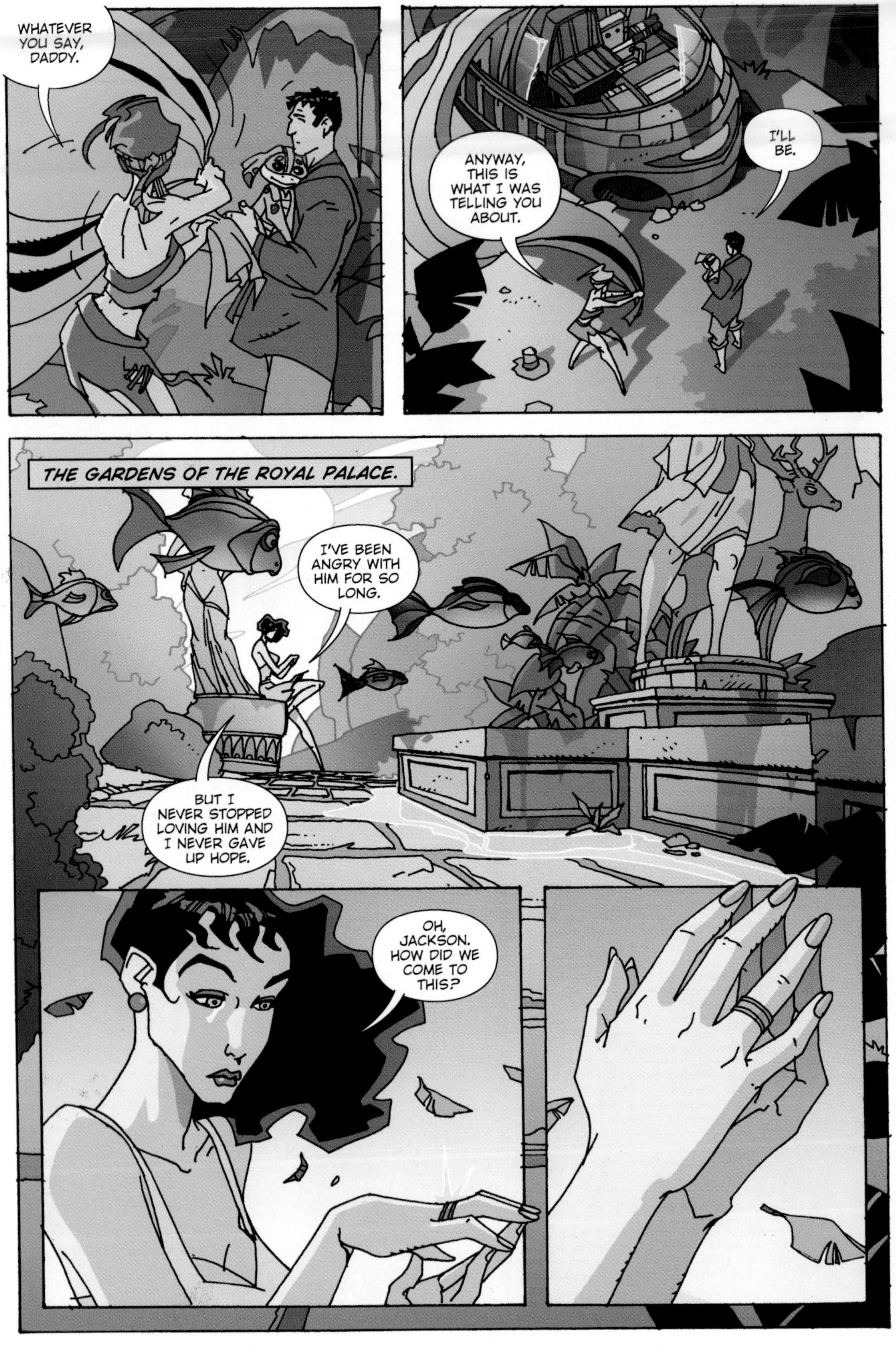
WHATEVER YOU SAY, DADDY.
ANYWAY, THIS IS WHAT I WAS TELLING YOU ABOUT.
I'LL BE.
THE GARDENS OF THE ROYAL PALACE.
I'VE BEEN ANGRY WITH HIM FOR SO LONG.
BUT I NEVER STOPPED LOVING HIM AND I NEVER GAVE UP HOPE.
OH, JACKSON. HOW DID WE COME TO THIS?

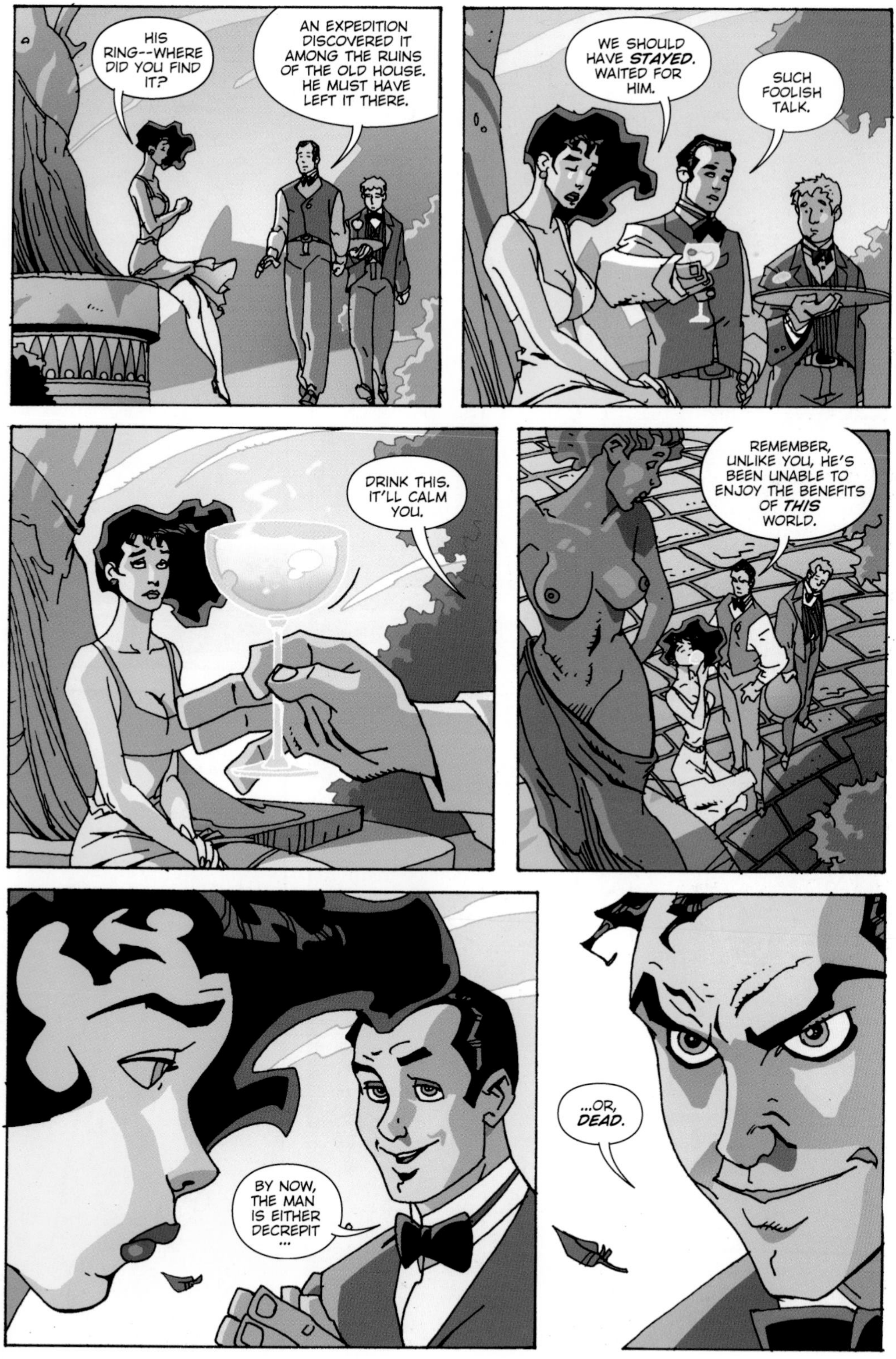
HIS RING--WHERE DID YOU FIND IT?
AN EXPEDITION DISCOVERED IT AMONG THE RUINS OF THE OLD HOUSE. HE MUST HAVE LEFT IT THERE.
WE SHOULD HAVE *STAYED.* WAITED FOR HIM.
SUCH FOOLISH TALK.
DRINK THIS. IT'LL CALM YOU.
REMEMBER, UNLIKE YOU, HE'S BEEN UNABLE TO ENJOY THE BENEFITS OF *THIS* WORLD.
BY NOW, THE MAN IS EITHER DECREPIT ...
...OR, *DEAD.*

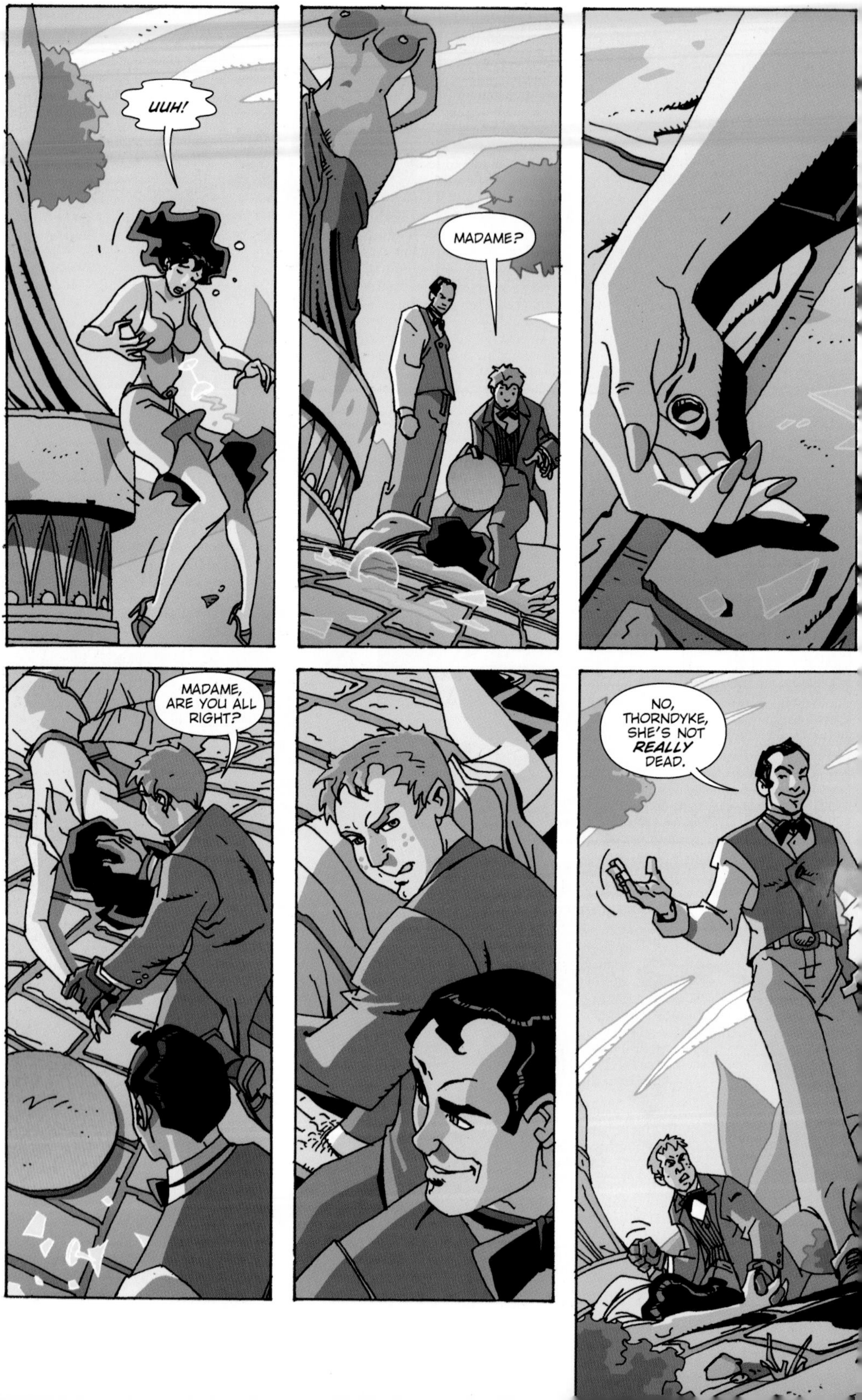
UUH!
MADAME?
MADAME, ARE YOU ALL RIGHT?
NO, THORNDYKE, SHE'S NOT *REALLY* DEAD.

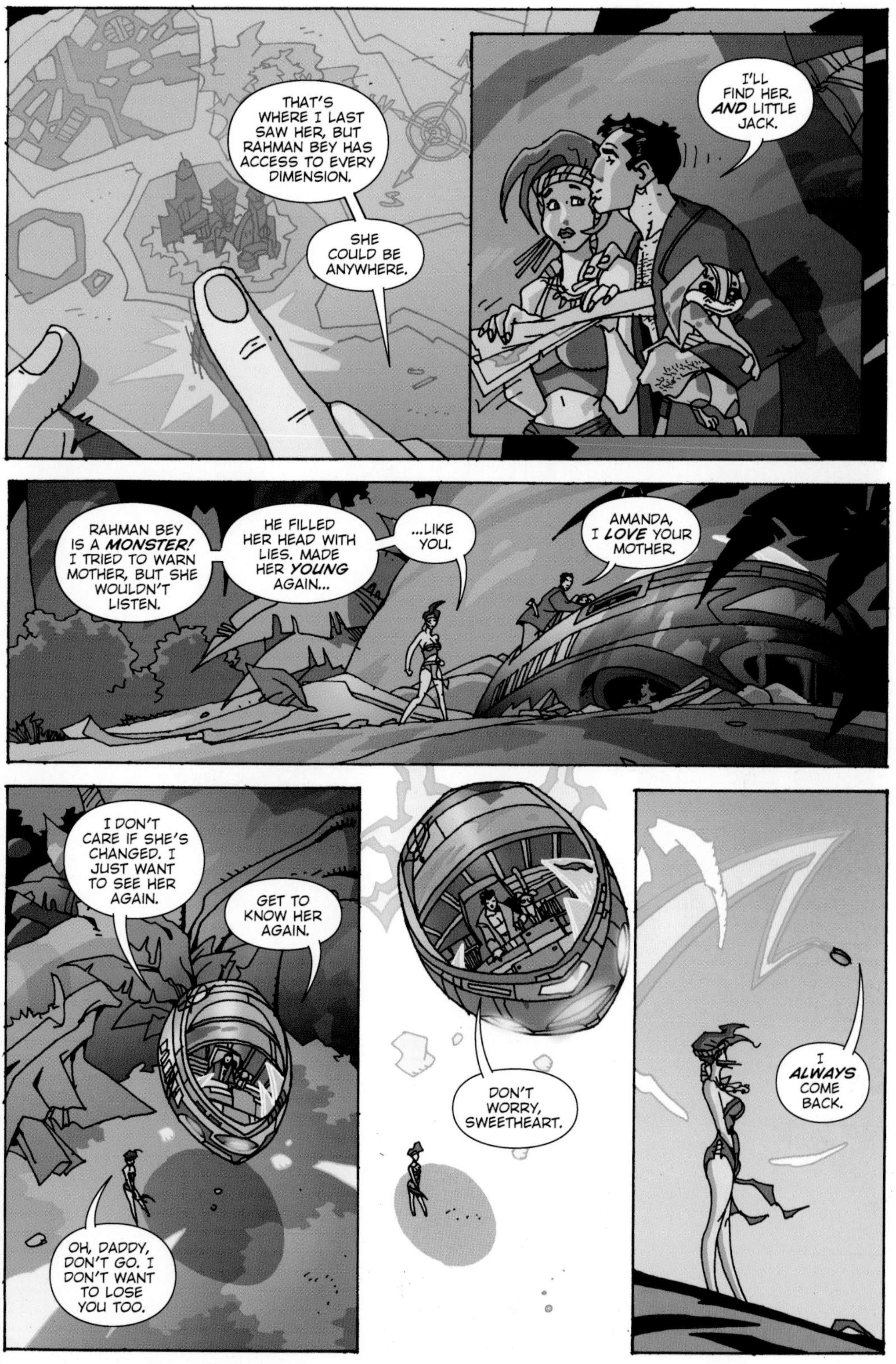
THAT'S WHERE I LAST SAW HER, BUT RAHMAN BEY HAS ACCESS TO EVERY DIMENSION.
SHE COULD BE ANYWHERE.
I'LL FIND HER. AND LITTLE JACK.
RAHMAN BEY IS A MONSTER! I TRIED TO WARN MOTHER, BUT SHE WOULDN'T LISTEN.
HE FILLED HER HEAD WITH LIES. MADE HER YOUNG AGAIN...
...LIKE YOU.
AMANDA, I LOVE YOUR MOTHER.
I DON'T CARE IF SHE'S CHANGED. I JUST WANT TO SEE HER AGAIN.
GET TO KNOW HER AGAIN.
OH, DADDY, DON'T GO. I DON'T WANT TO LOSE YOU TOO.
DON'T WORRY, SWEETHEART.
I ALWAYS COME BACK.

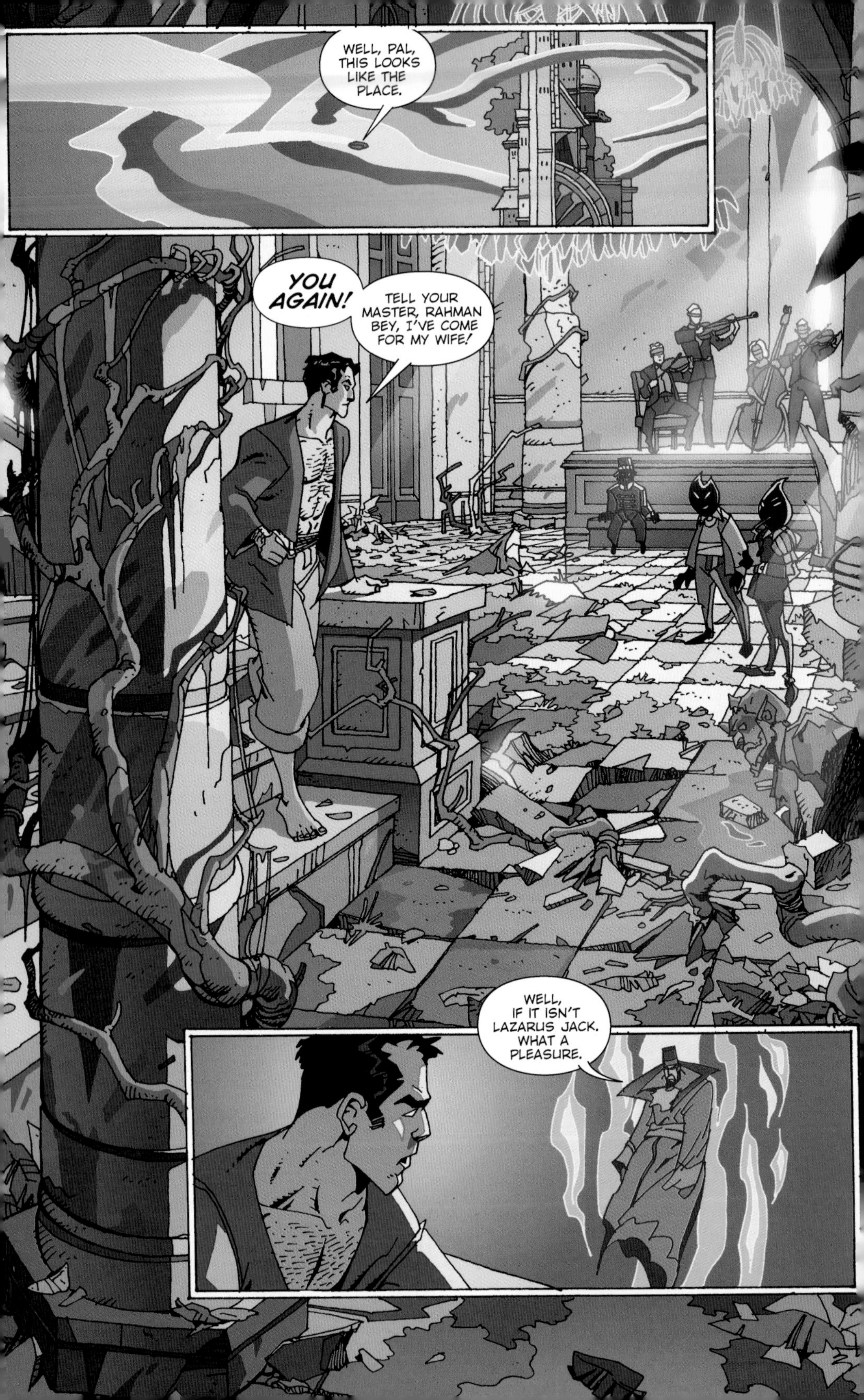
WELL, PAL, THIS LOOKS LIKE THE PLACE.
YOU AGAIN!
TELL YOUR MASTER, RAHMAN BEY, I'VE COME FOR MY WIFE!
WELL, IF IT ISN'T LAZARUS JACK. WHAT A PLEASURE.

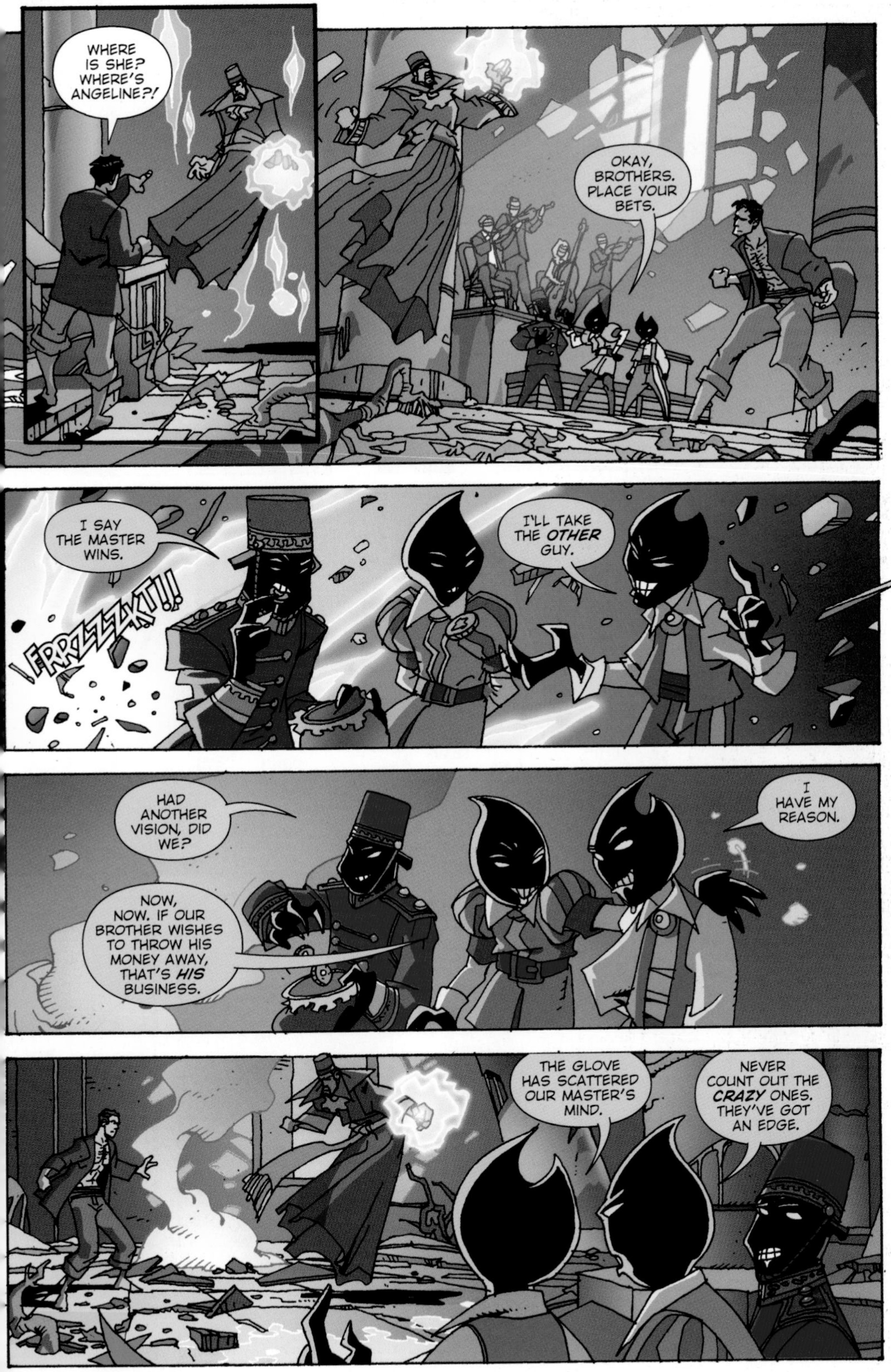
WHERE IS SHE? WHERE'S ANGELINE?!
OKAY, BROTHERS. PLACE YOUR BETS.
I SAY THE MASTER WINS.
I'LL TAKE THE *OTHER* GUY.
FRRZZZZKT!!
HAD ANOTHER VISION, DID WE?
I HAVE MY REASON.
NOW, NOW. IF OUR BROTHER WISHES TO THROW HIS MONEY AWAY, THAT'S *HIS* BUSINESS.
THE GLOVE HAS SCATTERED OUR MASTER'S MIND.
NEVER COUNT OUT THE *CRAZY* ONES. THEY'VE GOT AN EDGE.

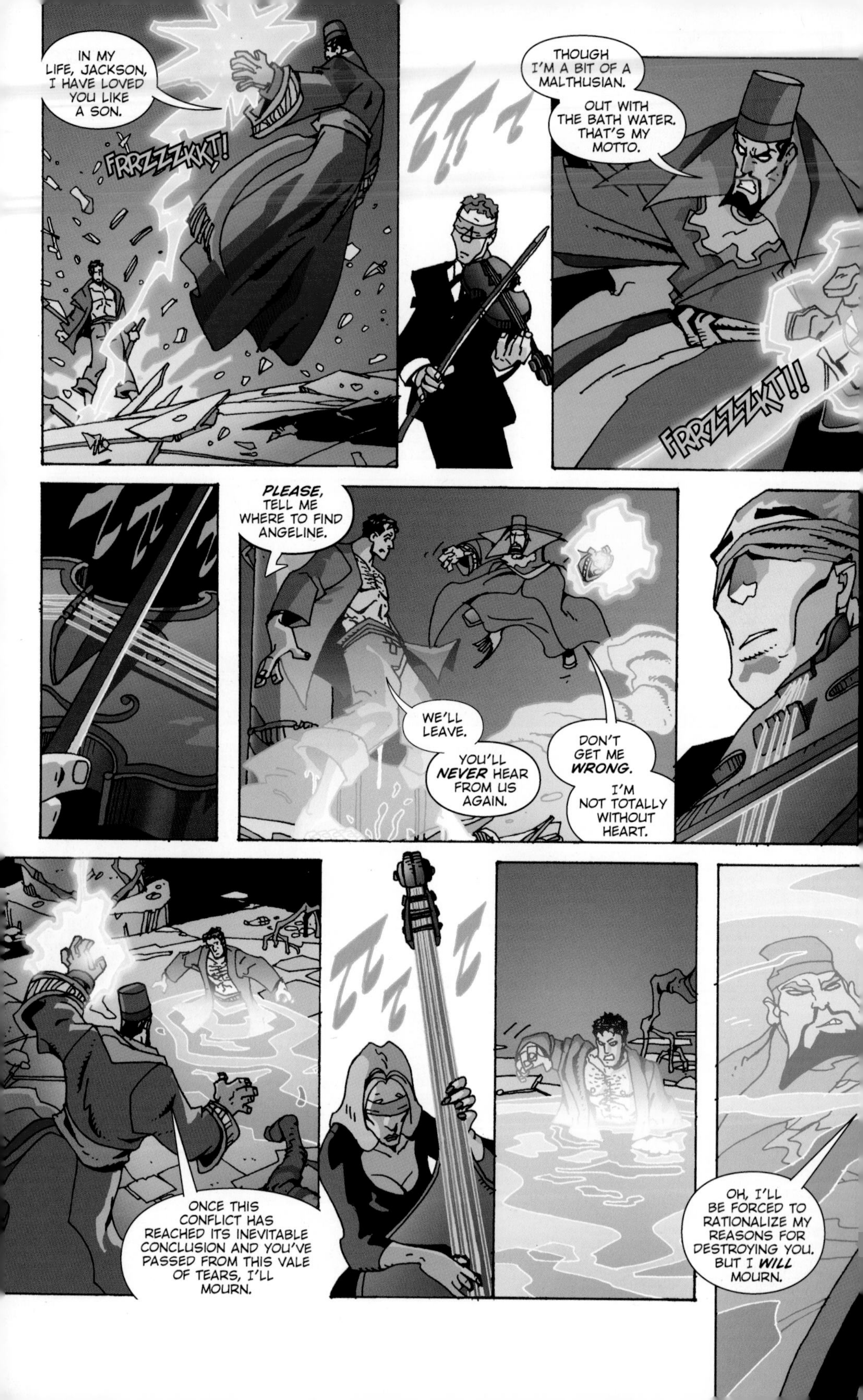

IN MY LIFE, JACKSON, I HAVE LOVED YOU LIKE A SON.
FRRZZZKKT!
THOUGH I'M A BIT OF A MALTHUSIAN.
OUT WITH THE BATH WATER. THAT'S MY MOTTO.
FRRZZZKKT!!
PLEASE, TELL ME WHERE TO FIND ANGELINE.
WE'LL LEAVE.
YOU'LL NEVER HEAR FROM US AGAIN.
DON'T GET ME WRONG.
I'M NOT TOTALLY WITHOUT HEART.
ONCE THIS CONFLICT HAS REACHED ITS INEVITABLE CONCLUSION AND YOU'VE PASSED FROM THIS VALE OF TEARS, I'LL MOURN.
OH, I'LL BE FORCED TO RATIONALIZE MY REASONS FOR DESTROYING YOU. BUT I WILL MOURN.

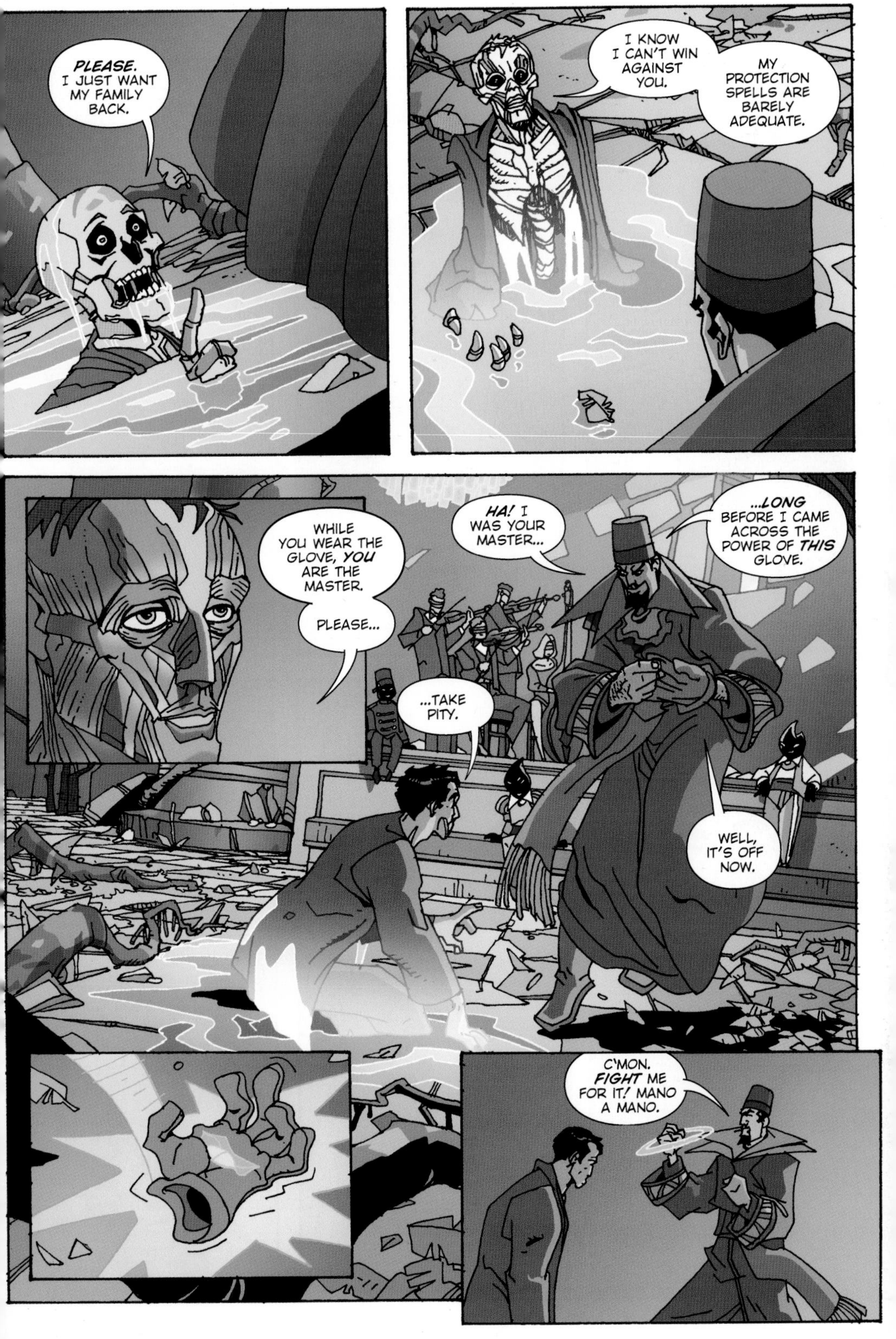

PLEASE. I JUST WANT MY FAMILY BACK.
I KNOW I CAN'T WIN AGAINST YOU.
MY PROTECTION SPELLS ARE BARELY ADEQUATE.
WHILE YOU WEAR THE GLOVE, YOU ARE THE MASTER.
PLEASE...
...TAKE PITY.
HA! I WAS YOUR MASTER...
...LONG BEFORE I CAME ACROSS THE POWER OF THIS GLOVE.
WELL, IT'S OFF NOW.
C'MON. FIGHT ME FOR IT! MANO A MANO.

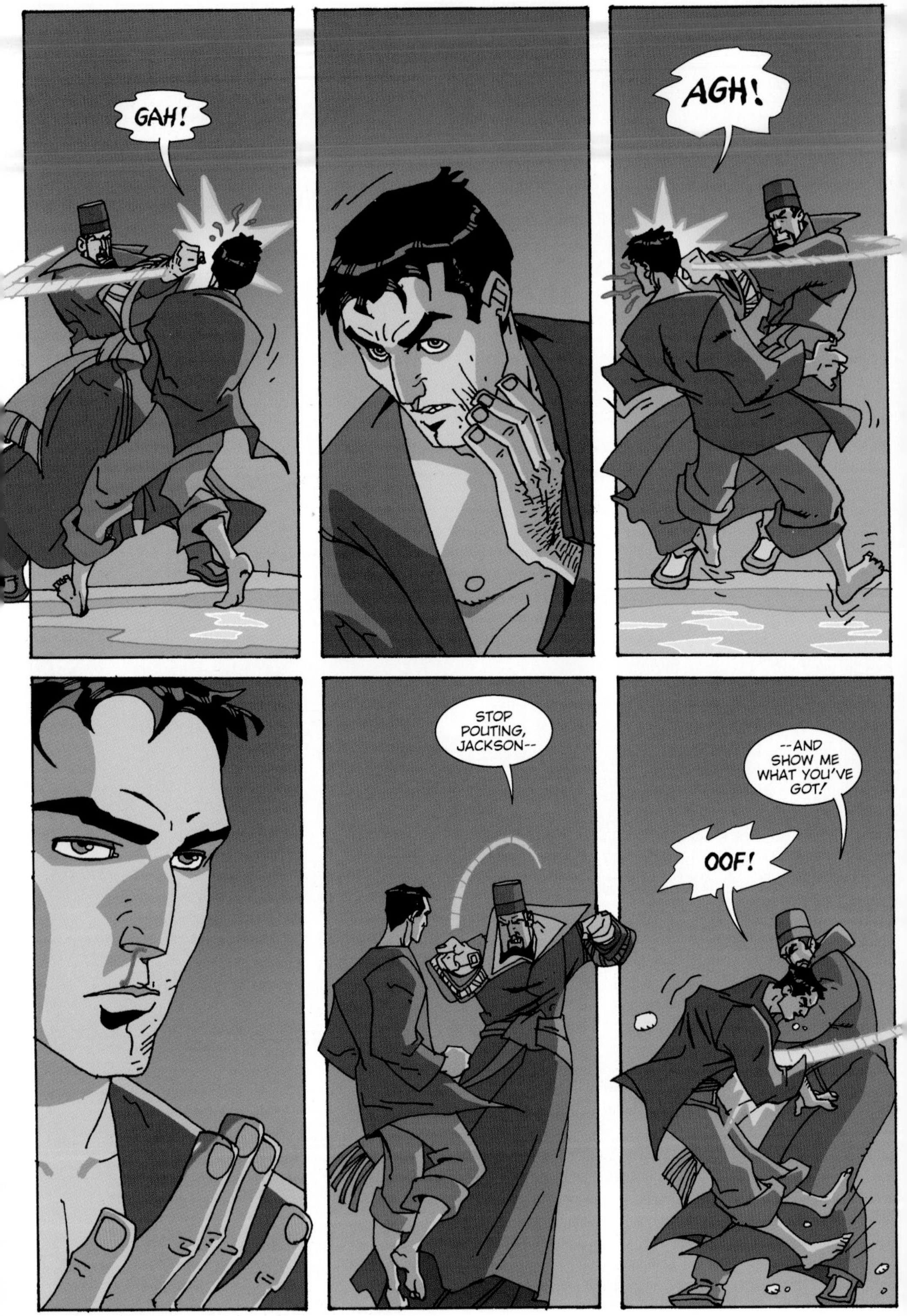
GAH!
AGH!
STOP POUTING, JACKSON--
--AND SHOW ME WHAT YOU'VE GOT!
OOF!

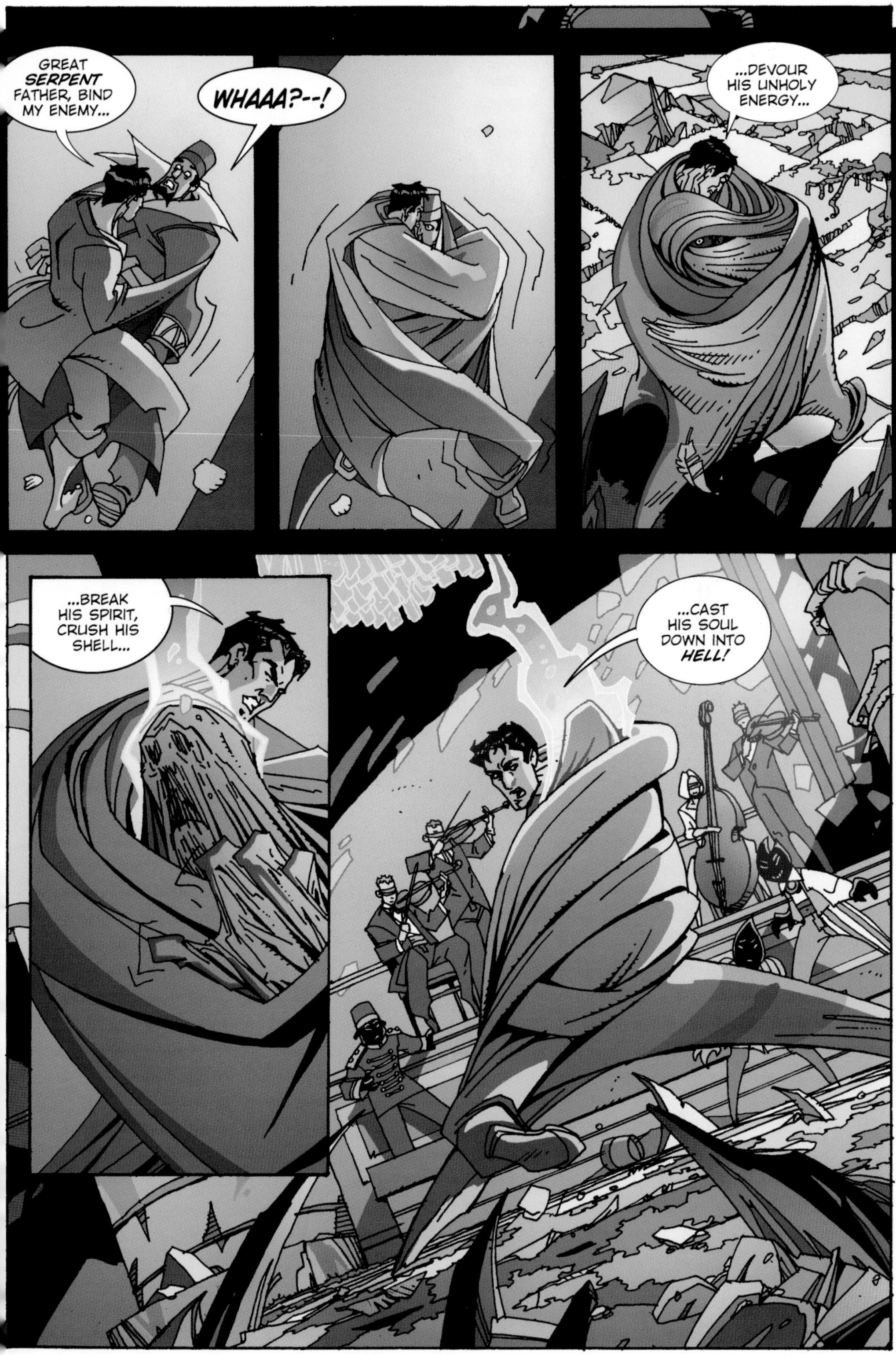
GREAT SERPENT FATHER, BIND MY ENEMY...
WHAAA?--!
...DEVOUR HIS UNHOLY ENERGY...
...BREAK HIS SPIRIT, CRUSH HIS SHELL...
...CAST HIS SOUL DOWN INTO HELL!

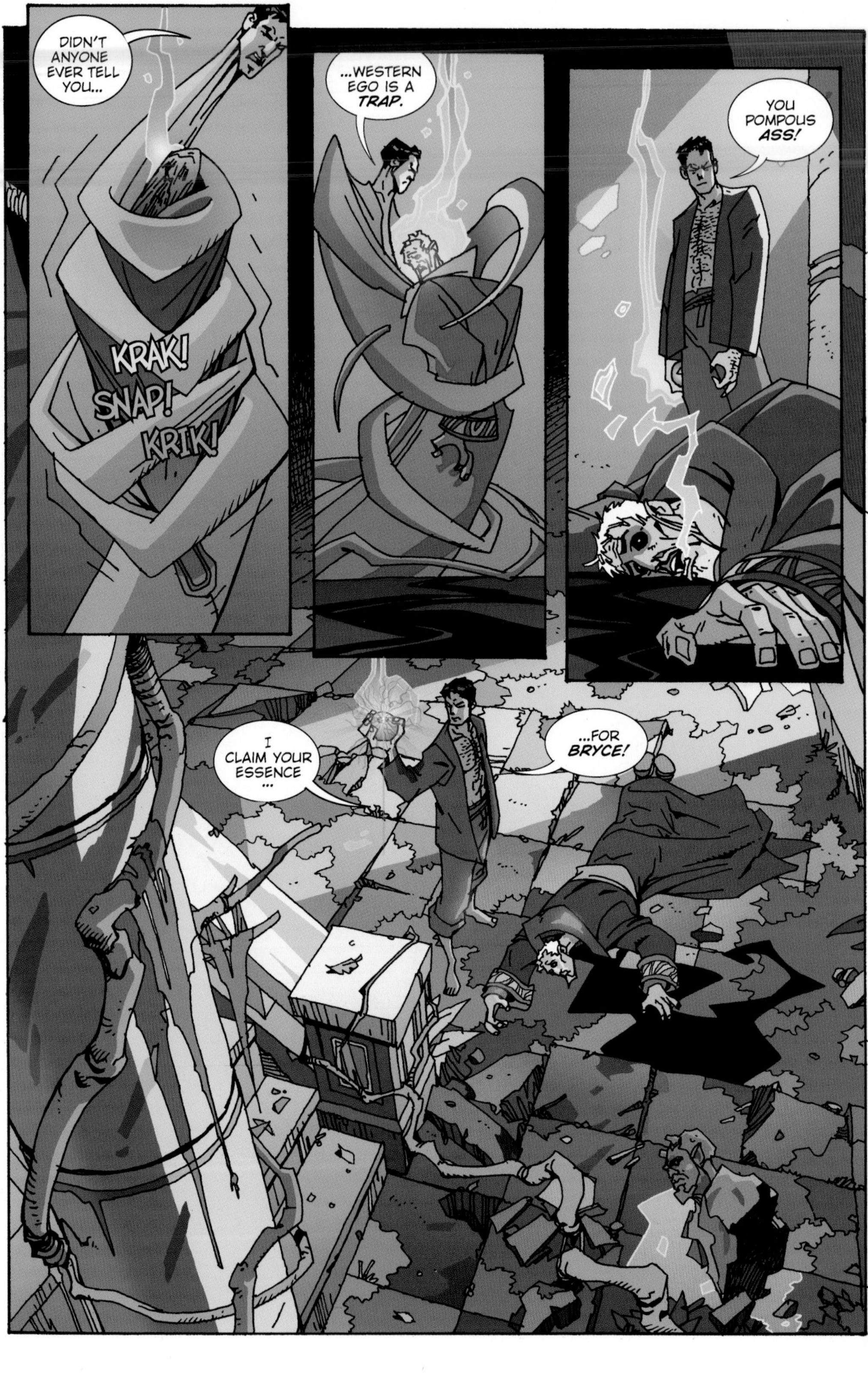
DIDN'T ANYONE EVER TELL YOU...
KRAK!
SNAP!
KRIK!
...WESTERN EGO IS A *TRAP.*
YOU POMPOUS *ASS!*
I CLAIM YOUR ESSENCE ...
...FOR *BRYCE!*

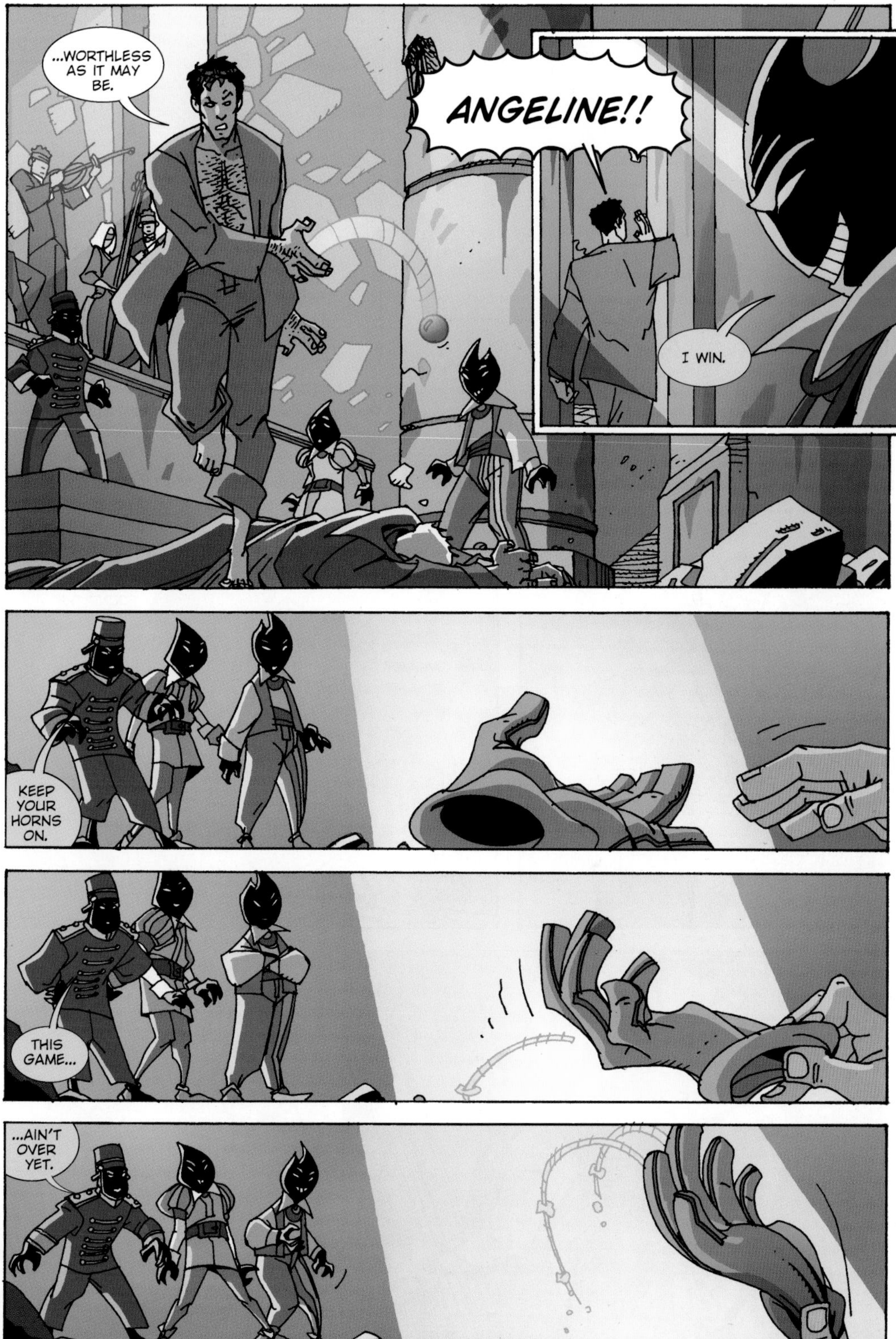
...WORTHLESS AS IT MAY BE.
ANGELINE!!
I WIN.
KEEP YOUR HORNS ON.
THIS GAME...
...AIN'T OVER YET.

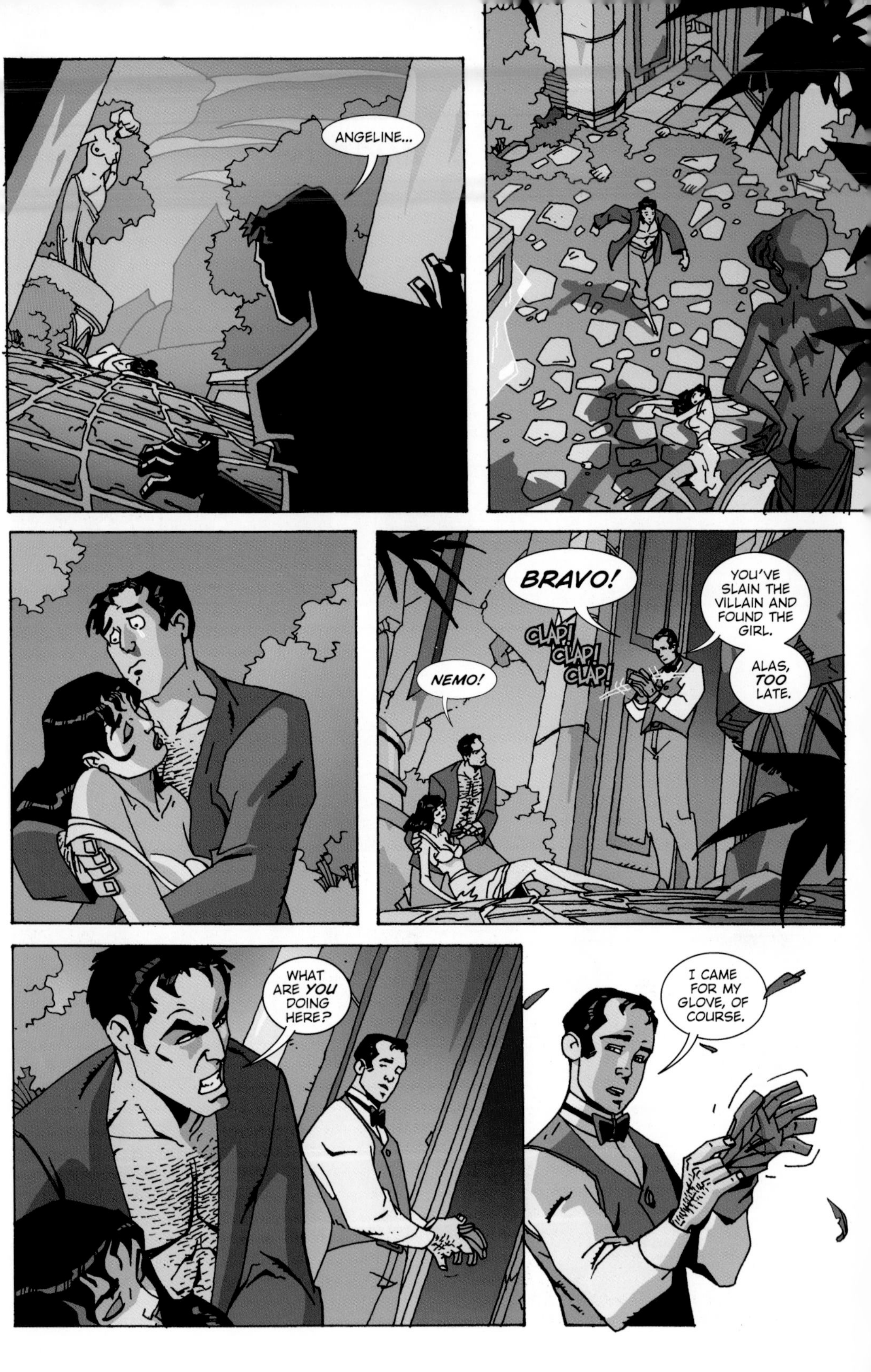
ANGELINE...
BRAVO!
CLAP! CLAP! CLAP!
YOU'VE SLAIN THE VILLAIN AND FOUND THE GIRL.
ALAS, TOO LATE.
NEMO!
WHAT ARE YOU DOING HERE?
I CAME FOR MY GLOVE, OF COURSE.

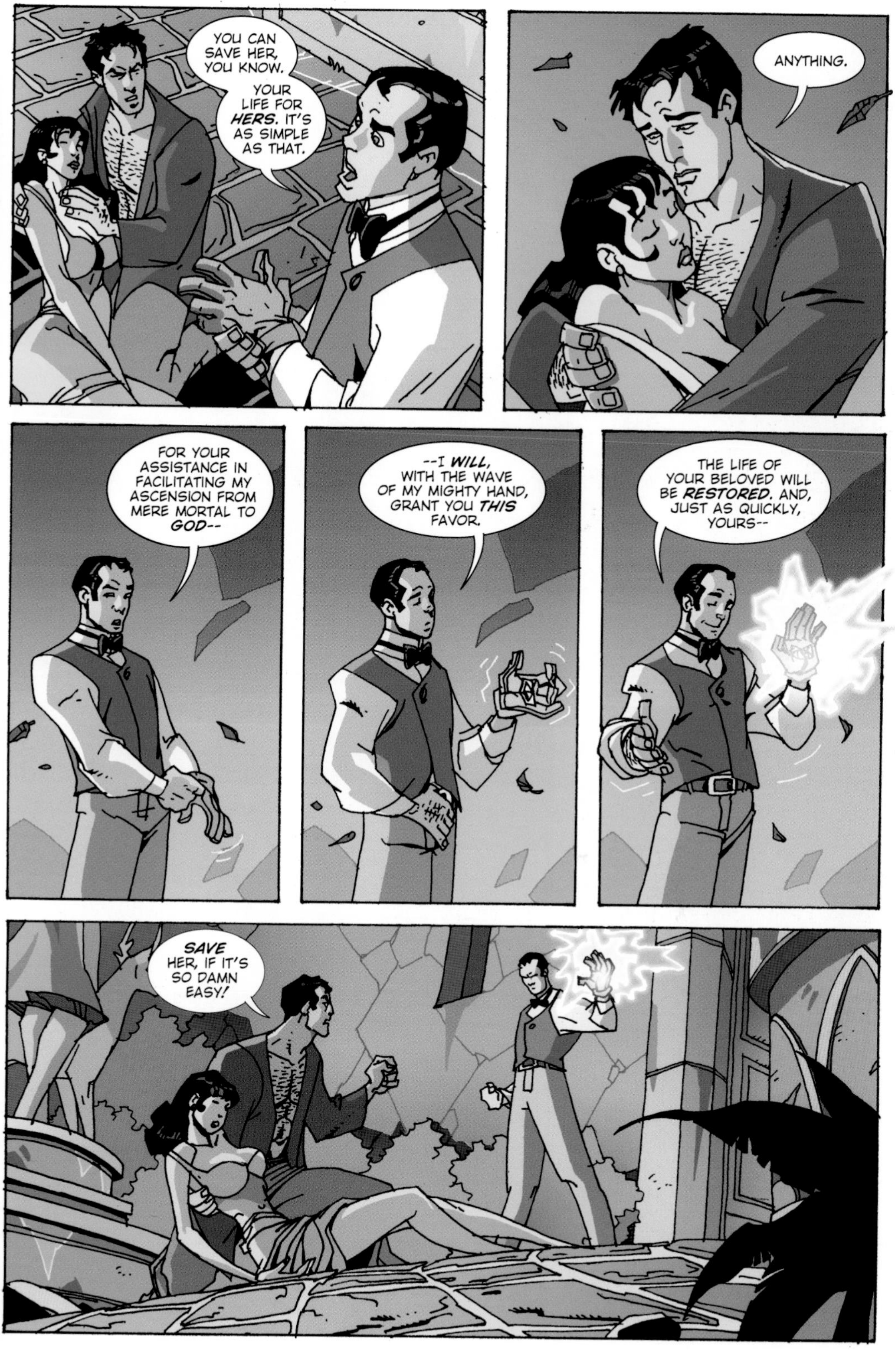
YOU CAN SAVE HER, YOU KNOW.
YOUR LIFE FOR **HERS**. IT'S AS SIMPLE AS THAT.
ANYTHING.
FOR YOUR ASSISTANCE IN FACILITATING MY ASCENSION FROM MERE MORTAL TO ***GOD***--
--I ***WILL***, WITH THE WAVE OF MY MIGHTY HAND, GRANT YOU ***THIS*** FAVOR.
THE LIFE OF YOUR BELOVED WILL BE ***RESTORED***. AND, JUST AS QUICKLY, YOURS--
SAVE HER, IF IT'S SO DAMN EASY*!*

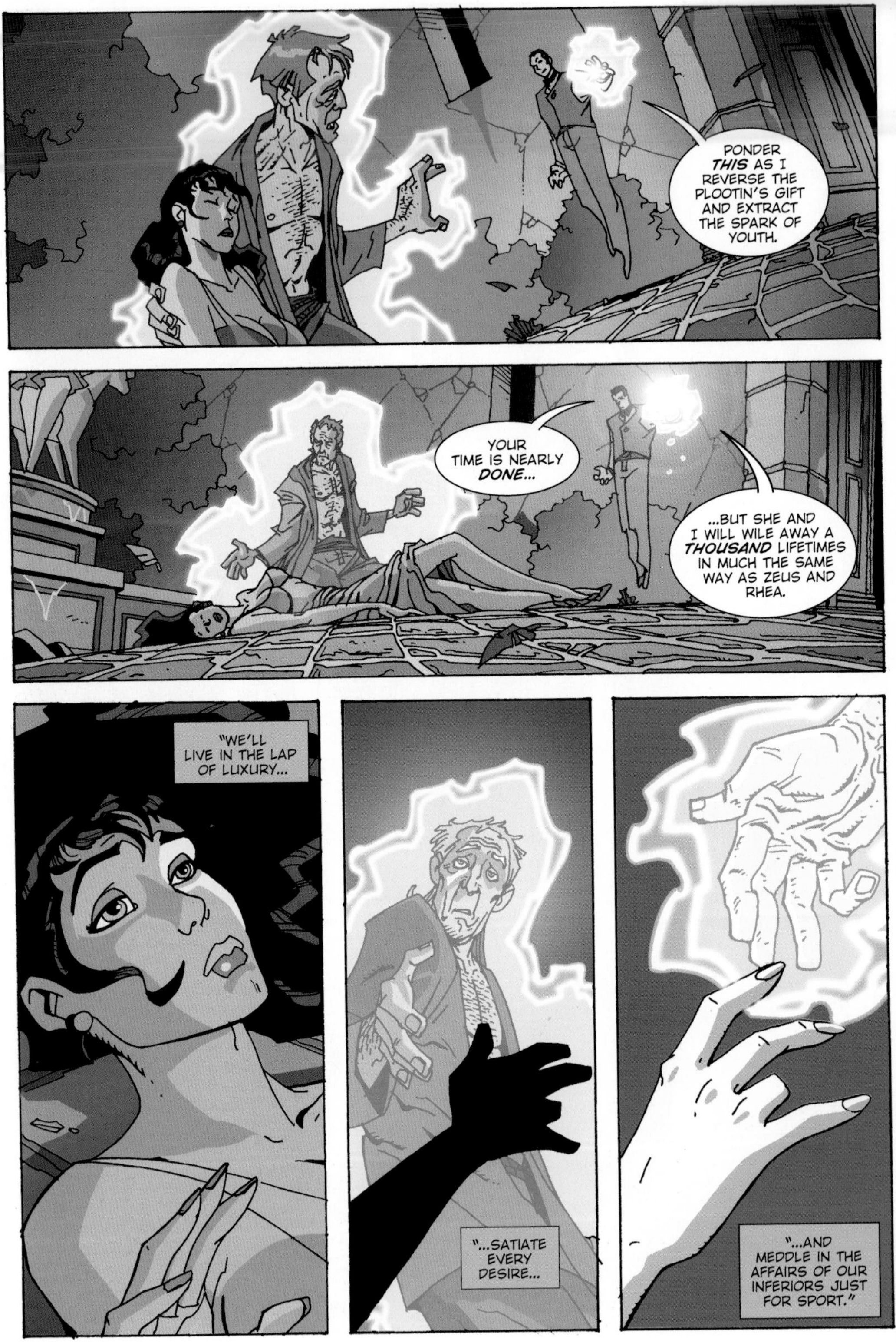
PONDER THIS AS I REVERSE THE PLOOTIN'S GIFT AND EXTRACT THE SPARK OF YOUTH.
YOUR TIME IS NEARLY DONE...
...BUT SHE AND I WILL WILE AWAY A THOUSAND LIFETIMES IN MUCH THE SAME WAY AS ZEUS AND RHEA.
"WE'LL LIVE IN THE LAP OF LUXURY...
"...SATIATE EVERY DESIRE...
"...AND MEDDLE IN THE AFFAIRS OF OUR INFERIORS JUST FOR SPORT."

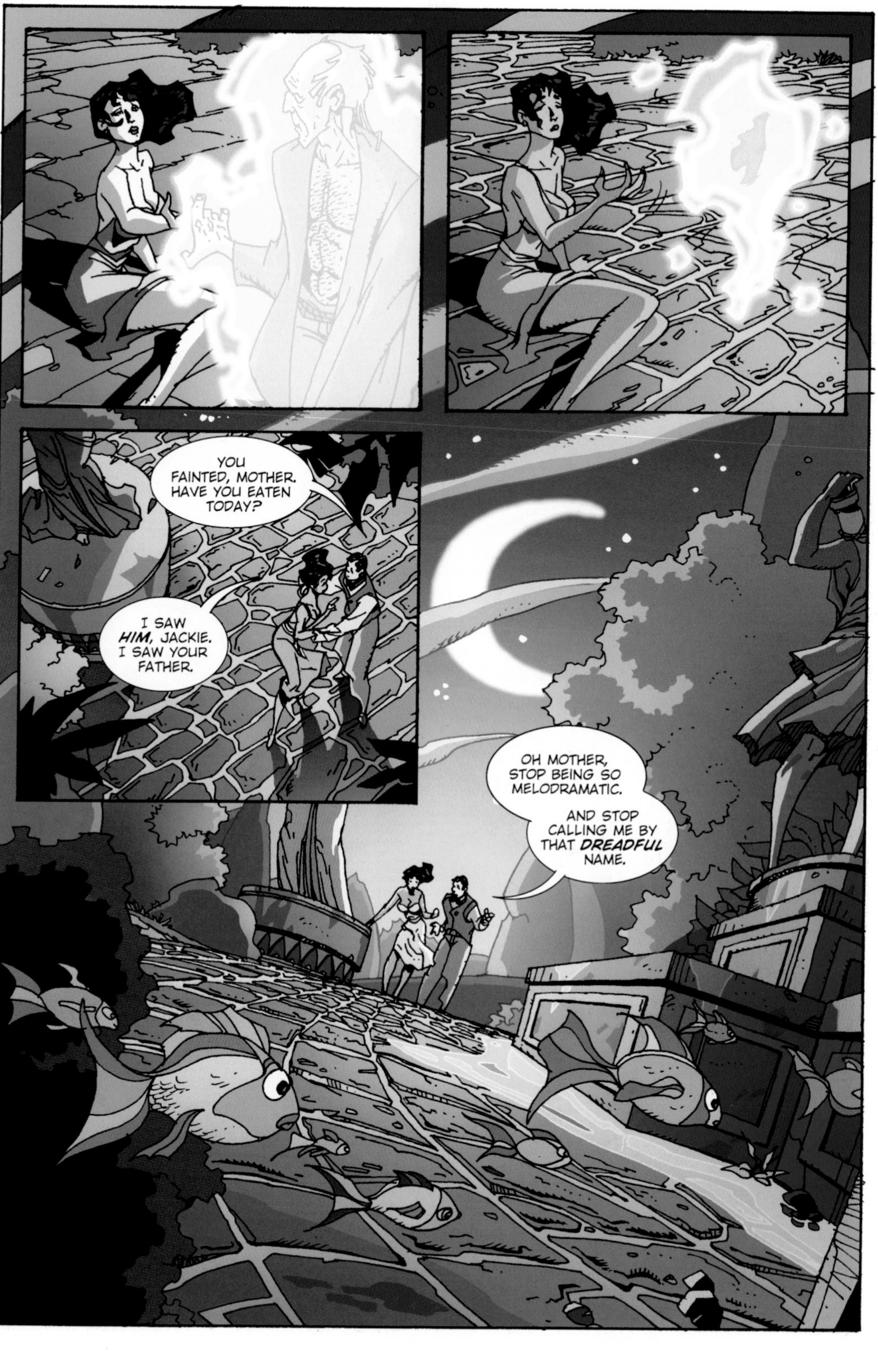
YOU FAINTED, MOTHER. HAVE YOU EATEN TODAY?
I SAW ***HIM***, JACKIE. I SAW YOUR FATHER.
OH MOTHER, STOP BEING SO MELODRAMATIC.
AND STOP CALLING ME BY THAT ***DREADFUL*** NAME.

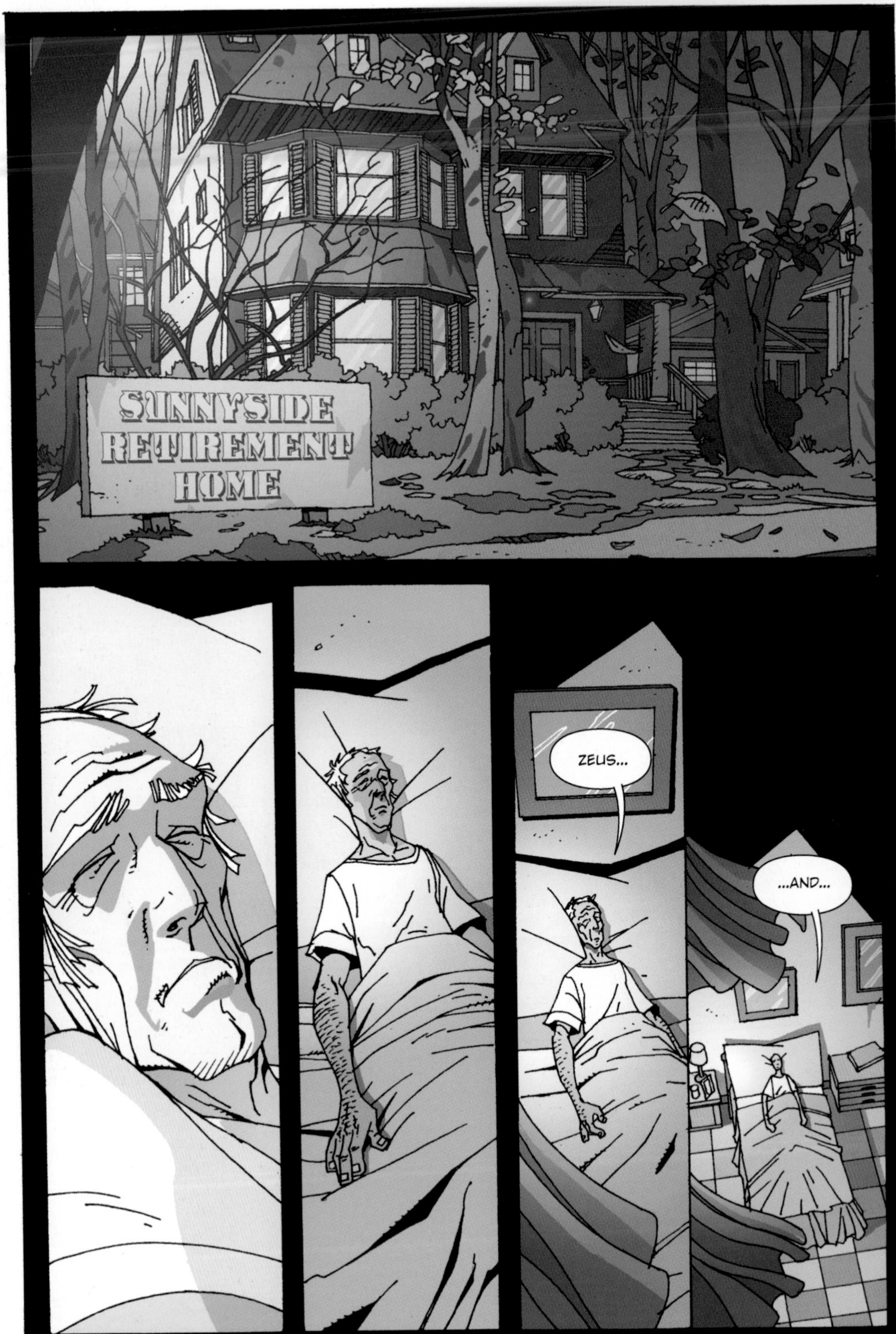
SUNNYSIDE RETIREMENT HOME
ZEUS...
...AND...

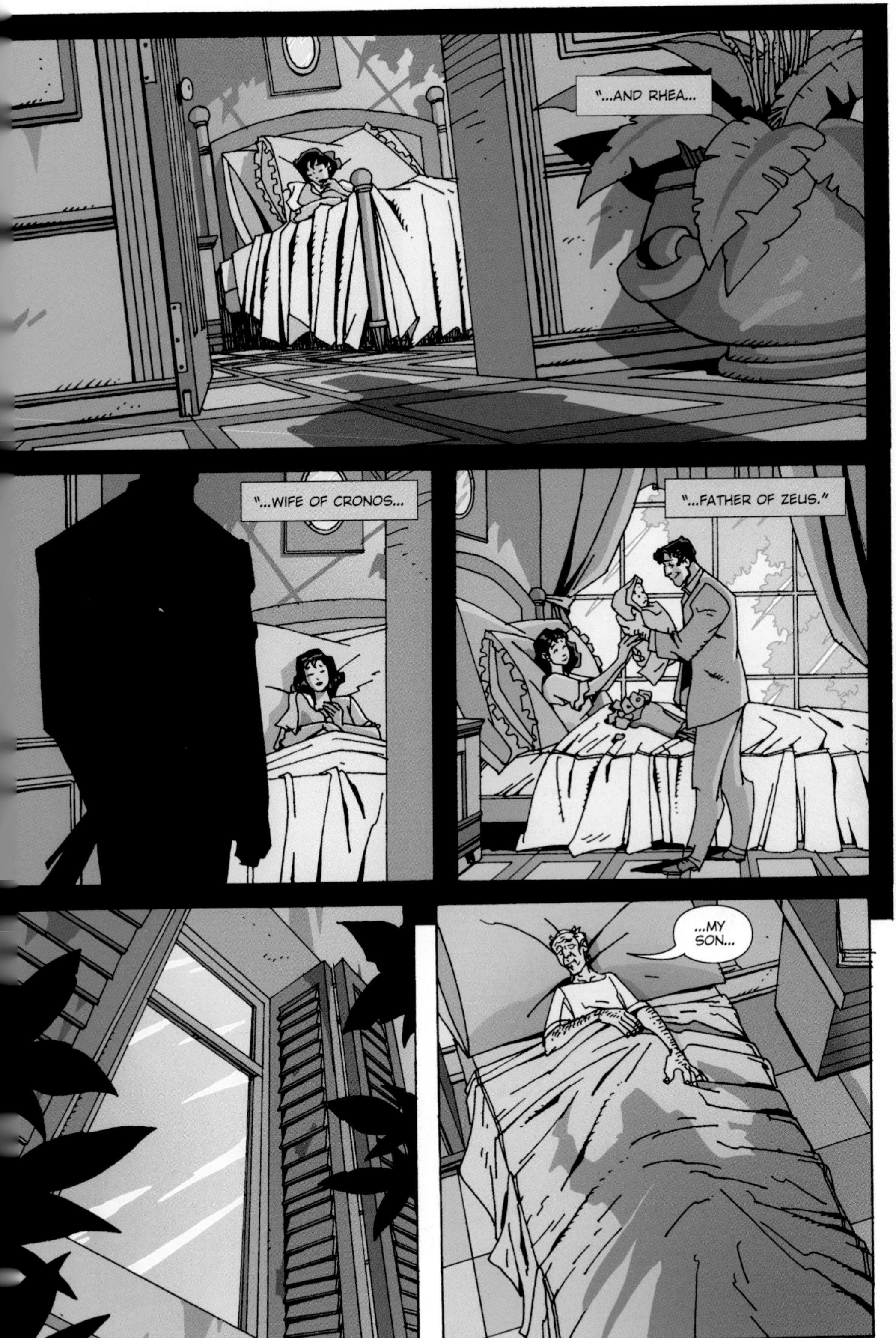
"...AND RHEA...
"...WIFE OF CRONOS...
"...FATHER OF ZEUS."
...MY SON...

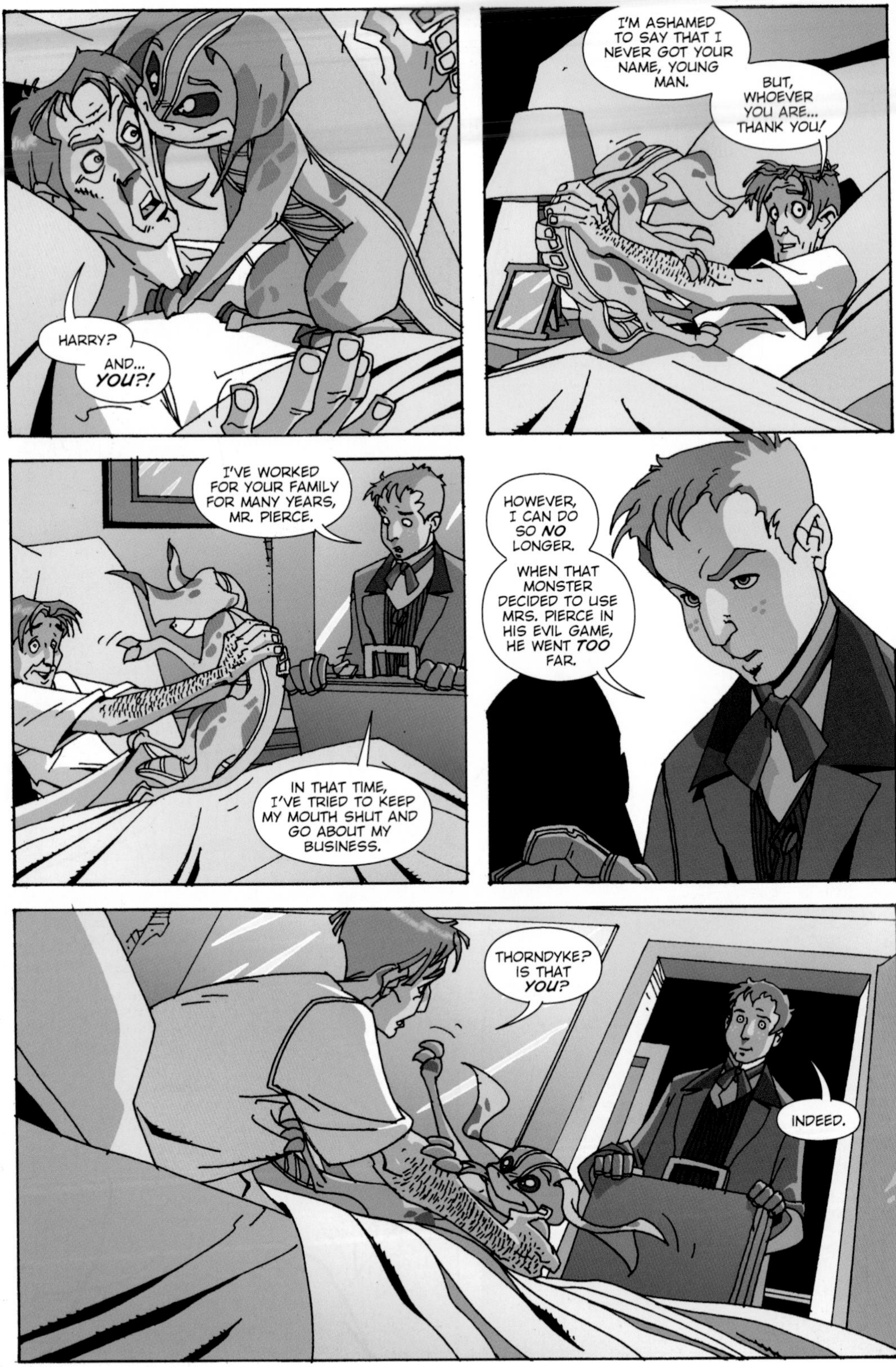
HARRY?
AND... ***YOU?!***
I'M ASHAMED TO SAY THAT I NEVER GOT YOUR NAME, YOUNG MAN.
BUT, WHOEVER YOU ARE... THANK YOU!
I'VE WORKED FOR YOUR FAMILY FOR MANY YEARS, MR. PIERCE.
IN THAT TIME, I'VE TRIED TO KEEP MY MOUTH SHUT AND GO ABOUT MY BUSINESS.
HOWEVER, I CAN DO SO ***NO*** LONGER.
WHEN THAT MONSTER DECIDED TO USE MRS. PIERCE IN HIS EVIL GAME, HE WENT ***TOO*** FAR.
THORNDYKE? IS THAT ***YOU?***
INDEED.

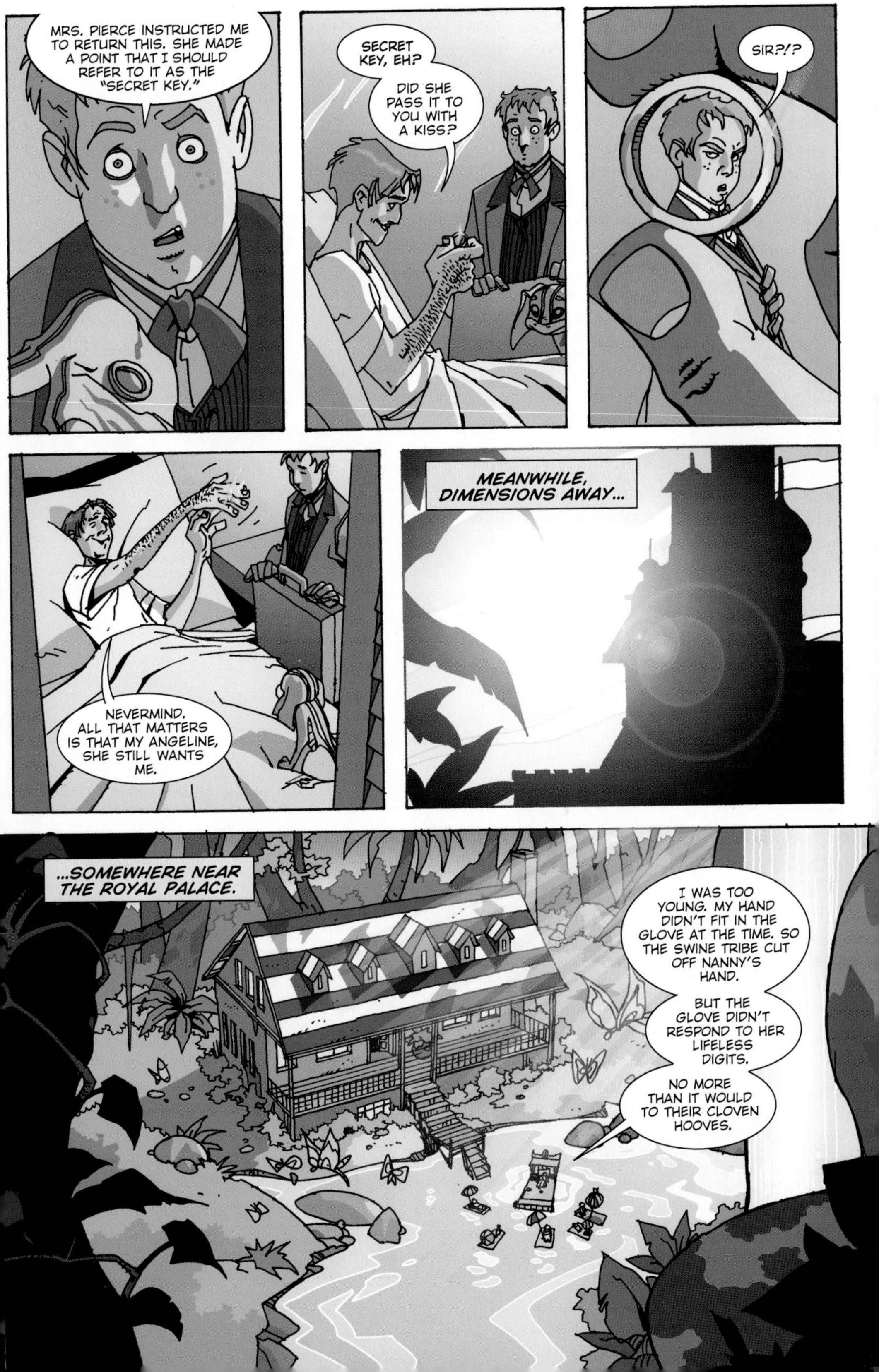
MRS. PIERCE INSTRUCTED ME TO RETURN THIS. SHE MADE A POINT THAT I SHOULD REFER TO IT AS THE "SECRET KEY."
SECRET KEY, EH?
DID SHE PASS IT TO YOU WITH A KISS?
SIR?!?
NEVERMIND. ALL THAT MATTERS IS THAT MY ANGELINE, SHE STILL WANTS ME.
MEANWHILE, DIMENSIONS AWAY...
...SOMEWHERE NEAR THE ROYAL PALACE.
I WAS TOO YOUNG. MY HAND DIDN'T FIT IN THE GLOVE AT THE TIME. SO THE SWINE TRIBE CUT OFF NANNY'S HAND.
BUT THE GLOVE DIDN'T RESPOND TO HER LIFELESS DIGITS.
NO MORE THAN IT WOULD TO THEIR CLOVEN HOOVES.

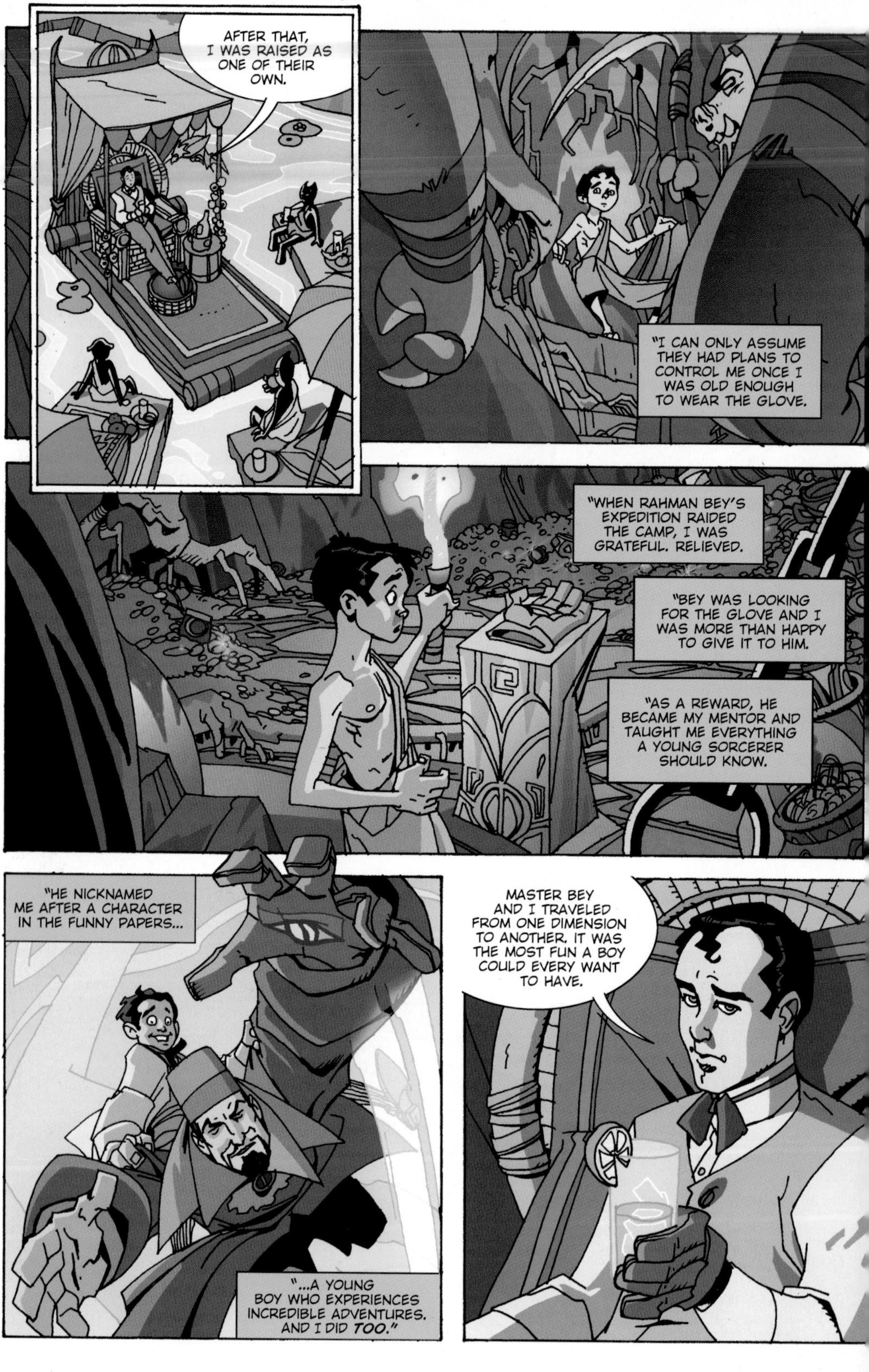
AFTER THAT, I WAS RAISED AS ONE OF THEIR OWN.
"I CAN ONLY ASSUME THEY HAD PLANS TO CONTROL ME ONCE I WAS OLD ENOUGH TO WEAR THE GLOVE.
"WHEN RAHMAN BEY'S EXPEDITION RAIDED THE CAMP, I WAS GRATEFUL. RELIEVED.
"BEY WAS LOOKING FOR THE GLOVE AND I WAS MORE THAN HAPPY TO GIVE IT TO HIM.
"AS A REWARD, HE BECAME MY MENTOR AND TAUGHT ME EVERYTHING A YOUNG SORCERER SHOULD KNOW.
"HE NICKNAMED ME AFTER A CHARACTER IN THE FUNNY PAPERS...
"...A YOUNG BOY WHO EXPERIENCES INCREDIBLE ADVENTURES. AND I DID *TOO*."
MASTER BEY AND I TRAVELED FROM ONE DIMENSION TO ANOTHER. IT WAS THE MOST FUN A BOY COULD EVERY WANT TO HAVE.

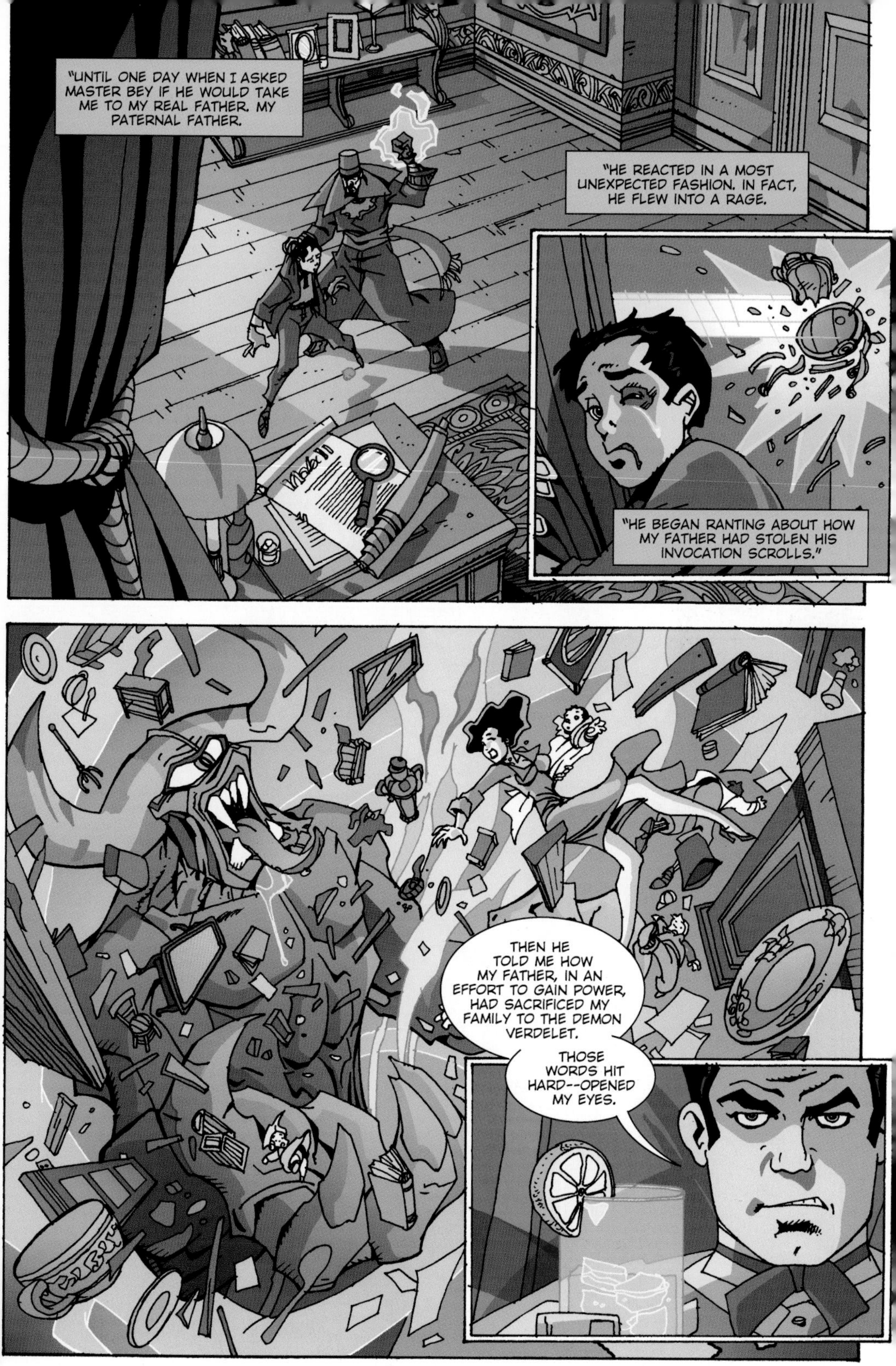
"UNTIL ONE DAY WHEN I ASKED MASTER BEY IF HE WOULD TAKE ME TO MY REAL FATHER. MY PATERNAL FATHER.
"HE REACTED IN A MOST UNEXPECTED FASHION. IN FACT, HE FLEW INTO A RAGE.
"HE BEGAN RANTING ABOUT HOW MY FATHER HAD STOLEN HIS INVOCATION SCROLLS."
THEN HE TOLD ME HOW MY FATHER, IN AN EFFORT TO GAIN POWER, HAD SACRIFICED MY FAMILY TO THE DEMON VERDELET.
THOSE WORDS HIT HARD--OPENED MY EYES.

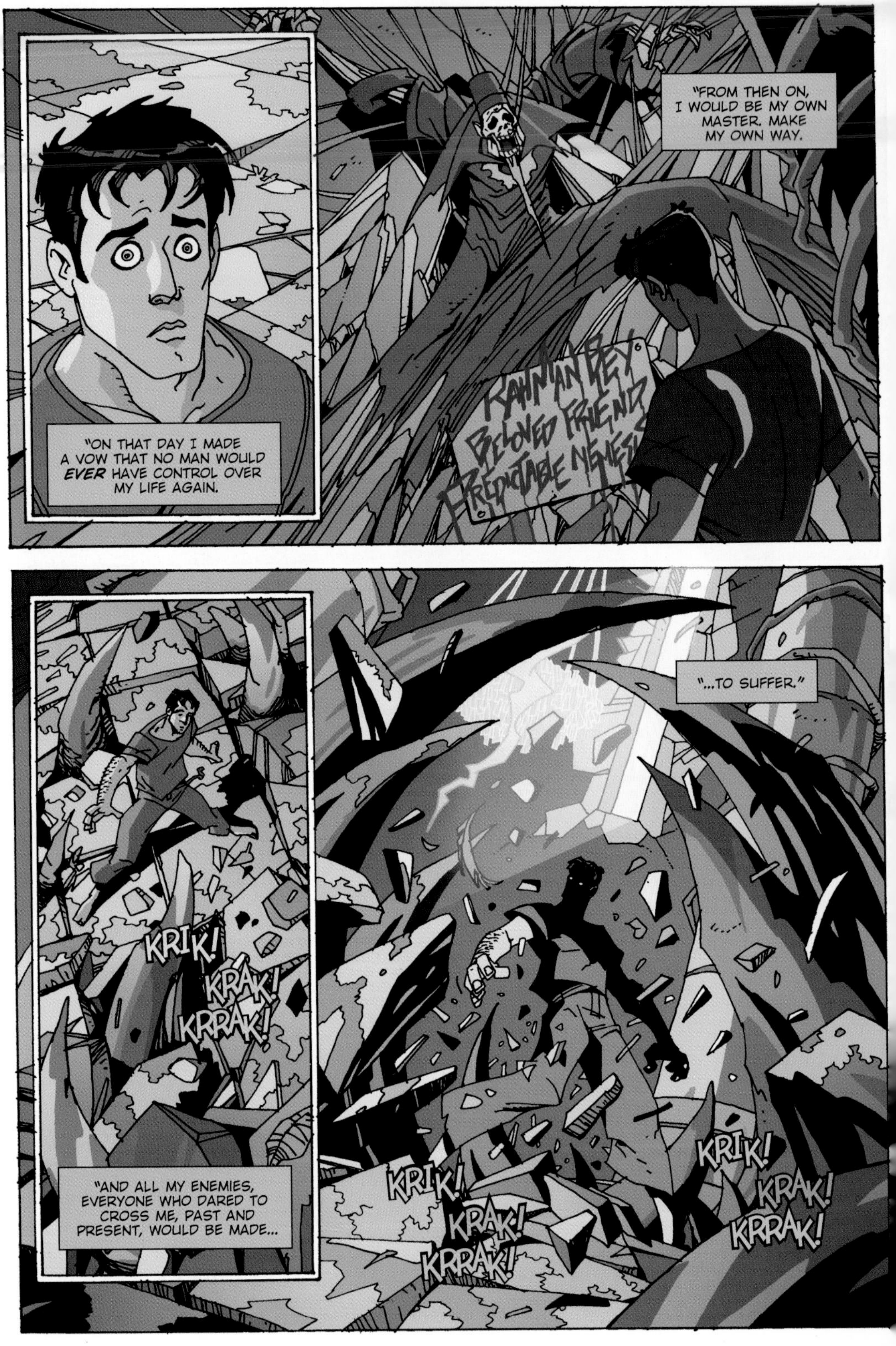
"ON THAT DAY I MADE A VOW THAT NO MAN WOULD *EVER* HAVE CONTROL OVER MY LIFE AGAIN.
"FROM THEN ON, I WOULD BE MY OWN MASTER. MAKE MY OWN WAY.
KRIK!
KRAK!
KRRAK!
"AND ALL MY ENEMIES, EVERYONE WHO DARED TO CROSS ME, PAST AND PRESENT, WOULD BE MADE...
"...TO SUFFER."
KRIK!
KRAK!
KRRAK!
KRIK!
KRAK!
KRRAK!

AN ORGANIC PRISON.

INTERESTING.

I THINK I HAVE JUST THE SPELL.

LIKE THE SUN SETS IN THE WEST...

...PASS THIS VESSEL THROUGH THE ASTRAL PLANE.

RISING IN THE EAST... ...CORPOREAL ONCE AGAIN.

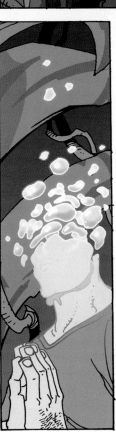

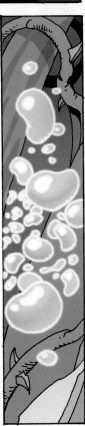

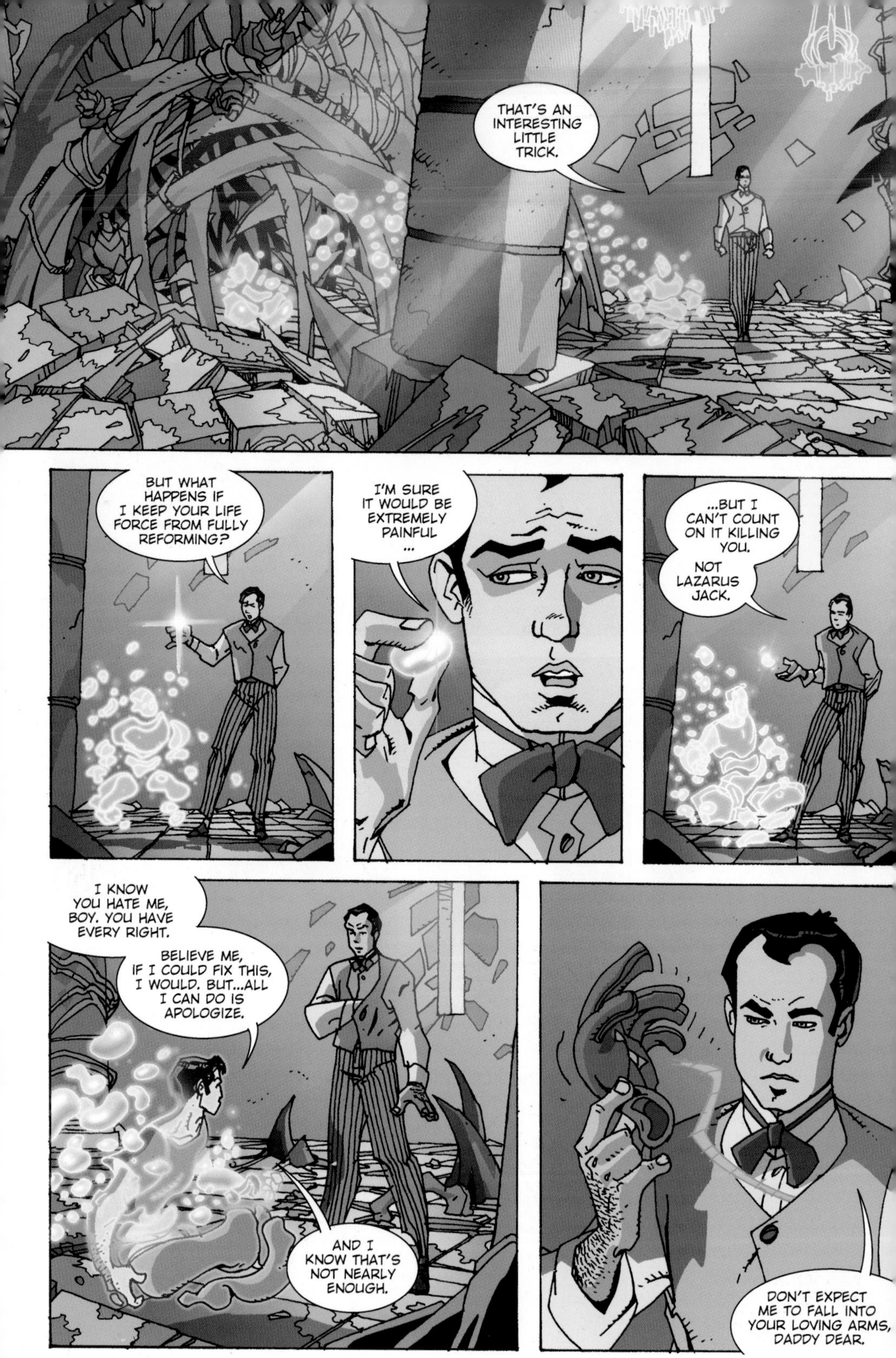
THAT'S AN INTERESTING LITTLE TRICK.
BUT WHAT HAPPENS IF I KEEP YOUR LIFE FORCE FROM FULLY REFORMING?
I'M SURE IT WOULD BE EXTREMELY PAINFUL ...
...BUT I CAN'T COUNT ON IT KILLING YOU.
NOT LAZARUS JACK.
I KNOW YOU HATE ME, BOY. YOU HAVE EVERY RIGHT.
BELIEVE ME, IF I COULD FIX THIS, I WOULD. BUT...ALL I CAN DO IS APOLOGIZE.
AND I KNOW THAT'S NOT NEARLY ENOUGH.
DON'T EXPECT ME TO FALL INTO YOUR LOVING ARMS, DADDY DEAR.

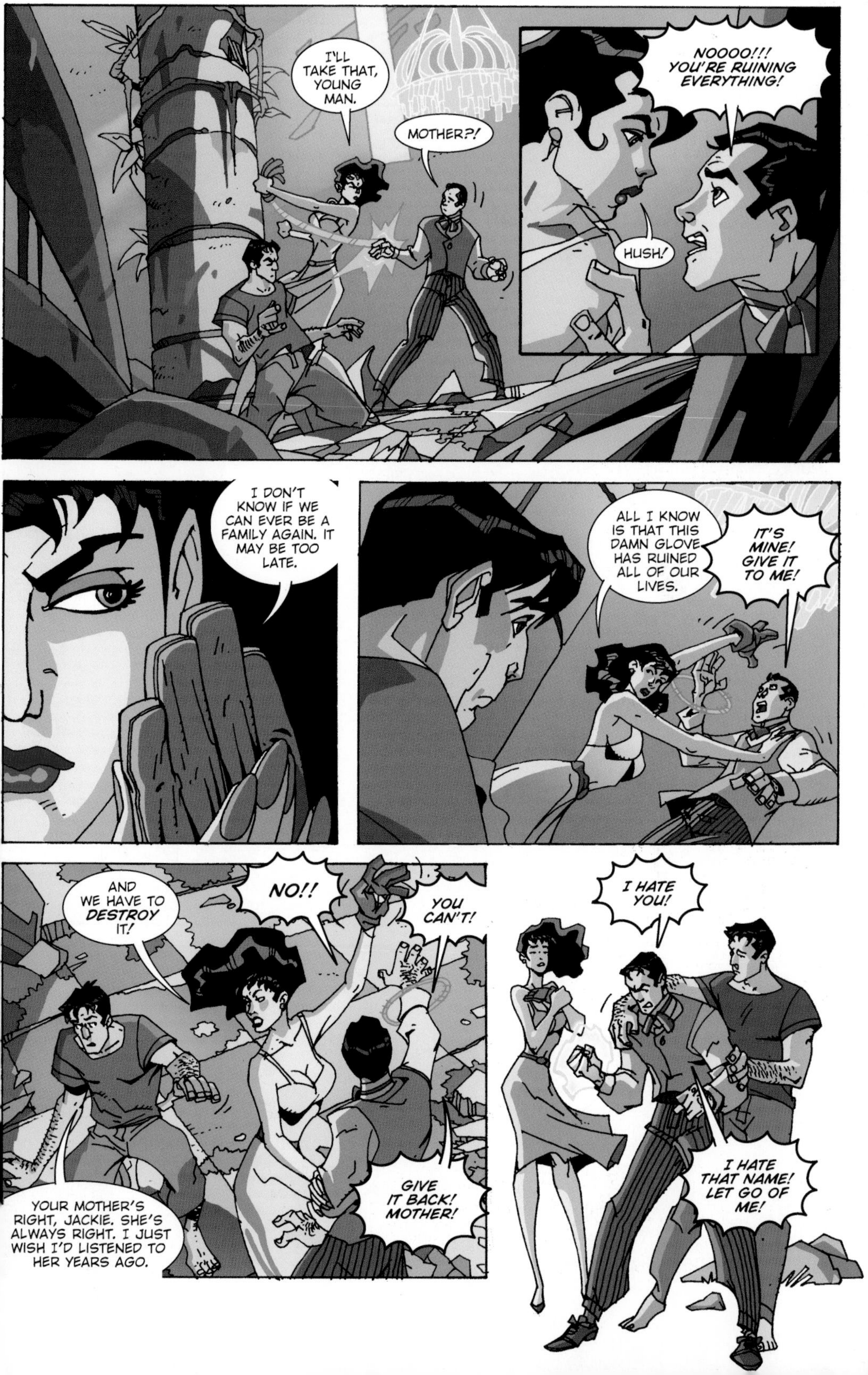

I'LL TAKE THAT, YOUNG MAN.
MOTHER?!
NOOOO!!! YOU'RE RUINING EVERYTHING!
HUSH!
I DON'T KNOW IF WE CAN EVER BE A FAMILY AGAIN. IT MAY BE TOO LATE.
ALL I KNOW IS THAT THIS DAMN GLOVE HAS RUINED ALL OF OUR LIVES.
IT'S MINE! GIVE IT TO ME!
AND WE HAVE TO DESTROY IT!
NO!!
YOU CAN'T!
YOUR MOTHER'S RIGHT, JACKIE. SHE'S ALWAYS RIGHT. I JUST WISH I'D LISTENED TO HER YEARS AGO.
GIVE IT BACK! MOTHER!
I HATE YOU!
I HATE THAT NAME! LET GO OF ME!

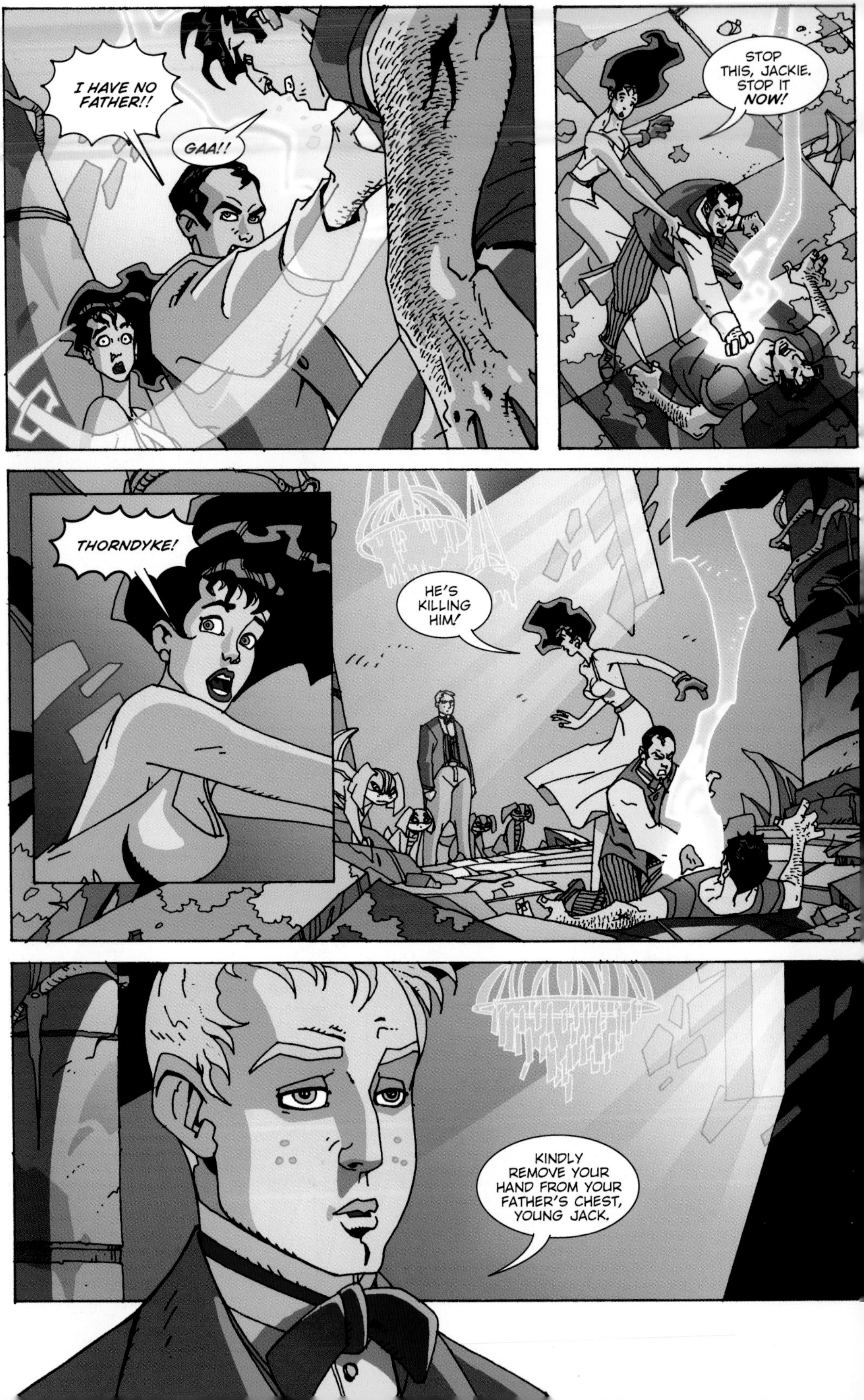
I HAVE NO FATHER!!
GAA!!
STOP THIS, JACKIE. STOP IT NOW!
THORNDYKE!
HE'S KILLING HIM!
KINDLY REMOVE YOUR HAND FROM YOUR FATHER'S CHEST, YOUNG JACK.

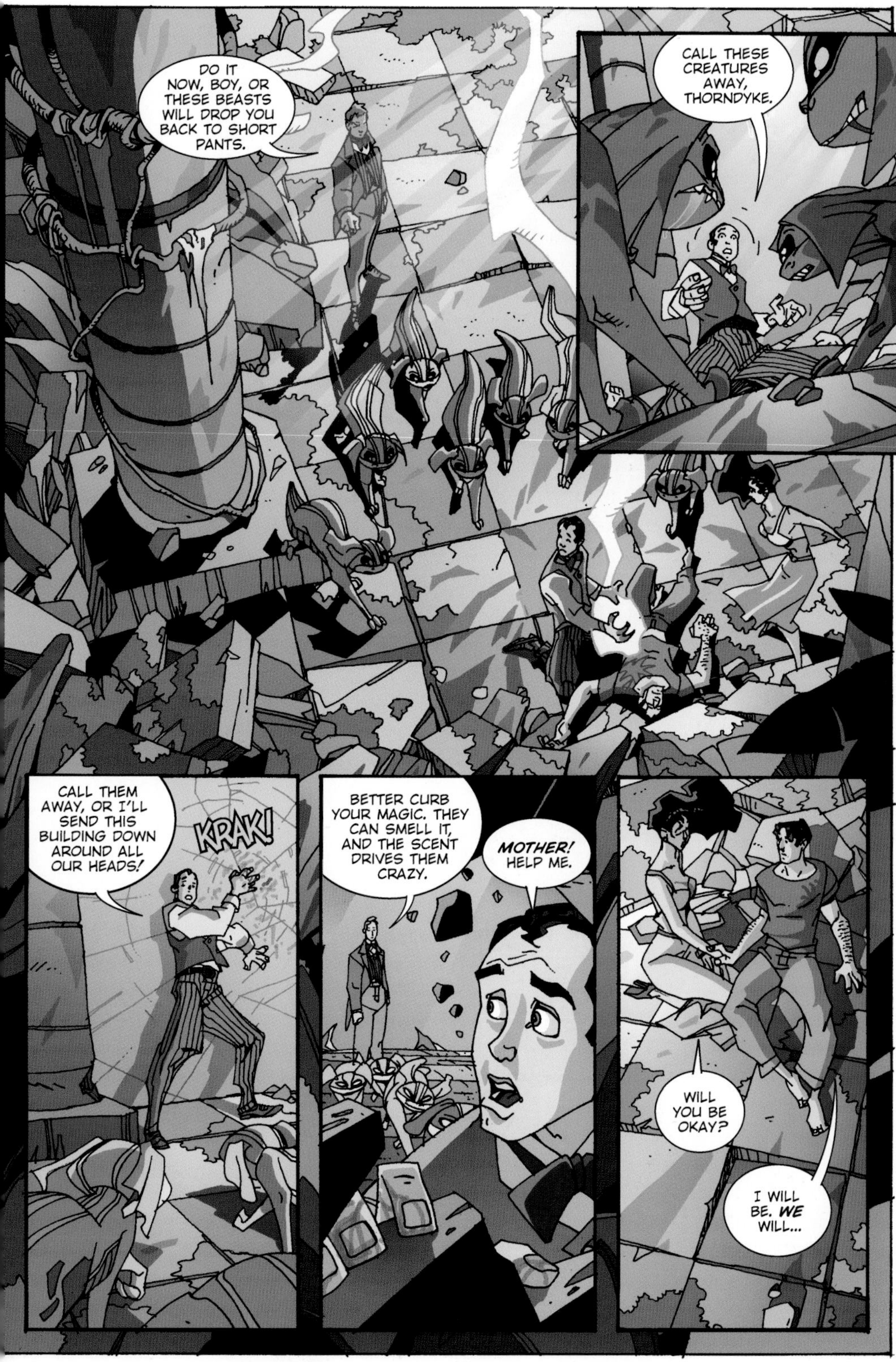
DO IT NOW, BOY, OR THESE BEASTS WILL DROP YOU BACK TO SHORT PANTS.
CALL THESE CREATURES AWAY, THORNDYKE.
CALL THEM AWAY, OR I'LL SEND THIS BUILDING DOWN AROUND ALL OUR HEADS!
KRAK!
BETTER CURB YOUR MAGIC. THEY CAN SMELL IT, AND THE SCENT DRIVES THEM CRAZY.
MOTHER! HELP ME.
WILL YOU BE OKAY?
I WILL BE. WE WILL...

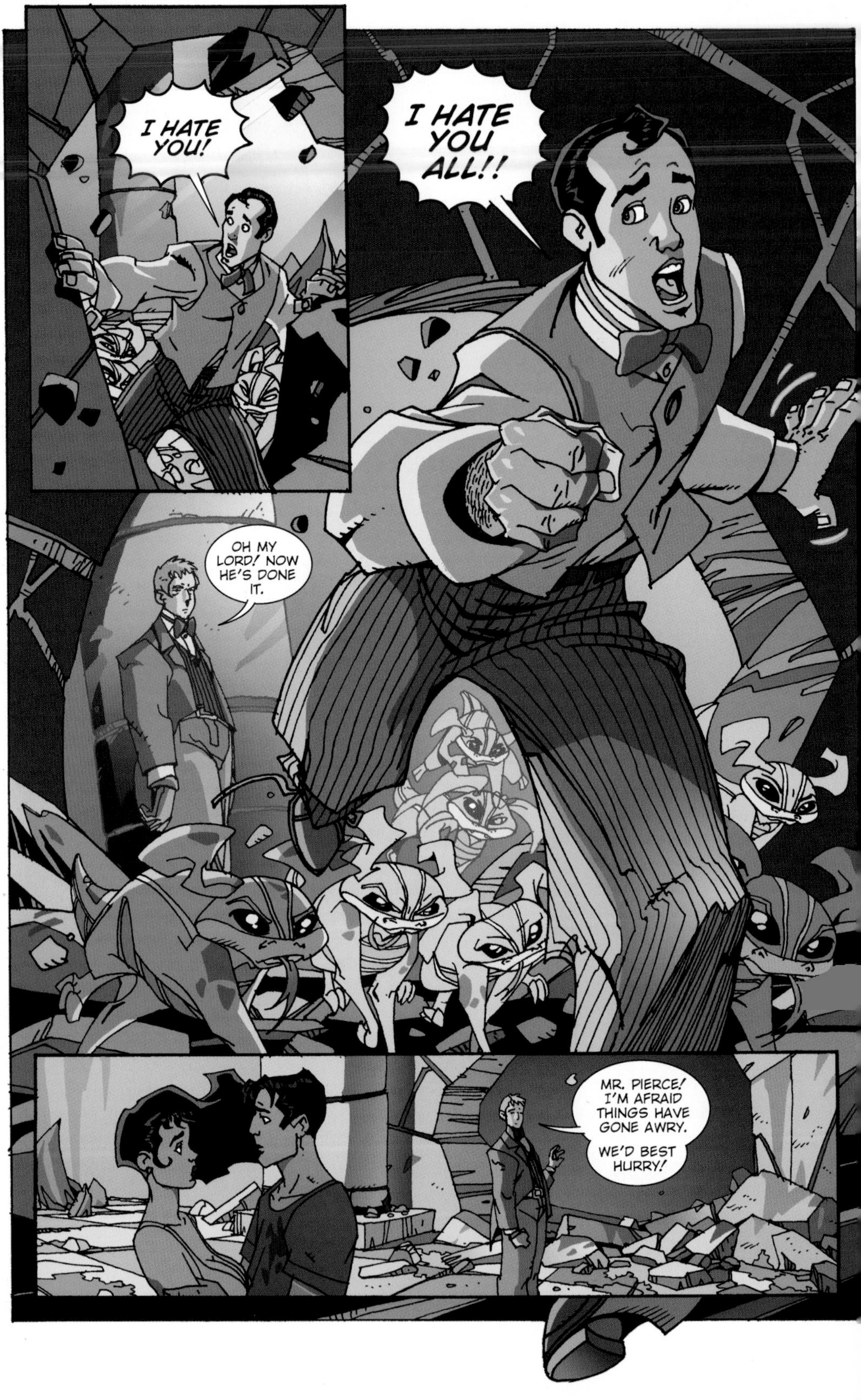
I HATE YOU!
I HATE YOU ALL!!
OH MY LORD! NOW HE'S DONE IT.
MR. PIERCE! I'M AFRAID THINGS HAVE GONE AWRY.
WE'D BEST HURRY!

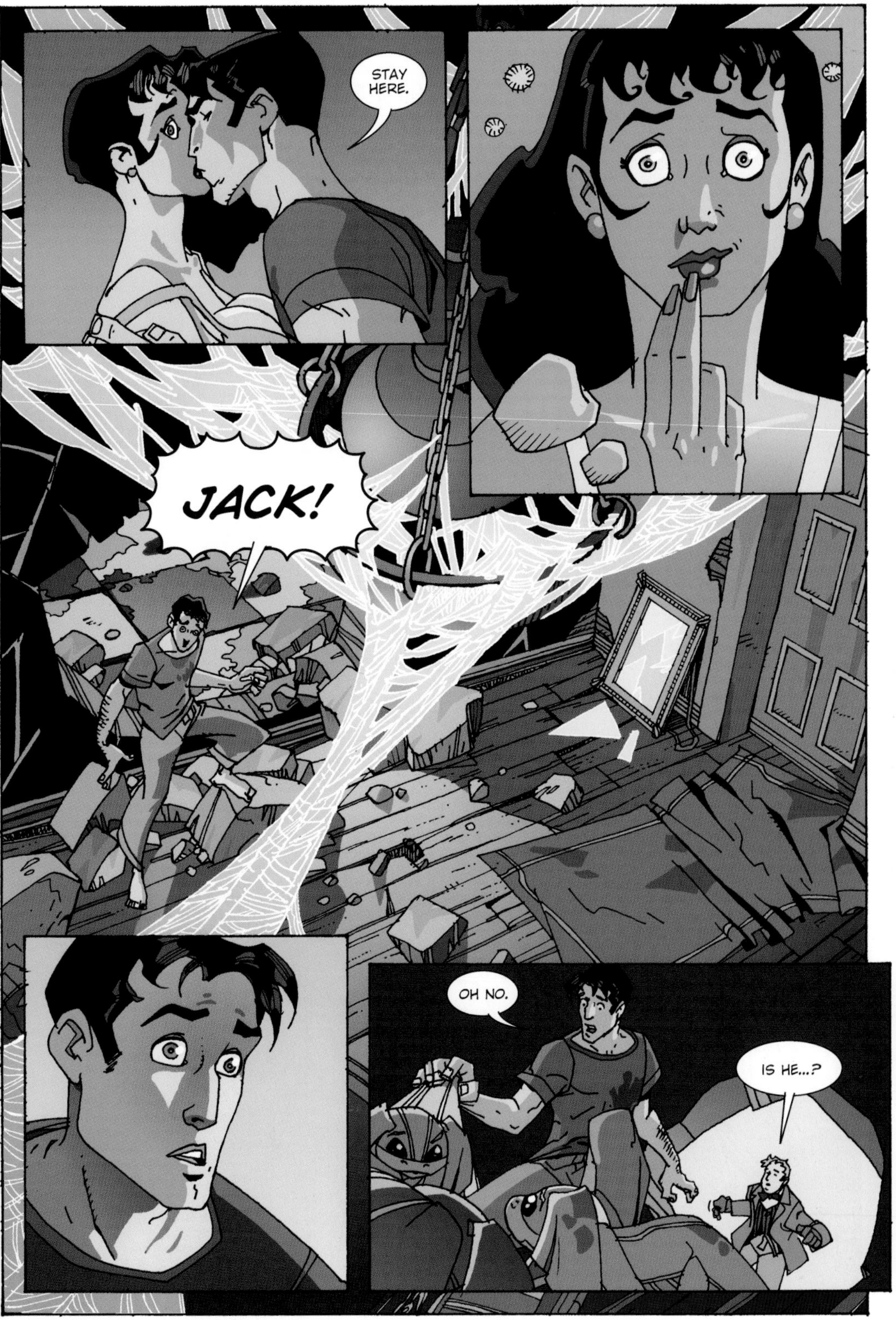
STAY HERE.
JACK!
OH NO.
IS HE...?

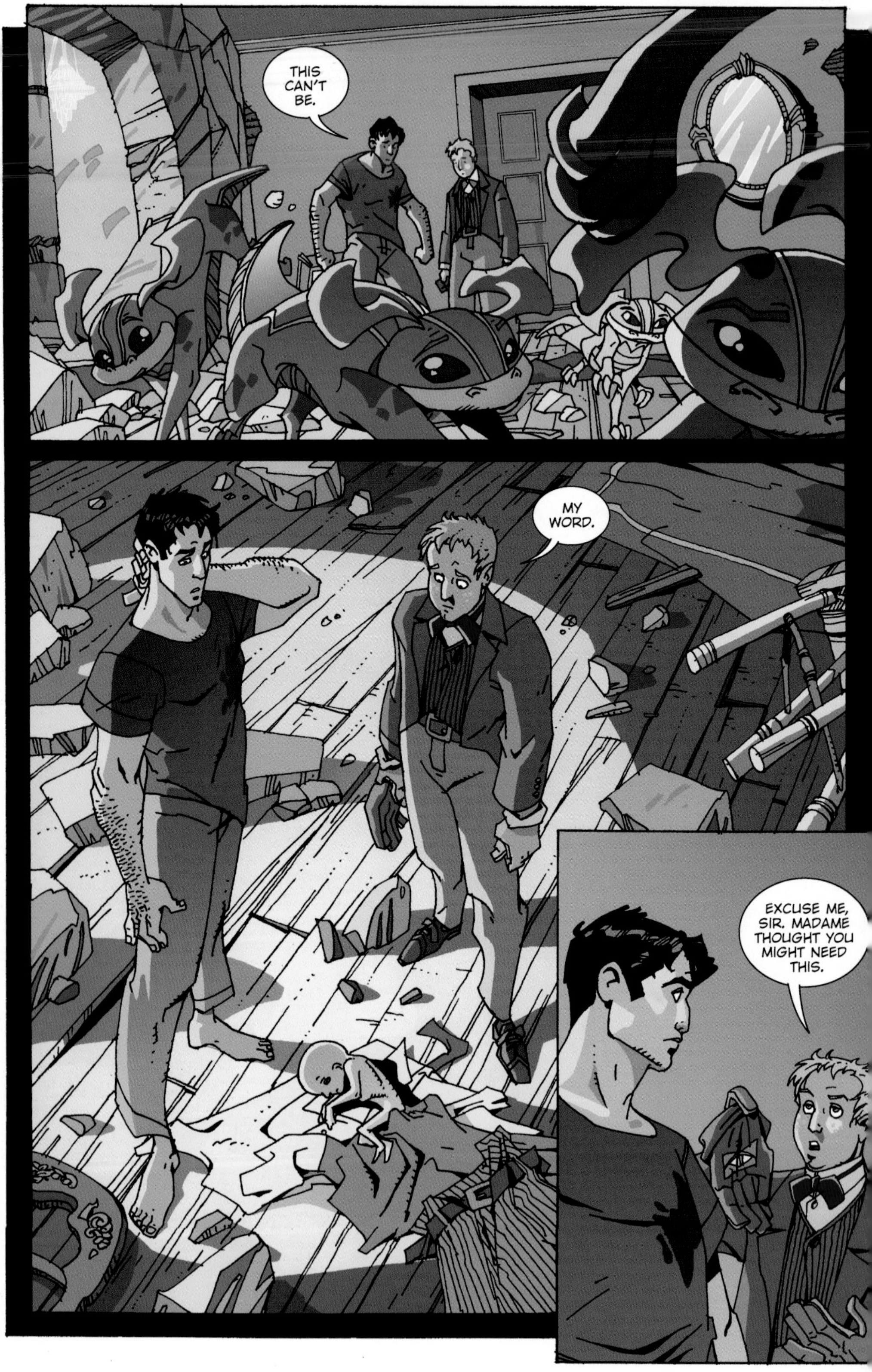
THIS CAN'T BE.
MY WORD.
EXCUSE ME, SIR. MADAME THOUGHT YOU MIGHT NEED THIS.

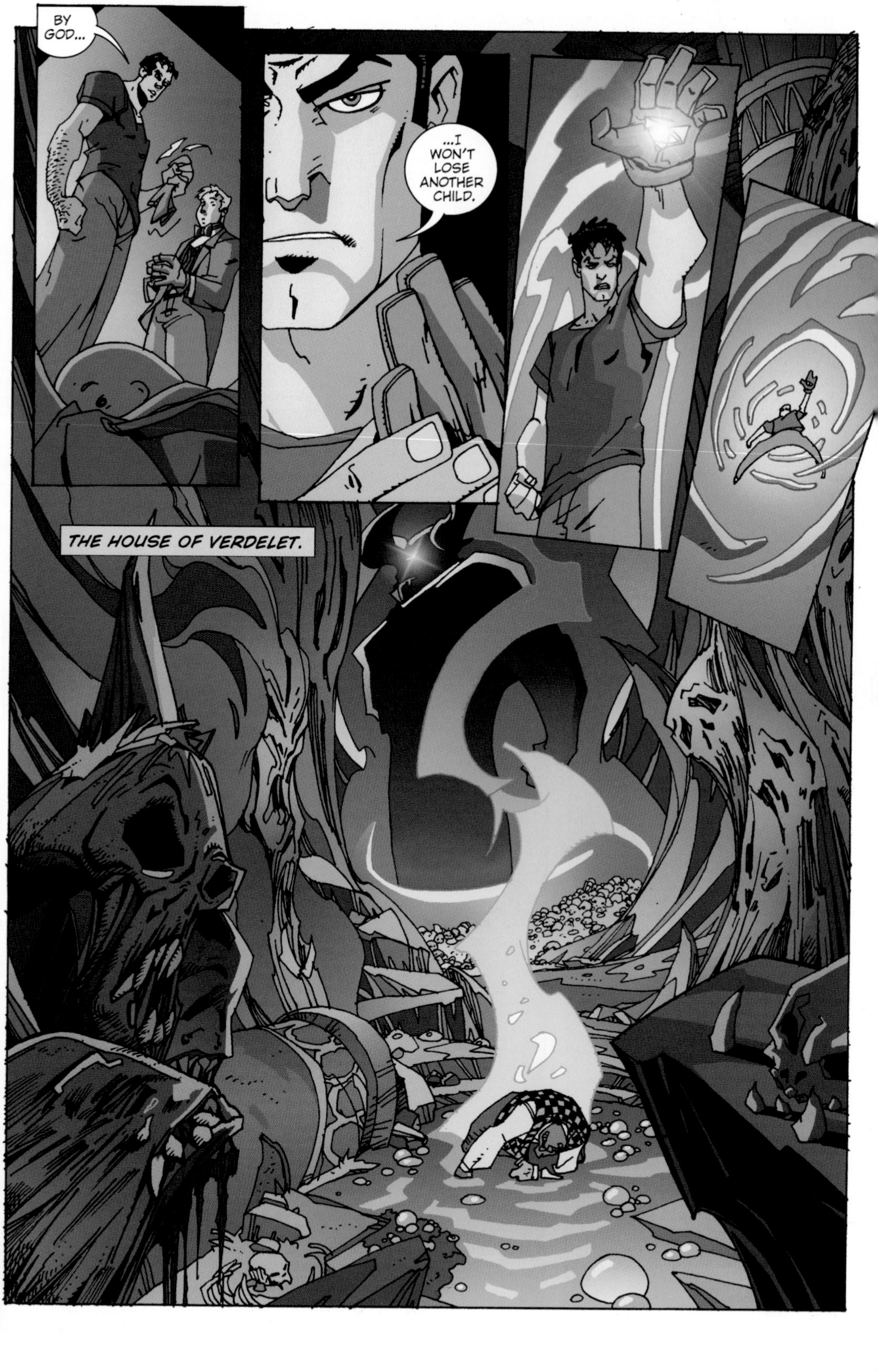
BY GOD...
...I WON'T LOSE ANOTHER CHILD.
THE HOUSE OF VERDELET.

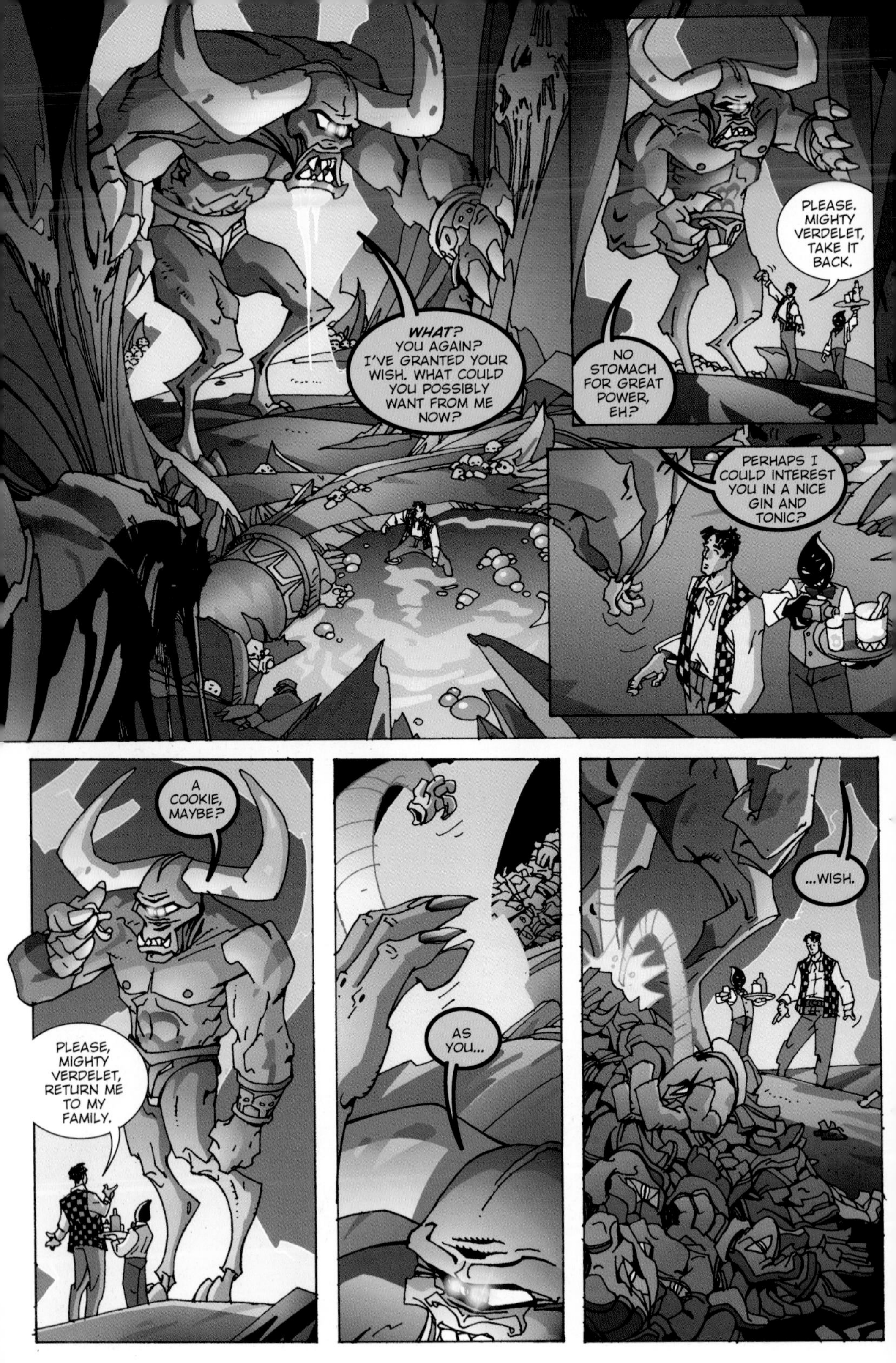
WHAT? YOU AGAIN? I'VE GRANTED YOUR WISH. WHAT COULD YOU POSSIBLY WANT FROM ME NOW?
PLEASE. MIGHTY VERDELET, TAKE IT BACK.
NO STOMACH FOR GREAT POWER, EH?
PERHAPS I COULD INTEREST YOU IN A NICE GIN AND TONIC?
A COOKIE, MAYBE?
PLEASE, MIGHTY VERDELET, RETURN ME TO MY FAMILY.
AS YOU...
...WISH.

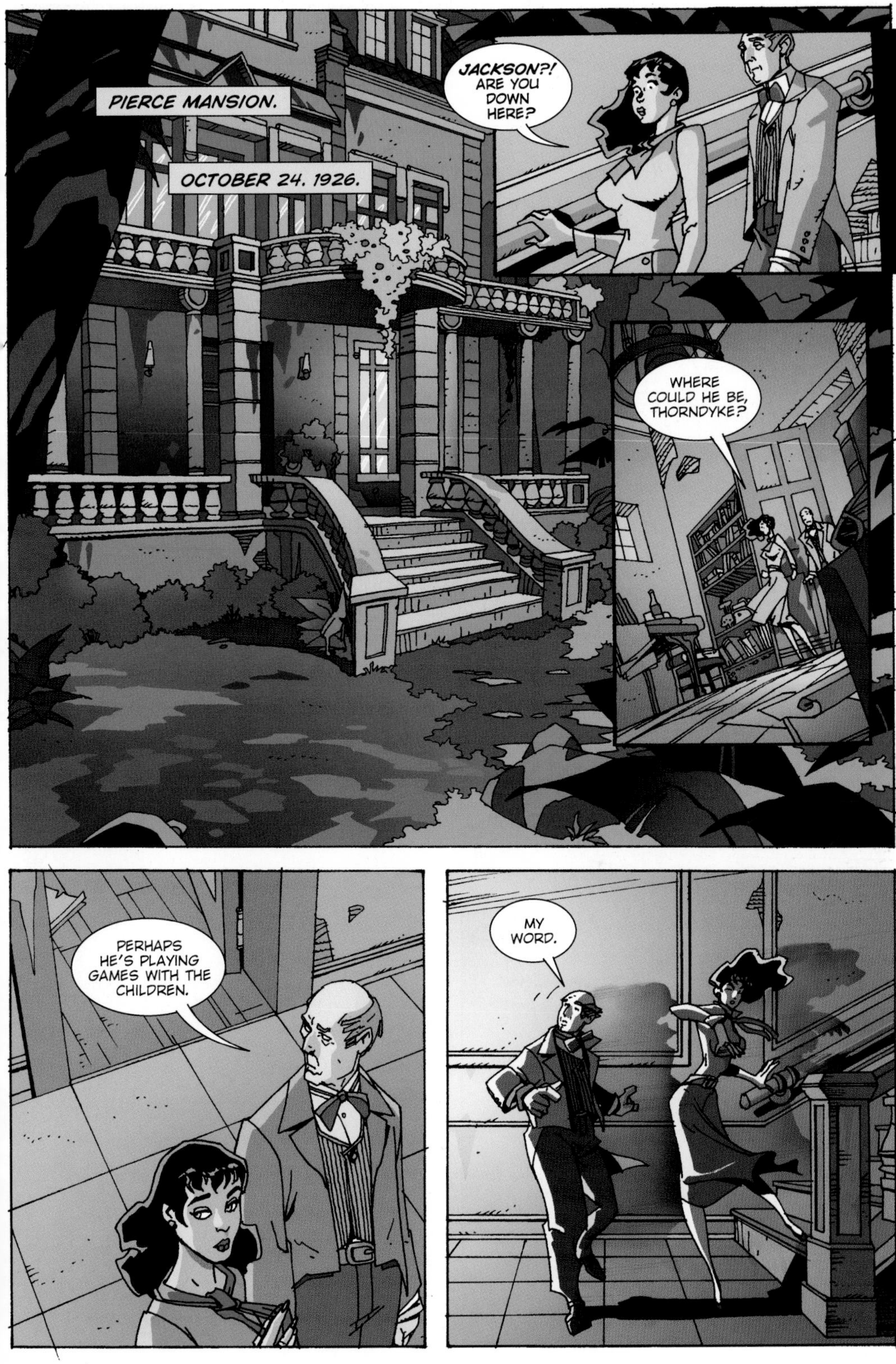
PIERCE MANSION.
OCTOBER 24. 1926.
JACKSON?! ARE YOU DOWN HERE?
WHERE COULD HE BE, THORNDYKE?
PERHAPS HE'S PLAYING GAMES WITH THE CHILDREN.
MY WORD.

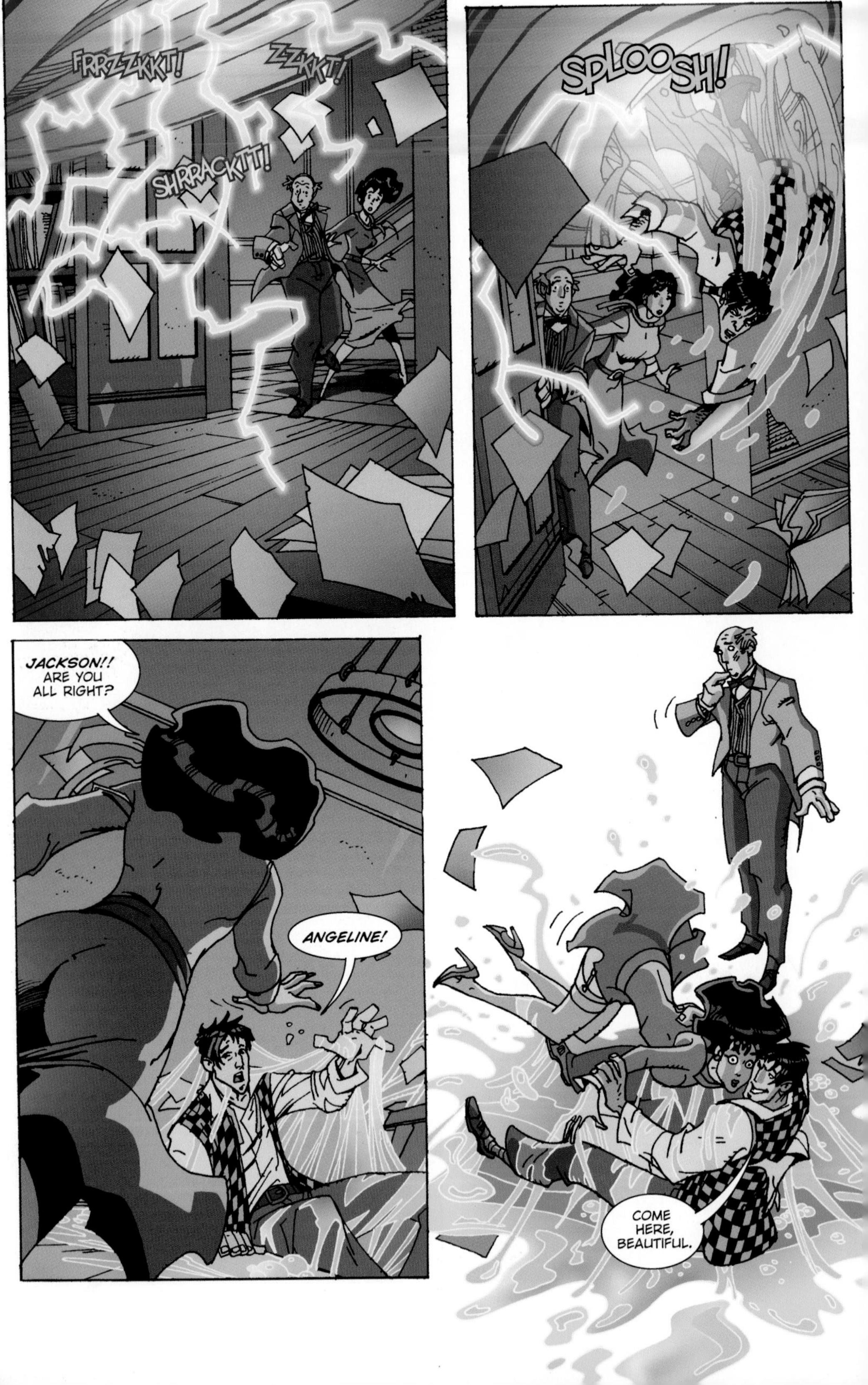
FRRZZAKKT!
ZZAKKT!
SHRRACKTTT!
SPLOOSH!
JACKSON!! ARE YOU ALL RIGHT?
ANGELINE!
COME HERE, BEAUTIFUL.

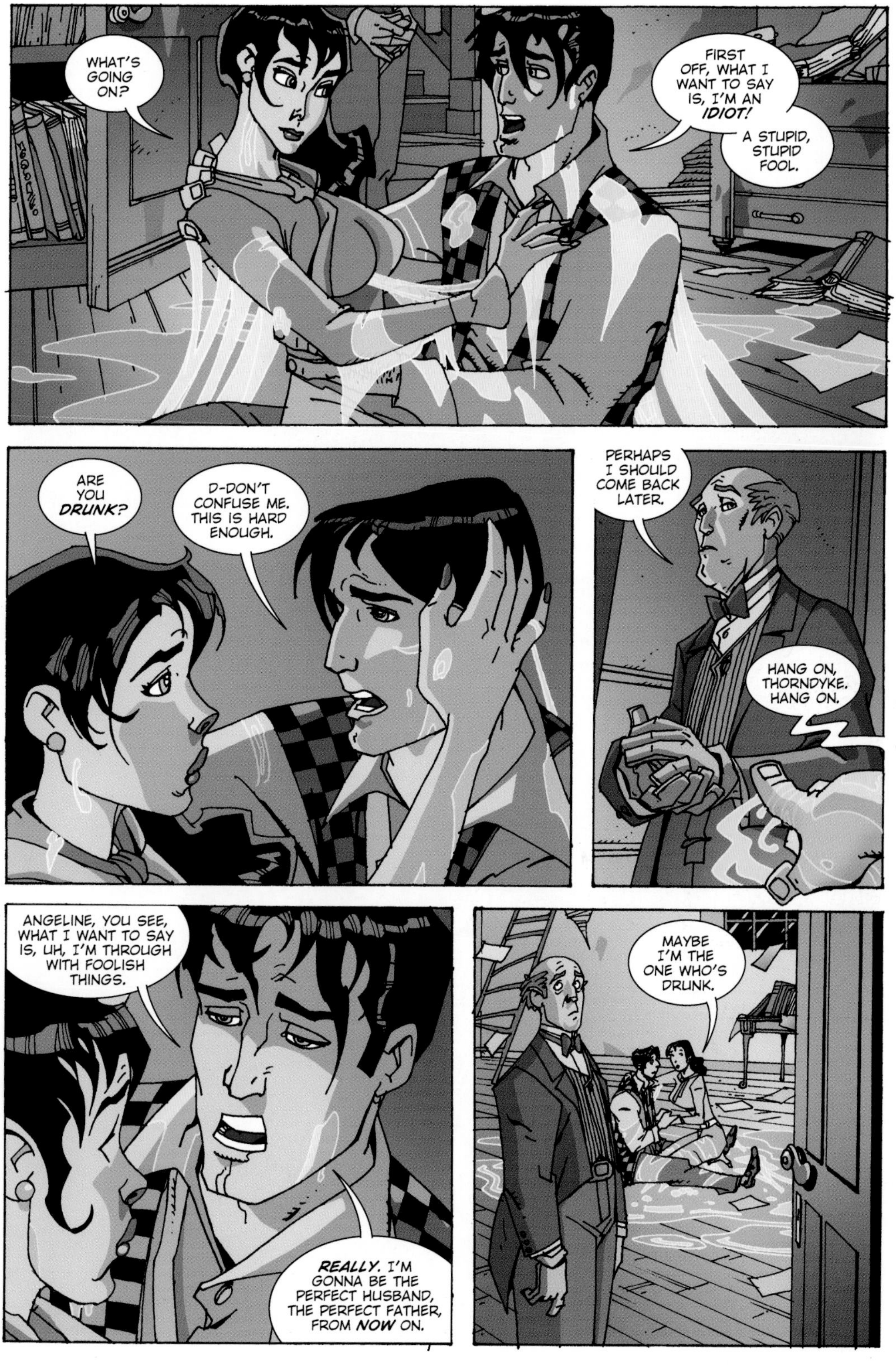
WHAT'S GOING ON?
FIRST OFF, WHAT I WANT TO SAY IS, I'M AN *IDIOT!*
A STUPID, STUPID FOOL.
ARE YOU *DRUNK?*
D-DON'T CONFUSE ME. THIS IS HARD ENOUGH.
PERHAPS I SHOULD COME BACK LATER.
HANG ON, THORNDYKE. HANG ON.
ANGELINE, YOU SEE, WHAT I WANT TO SAY IS, UH, I'M THROUGH WITH FOOLISH THINGS.
REALLY. I'M GONNA BE THE PERFECT HUSBAND, THE PERFECT FATHER, FROM *NOW* ON.
MAYBE I'M THE ONE WHO'S DRUNK.

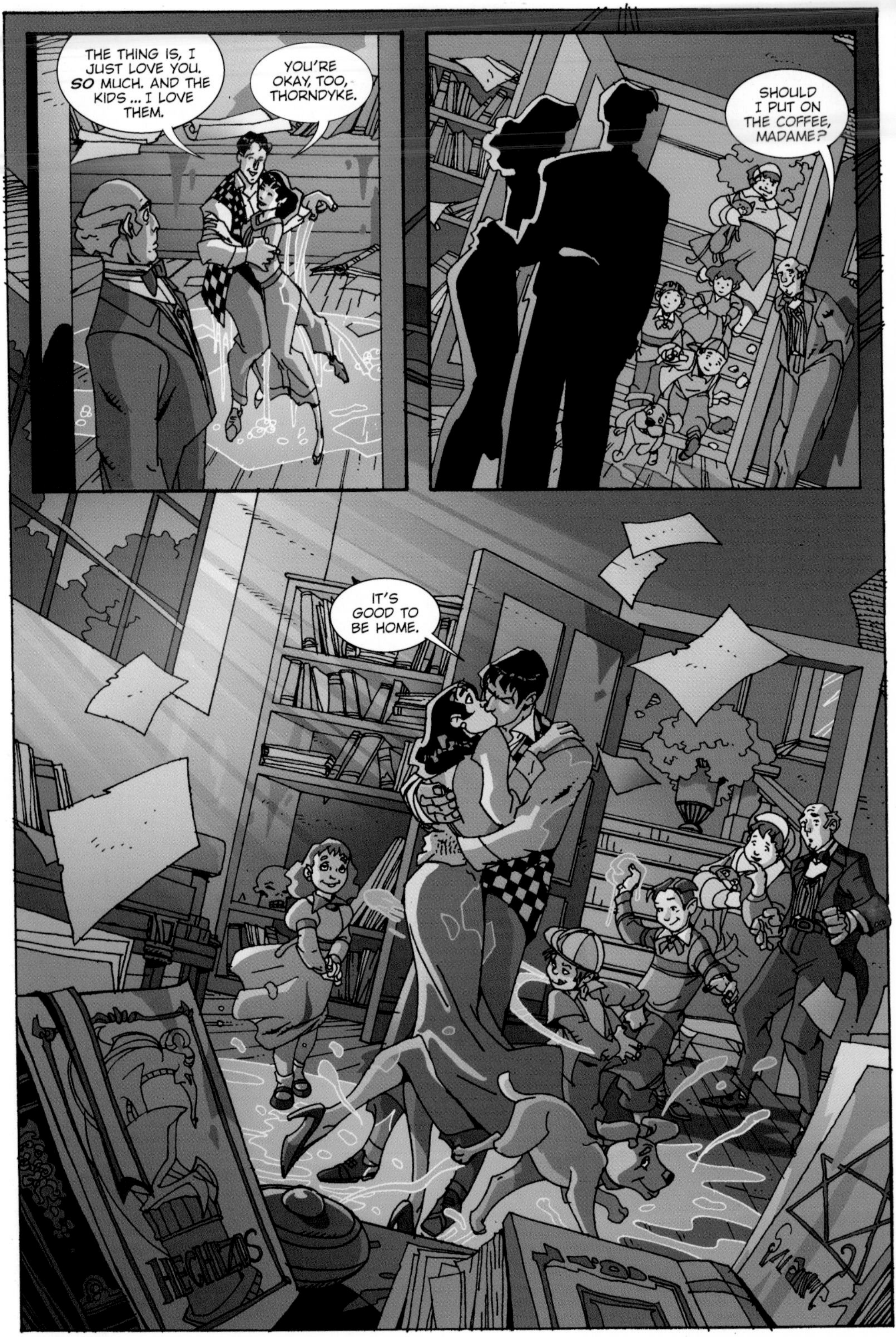
THE THING IS, I JUST LOVE YOU. SO MUCH. AND THE KIDS ... I LOVE THEM.
YOU'RE OKAY, TOO, THORNDYKE.
SHOULD I PUT ON THE COFFEE, MADAME?
IT'S GOOD TO BE HOME.
HECHIZOS

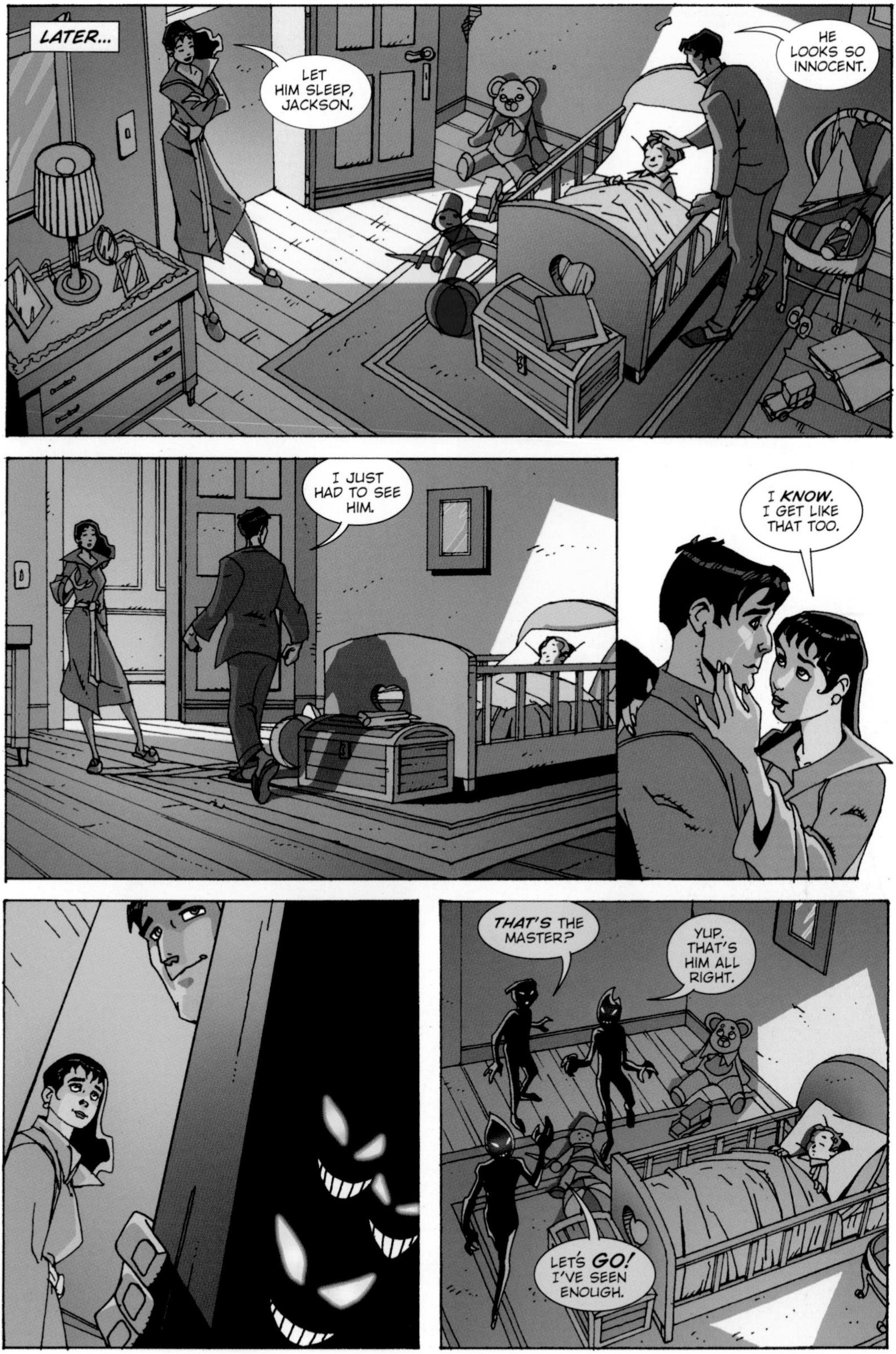
LATER...
LET HIM SLEEP, JACKSON.
HE LOOKS SO INNOCENT.
I JUST HAD TO SEE HIM.
I KNOW. I GET LIKE THAT TOO.
THAT'S THE MASTER?
YUP. THAT'S HIM ALL RIGHT.
LET'S GO! I'VE SEEN ENOUGH.

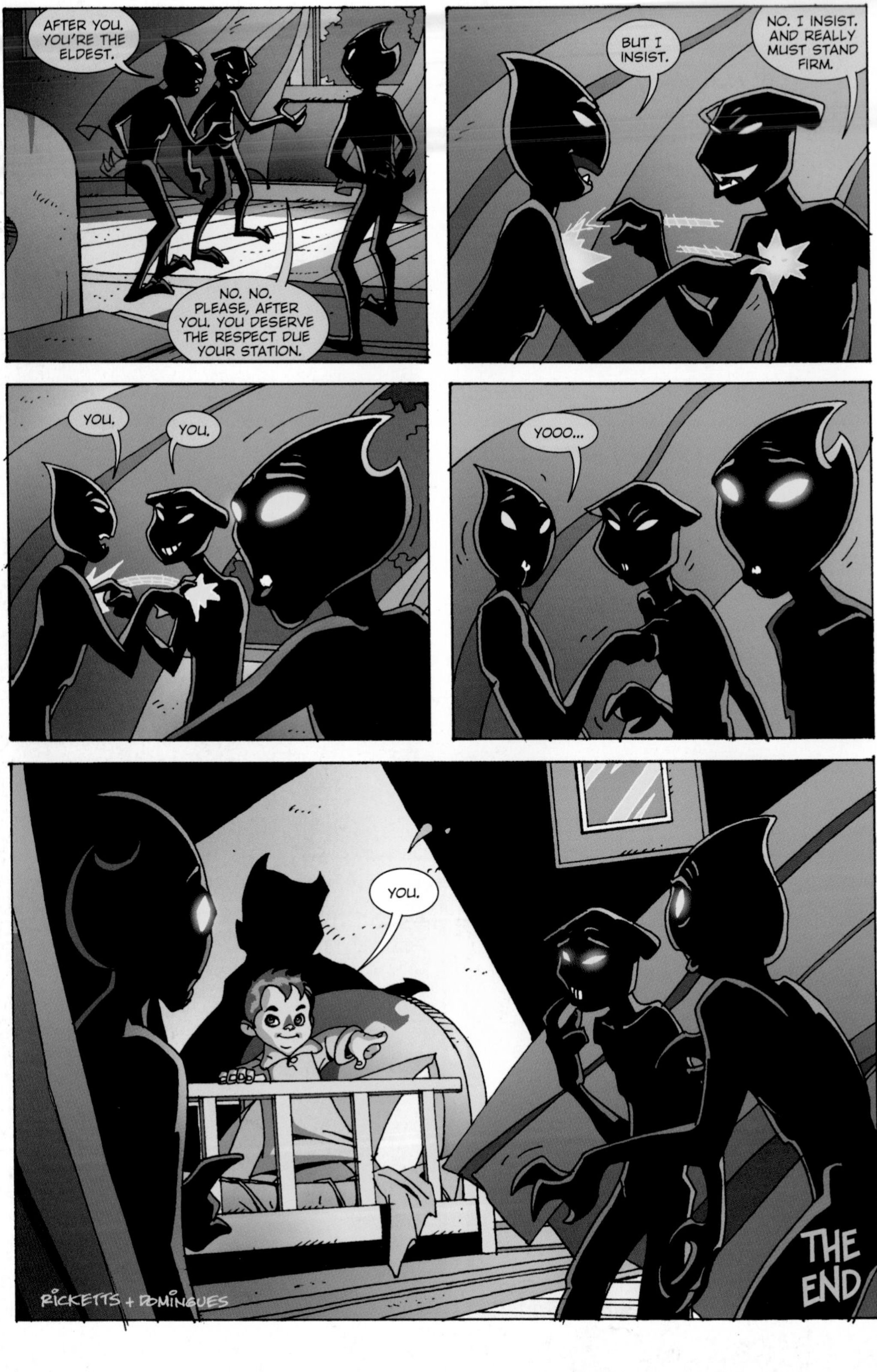
AFTER YOU. YOU'RE THE ELDEST.
NO. NO. PLEASE, AFTER YOU. YOU DESERVE THE RESPECT DUE YOUR STATION.
BUT I INSIST.
NO. I INSIST. AND REALLY MUST STAND FIRM.
YOU.
YOU.
YOOO...
YOU.
THE END
RICKETTS + DOMINGUES

SINCE 1990

HORACIO DOMINGUES

HAS BEEN ILLUSTRATING BOOKS WRITTEN BY CARLOS TRILLO
FOR THE
EUROPEAN MARKET

HIS WORKS INCLUDE **Hyter De Flok** AND **Aileen**

FOR FRENCH PUBLISHER ALBIN MICHEL

as well as

WHY THE KNIGHT HAS DISAPPEARED AND MURDER IN THE FAERIE WORLD
FOR SAF COMICS

MARK RICKETTS

IS THE ACCLAIMED WRITER OF THE GRAPHIC NOVEL

NOWHERESVILLE

AND THE WINNER OF THE

2000 KLASKY CSUPO SCREENWRITING COMPETITION

HE HAS BEEN DESCRIBED AS "A POWERFUL STORYTELLER"

BY DON McPHERSON OF THE FOURTH RAIL

AND PRAISED FOR HAVING
"A KEEN EYE FOR THE DARK PLACES AND A SHARP EAR
FOR THE
BEAT OF SPEECH"

BY 100 BULLETS AUTHOR BRIAN AZZARELLO

MIKE MIGNOLA JILL THOMPSON EVAN DORKIN SEAN PHILLIPS
SCOTT MORSE TONY MILLIONAIRE GARY GIANNI AND OTHERS
The Dark Horse Book of
Witchcraft

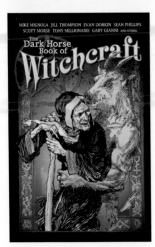

THE DARK HORSE BOOK OF WITCHCRAFT HC

By Mike Mignola, Mark Ricketts, Evan Dorkin, Jill Thompson, and others. Cover by Gary Gianni

Following the success of *The Dark Horse Book of Hauntings*, Dark Horse returns with another collection of bizarre tales by Eisner Award-winning artists Mike Mignola, Mark Ricketts, Gary Gianni, Evan Dorkin, Jill Thompson, and Scott Morse. *The Dark Horse Book of Witchcraft* conjures up weird tales of horror and magic the likes of which one seldom sees in the comics medium.

Hardcover, 96 pages, Full color
$14.95, ISBN: 1-59307-108-6

MIKE MIGNOLA'S
HELLBOY
WEIRD TALES
Volume One

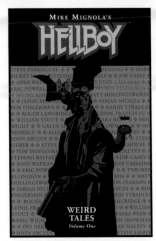

HELLBOY: WEIRD TALES VOLUME ONE

by Mark Ricketts, Eric Wight, Joe Casey, John Cassaday, Alex Maleev, Eric Powell, and others. Cover by Mike Mignola

Some of the top writers and artists in today's world of comics provide their take on Hellboy and the B.P.R.D. Old-fashioned pulp fun featuring one of the greatest heroes of modern comics.

Softcover, 128 pages, Full color
$17.95, ISBN: 1-56971-622-6

THE GOON
NOTHIN' BUT MISERY
by Eric Powell

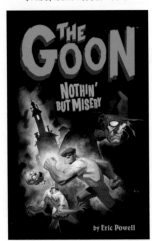

THE GOON, VOLUME 1: NOTHIN' BUT MISERY

By Eric Powell

An insane priest is building an army of the undead, and only one man can put them in their place: the Goon. This volume collects *The Goon* issues 1-4 and *The Goon Color Special*, originally published by Albatross Exploding Funny Books; presented in full-color for the first time.

Wizard Magazine says, "Every comic should be this much fun to read!"

Softcover, 136 pages, Full color
$15.95, ISBN: 1-56971-998-5

Scarlet Traces
Ian Edginton ◦ D'Israeli

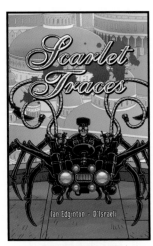

SCARLET TRACES

By Ian Edginton and D'Israeli

A decade after the Martians' failed invasion of the British Isles, the United Kingdom's monopoly of the Martian heat-ray has assured their dominance over two-thirds of the Earth's surface. However, there is something rotten at the heart of the Empire... *Scarlet Traces* brings readers a fantastic combination of mystery, horror, and science fiction.

Hardcover, 88 pages, Full color
$14.95, ISBN: 1-56971-940-3

AVAILABLE AT YOUR LOCAL COMICS SHOP OR BOOKSTORE

To find a comics shop in your area, call 1-888-266-4226

For more information or to order direct visit darkhorse.com or call 1-800-862-0052 • Mon.-Sat. 9 A.M. to 5 P.M. Pacific Time

***Prices and availability subject to change without notice**

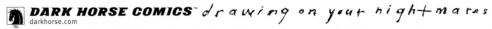

DARK HORSE COMICS™ *drawing on your nightmares*
darkhorse.com